Technical Guide to
Hotel Operation

SECOND EDITION

Technical Guide to
Hotel Operation

SECOND EDITION

BK CHAKRAVARTI PhD

Department of Hotel Management and Catering Technology
Birla Institute of Technology (Deemed University), Mesra, Ranchi
Former Principal, IHM, Patna
Former Director, Bihar State Tourism Development Corporation
Former Visiting Lecturer, University of Calcutta

CBS

CBS Publishers & Distributors Pvt Ltd

New Delhi • Bengaluru • Chennai • Kochi • Mumbai • Pune
Hyderabad • Kolkata • Nagpur • Patna

Technical Guide to
Hotel Operation
SECOND EDITION

ISBN: 978-81-239-2350-5

Published by Satish Kumar Jain for

CBS Publishers & Distributors Pvt Ltd
4819/XI Prahlad Street, 24 Ansari Road, Daryaganj, New Delhi 110 002, India.
Ph: 23289259, 23266861, 23266867   Fax: 011-23243014   Website: www.cbspd.com
                                                                                              e-mail: delhi@cbspd.com; cbspubs@airtelmail.in

Corporate Office: 204 FIE, Industrial Area, Patparganj, Delhi 110 092
Ph: 4934 4934   Fax: 4934 4935   e-mail: publishing@cbspd.com; publicity@cbspd.com

Branches

- **Bengaluru:** Seema House 2975, 17th Cross, K.R. Road,
  Banasankari 2nd Stage, Bengaluru 560 070, Karnataka
  Ph: +91-80-26771678/79   Fax: +91-80-26771680   e-mail: bangalore@cbspd.com
- **Chennai:** 20, West Park Road, Shenoy Nagar, Chennai 600 030, Tamil Nadu
  Ph: +91-44-26260666, 26208620   Fax: +91-44-42032115   e-mail: chennai@cbspd.com
- **Kochi:** 36/14 Kalluvilakam, Lissie Hospital Road, Kochi 682 018, Kerala
  Ph: +91-484-4059061-65   Fax: +91-484-4059065   e-mail: kochi@cbspd.com
- **Mumbai:** 83-C, Dr E Moses Road, Worli, Mumbai-400018, Maharashtra
  Ph: +91-9833017933   e-mail: mumbai@cbspd.com
- **Pune:** Bhuruk Prestige, Sr. No. 52/12/2+1+3/2 Narhe, Haveli
  (Near Katraj-Dehu Road Bypass), Pune 411 041, Maharashtra
  Ph: +91-20-64704058, 64704059, 32392277 Fax: +91-20-24300160   e-mail: pune@cbspd.com

Representatives

- **Hyderabad**   0-9885175004
- **Nagpur**   0-9021734563
- **Kolkata**   0-9831437309, 0-9051152362
- **Patna**   0-9334159340
- **Vijayawada**   0-9000660880

Printed at India Binding House, Noida, UP

Preface to the Second Edition

The first edition of *Technical Guide to Hotel Operation* was published in 1990. The book made a very good impact among the hospitality professionals all over the country and almost all the copies first published were exhausted in a short time. Unfortunately, I could not find time to review the book for further publication in the following years.

Recently, with the encouragement of CBS Publishers & Distributors, New Delhi, and specially from Mr YN Arjuna, Senior Director, I opened my pen to revise the book thoroughly for the present edition. Two new chapters, namely, "Bar Operation in Hotel" and "Computer in Hotel Industry" have been added for contemporary interest.

The volume is handy and has all the required practical information for day-to-day hotel operation as well as provides knowledge and guidelines for the would-be hotel entrepreneurs. The present volume should be of value to the students and teachers as well as all those engaged in the hotel management and catering studies.

Here, I take the opportunity to extend my thanks to Mr SK Jain and his team at CBS P&D, New Delhi, for bringing out this book up to international standards and in an excellent design and format.

Dr BK Chakravarti

Preface to the First Edition

My objective in the preparation of this book is to provide guidelines and comprehensive details of the hotel catering business. My long experience and contact with the people reveal that, there is not a single volume in the hotel industry's library wherein all the essentials from the starting of the hotel to 'day-to-day' operation of it can be available in one publication.

Every effort has been made to incorporate up-to-date data and text useful for the future hotel entrepreneurs as well as for those already in the business.

The need for a book of this type is felt almost everyday for people like us in the catering schools, for those who wish to improve the business of hotel catering and also for the new entrepreneurs of this lucrative hotel trade.

If the people of the trade and the students of the hotel schools feel themselves benefited after reading the book , then I shall not only feel myself rewarded but also the labour and encouragement of many well-wishers in the preparation of the book would be rewarded.

While writing this book, I consulted several people of the industry and many frontline experts in the country and abroad for whose advice and help, I am grateful. I also thank my staff for their effort in collecting diagrams and reference materials, etc. for the book.

I am specially grateful to my wife, 'Subba' who acted as a constant source of inspiration and encouragement in the production of this book. Finally, I am grateful to the publisher who could bring the book at a very short time exerting great interest.

Dr BK Chakravarti

Contents

5. Sanitation, Safety and Security in Hotels   44

6. Front Office (Guest Reception Department)   58

7. Housekeeping Department of the Hotel   72

8. Food and Beverage Department of Hotels   85

techniques 104; Quality—estimation, portioning and pricing of dishes 106; Costing procedure of food 108; Pricing based on costs 109; Pricing based on return 109; Controlling neasures for the prevention of loss in food preparation 109; Staffing pattern in hotel kitchen 110

11. Computer in the Hotel Industry 161

Why use a computer system? 163; Computer hardware 164; Brief history of computers 164; Hardware in the hospitality industry 166; Hotel computer 167; Global distribution systems (GDS) 168; Advanced deposits 168; Travel agent commission 168; Reservation systems operation 169; Property management systems (PMS) 169; Registration 170; Housekeeping 170; Guest accounting 171; Night audit 171; Case example: Using computerized systems in small hotels 172; Ancillary systems 173; Telephone systems 173; Electronic door-locking systems 174; Energy management systems (EMS) 174; In room guest services 174

Appendices

List of Figures

List of Tables

Hotel Industry in India

Hotel-keeping is an international industry. The concept of modern hotel business in India started late compared to the hotel business elsewhere in Europe and America. In India, we have been operating the hotel business more or less in the Western style, particularly in the American style in recent times. Hotels serve for guests from all parts of the country and also from all parts of the world and often employ staff from various states and nationalities. It is a common sight to find businessmen and tourists from Japan, the UK and the USA attending symposia in New Delhi, Mumbai or Kolkata and tourists from all parts of the world visit India throughout the year. Every hotel, small or large, has its own special atmosphere and ambience; for instance, the quality, ambience and grandeur of Ashoka Hotel, New Delhi, Taj, Mumbai and Grand of Kolkata are legendary.

Within India, in the last few years, many fine hotels have been built. The new hotel era was first dominated in New Delhi by the Oberoi Group. ITC, ITDC and other large luxurious groups of hotels quickly followed. Leela Penta, Holiday Inn, Comfort Inn, Fortune, Ginger, Park, Sarovar, etc. in places even outside the Indian capital are some of the finest hotels of the country. Keeping with this trend, the hotel business proliferated throughout India and State Tourism Corporations also added many

establishments for providing food and accommodation to the growing tourists and business traffic. Today, whilst the building costs in the hotel sector are certainly substantial, the industry has gradually become more attractive to private investors with assurance of financial incentives from government. In spite of the rapid growth in the hotel business in India, only about 90,000 hotel rooms of approved quality are now available and by 2020 our need will be around 2 lacs rooms for an estimated 10 million tourists from abroad. In addition, Indian Railways alone move about million people everyday over a route length of more than 80 thousand km. Besides, 4–5 millions also cover a road distance of 15,34,265 km. Thus, in addition to hotels, motels, yatrikas, yatrinivas will also be opened to the tourists in future years. It may also be mentioned that the hotel industry is not in the hands of large chains only. Indeed, 3/4th of hotels all over the country have less than 25 rooms and are in the hands of smaller operators which means that hotel-keeping still has strongly individualistic style.

History of hotels, motels dates back to the ages of inns, sarai, dharamsalas, etc. The true hotel construction took shape after the introduction of railways in our country. The quality of hotel operations also varied within changing times and with the availability of modern technological gadgets. Computers and other electronic devices are now being introduced fast in the hotel operations.

Some of the interesting historical milestones in the growth of the hotel industry are given below.

- Indoor plumbing was introduced in the hotel industry first in the year 1834.
- Steam elevators were first used in hotel in 1853.
- The Netherland Hotel in NY city was the first to have telephones in the rooms in 1894.
- The Waldorf Astoria was built in New York City in 1896. The original hotel was demolished in 1929 for Empire State Building. The new Waldorf Astoria was built in 1931 at its present location of Park Avenue.
- The legal significance of the term 'hotel' as defined in the Hotel Proprietor's Act 1956 of the UK identified it as a place obliged to receive, lodge and serve travellers for reasonable prices without previous contract unless there are reasonable grounds for refusal. But in practice, many types of establishments are often described or, referred to as hotels. The latin word *hospitium*, the hall in a medieval monastery where guests were given hospitality, became 'Hospice', then 'hostel' and eventually 'hotel'. Today people use the word 'hotel' to describe anything from a village dhaba to Ashoka in New Delhi.

Types of Hotels

The location of a hotel and the type of people it attracts are the two factors which make important differences in the style of one hotel against the style of the other. Big hotels find their greatest profitability in the sale of bedroom accommodation linked with function and conferences business. Many of the big city hotels in India, particularly in Chennai, offer services for conducting marriage ceremonies in their 'Madampam' with full catering facilities as additional source of revenue. In smaller cities, hotels are mainly located close to the railway stations, bus stands, central bazar as in India.

Hotels, in holiday and recreational areas (Resort hotels), usually involve themselves in the promotion of entertainment for their guests in foreign countries. But this trend is yet to be picked up by Indian hoteliers. Generally, the Resort hotel owner or manager must play the role of a creative host in a more intimate way for the guests.

The growing vehicular traffic and surface transport had resulted in the growth of many hotels in the country. But in our country, sufficient rooms and catering services are not available to the visitors compared to what is available in motels of Western countries. As a result, the quality of services such as catering, hygiene, sanitation, etc. need to be updated, if these establishments want to survive and grow for touristic benefits in India.

An expansion in air travel has stimulated hotel developments at airports. Hotels (airport hotels) at these locations compare well with large city hotels. Many of these are well equipped to deal flight catering, sophisticated demands of international conferences, exhibitions, etc. To attract this form of business, one must provide a wide range of equipment, vehicles, film projectors, overhead projectors closed circuit television, secretarial, printing and translation services along with well-developed quality food and accommodation services. Because of high building costs and a shortage of sites, hotels may be combined with other developments. In new structures, the basement, ground floor and even some other floor may house shops, offices and other business activities. An increasing number of hotels in all locations now provide facilities for group business and social group functions as well as individual travellers.

It is also a fact that big establishments tend to demand a greater degree of specification, whereas in case of the smaller hotels everyone from the manager (proprietor) downwards need, at time, to be all-rounder or multipurpose worker.

Hotel Building or the Premises for Hotel Business

Before considering any thing in detail, one must know that for any hotel operation a good building, satisfying the basic requirements of the hotel business must be available with the operators. In India, a suitable building on lease for running hotel is very difficult to obtain compared to the opportunities in developed countries. Most of the hotel business operators now have a difficult task to invest huge money in the premises construction fresh for operations. However, with the declaration of hotel as an industry, government financial institutions can be approached for funds on agreed interest terms. Funds can be raised from the public by way of release of shares and collecting term loans. Now, whatever may be the sources of fund, a good hotel business greatly depends upon the nature of the hotel premises (building and location in particular).

Global survey reveals that hotel buildings comprise small structures having 10–15 rooms to grand structures having more than 1000 rooms. In India, Ashoka, Oberoi Towers, Taj Palace, Taj Mahal Hotel, Maurya Sheraton, Hyatt Regency are some of the biggest hotels to name. Apart from these massive structures, we find a large number of palace hotels in India (Royal houses converted to hotels with large gardens and playgrounds). Swimming pools, tennis lawns exist for recreation. So, before conceiving the idea of constructing hotels, one has to plan suitably as regards to size, facilities to be offered, future expansion and trends of technology and consumer behaviour. All details are now handled by experts from the beginning of construction stage in close association with the promoters and proprietors. Budget, however, is one of the major considerations for incorporating latest technologies.

Whatever may be the case, for hotel plans, some basic factors are to be considered in the matter of choosing the site and for the civil structure of the hotel buildings. These are described below.

Locations

Location factor is essential for successful hotel business. Accessibility of hotel building by the staff and guest, its distance from the transport terminals and neighbourhood are important considerations. In spite of a fine structure, a badly located premise shall not be able to sustain the business competition or shall not be able to attract the required clients to run the business on profit.

Architecture of the Hotel Building

There is no specific rule regarding the style to be incorporated in the hotel architecture. But it is a common trend to incorporate local grandeur, contemporary building styles, simplicity, utility, efficiency, environment, vastu, etc. The architectural considerartion is largely influenced by the present trend. The hotel construction is largely influenced by the American style. More and more vertical structures are coming up. We are no longer interested to have hotels such as Ashoka and Taj Mahal any more in the country.

In-house Distribution of Hotel Space

Hotel works like a miniature townships within the building. Some of the bigger units are virtually self-contained communities having almost everything that is necessary for housing and servicing thousands of guest. Apart from the more obvious services of providing food, drink and overnight accommodation, large hotels have behind their scenes engineering departments to provide controlled climates, power and water. Their maintenance departments not only carry out major cleaning, but also take care of redecoration and even structural alteration. Some of the hotels even have their own silversmiths and many have furniture departments for upholstery repair. Hotels may be found with shops for hairdressers, travel agencies and other public service agencies that give the hotel foyer an air of sophisticated shopping arcade. The hotelier is concerned not only with the bedrooms and dinning rooms facilities, but also with the demand of his guests and other consumers as they may also seek entertainments, so orchestras, cabarets, conference facilities are also linked with the hotel services.

To provide space for all these, appropriate space distribution and space management are necessary for proper and efficient services. The productivity of hotel staff, security system, and time savings are closely related to the technical space planning at the time of hotel construction.

Hotel Space

Hotel space is broadly divided into two categories. Category one includes the public areas or public rooms such as hall, lounge, reception, cloakroom, television lounge, restaurants, playrooms, conference halls, etc. Impression made in these public rooms is important for other services by the hotels. This valuable impression can be achieved by remembering the practicality. Unnecessary distance, stuffy atmosphere, overcrowding, poor visibility, bad decor, must be avoided. Guest must not feel the sense of mixing with undesirable persons. Bulk of the hotel space is consumed for providing residential accommodation for bedrooms with private bathrooms. Thus, the physical requirement of the bedrooms during planning is important. Hotel and restaurant division of the Tourism Departments, Govt of India has laid down certain specifications for size, etc. for rooms and bathrooms of various categories of hotels, but certain other features are to be considered for practical hotel-keeping. The hotel guest increasingly regards his hotel bedrooms as a place where he may sit, use computer, telephone, eat and drink as well as sleep. The bed is, however, of prime importance. The furniture and placement of them within the room must be simple and practical to avoid inefficiency in cleaning. The main items of furniture to be looked at are beds, wardrobes, bedside table, luggage rack, seating, dressing or combined dressing-cum-writing table and mirrors. Because of rough use and frequent movement,

the strength of furniture must be of a good quality. Many other minor details of the sizes, relative distances, layout, etc. vary from establishment to establishment and from country to country. But the guests comfort and convenience should be the prime objective of room planning.

Space for Storage and Servicing

This also varies from hotel to hotel and from place to place. In general, there should be separate spaces for storage and servicing. Storage also can be divided into two large sections like that of dry storage (perishable). If business demands, spaces for wine storage and cold storage are to be planned. Stores ought to be near the supply entrance and are normally located close to the back-door. Good lighting, ventilation, clean floor, wide doors should be thought of carefully at the time of store planning. Shelves heights are often neglected causing the inconvenience for storage. Presently because of statutory regulations for storage of LPG-cylinders, adequate planning is to be made for gas storage.

Kitchen Space

The kitchen is the heart of hotel providing food to the registered guests as well as unregistered guests who come to the hotel only for eating and entertainment. The planning of the kitchen layout centres on the policy of food sales which is reflected on the menu. Kitchen is the expensive place of the hotel contrary to the common belief and the working of the kitchen is tiring. The kitchen area should lie between the store and the service area, should be near the dining area. The still room and wash-up area should also be located near the dinning areas. Depending upon the size, budget and policy of the establishments, many sophistications can be introduced in the kitchen plans, but the basic layout should be something as shown in Fig. 1.1. Hot air ventilation system, kitchen waste disposal system must be provided along with toilet and bathing facilities for the kitchen staff.

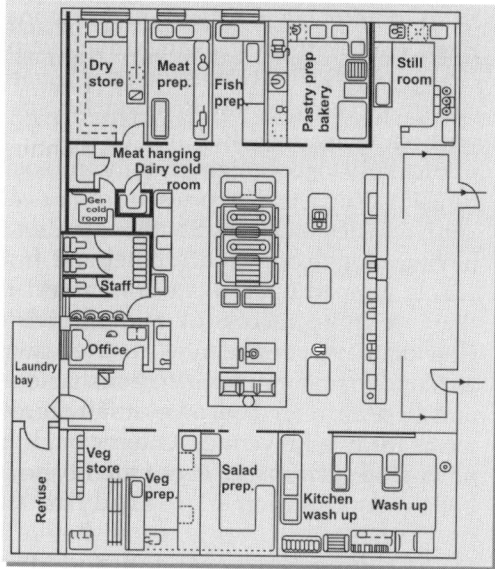

Fig. 1.1: Kitchen space layout

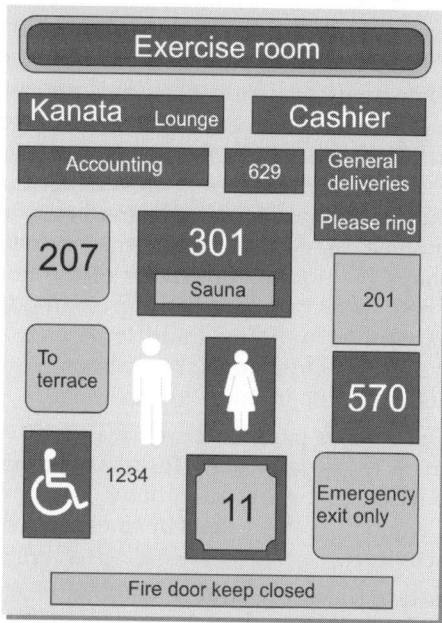

Fig. 1.2: Graphics patterns used in hotels

Hotel Graphics (Fig. 1.2)

Big hotels are places not only for eating, drinking and staying, but also for the finest ambience, aesthetics and pleasure to the eye. The quality of the total environment inside and outside the hotel depends upon types of materials selected for building the hotel, its decor, furnishing, fixtures, engineering aspects and landscape of the surroundings. Hotel graphics, i.e. various writing and signage used in hotels also form a part of aesthetics, decor and luxury in hotels. Hotel graphics cover a complete sign schedule for hotels from personalised name tags to exterior building identification. The required signage can be:

- Standard or custom made
- Cast or fabricated
- Laminated or engraved
- Attached or heat imprinted
- Silk screened or photoetched

It must be ensured that things are designed by experienced professionals based on specific need and choice avoiding repetition or duplication. Some of the items that are internationally used are listed below:

1. Polished brass letters
2. Polished brass poster stand
3. Antique bronze function board
4. Polished brass suite numbers
5. Polished brass meeting room slide system
6. Brass directional letters
7. Antique bronze plaque with polished brass letters
8. Cast bronze plaque
9. Laminated bronze letter/logo
10. Schedule board/brass or teak
11. Polished brass suite/room numbers
12. Antique bronze letters

Non-traditional Services Offered by Hotels

It may be mentioned that hotels can be constructed without the provision for restaurants or other food services. But the return of investment from sales of food and beverages is very high compared to the sale of accommodation only. Many hotels these days have started providing some non-traditional services.

1. **Shop items:** Depending on space, policy, etc. many good hotels operate on their own some utility shops within the hotel premises for revenue. The shops may also be let out to outside parties on agreed terms for revenue. In some categories of hotels, the existence of shops is must for the status of the hotels. These shops usually sell useful commodities as well as national handicrafts, etc. for travellers. Drugstores, bookshops, etc. are also common in many places.

2. **Outdoor or party catering:** It is a growing trend these days to ask for private catering parties to be organized by the hotels. Certain hotels do a good business out of this activity.

3. **Sale of bakery products:** The Great Eastern Hotel of Kolkata had a very good business other than its normal food and accommodation business by way of sale of its baking products. Hotels willing for such activity may opt for, depending upon manpower, space, market and policy in particular.

4. **Sale of meeting rooms for convention and secretarial service:** Hotels are very often quiet during the day and the main lounge, banquet halls, other large rooms may not be in full use for guests all the time. Thus, sales technique and changes in the working of hotel staff, these spaces can be sold as public rooms for large and small meetings with additional income to hotels. For letting out space for public meetings, conferences, seminars, workshops, etc. a very little investment is necessary. Some audio-visual aids, chairs, etc. which are generally required can be hired from outside agencies also. The benefits of meeting room sales also include the possibility of sales of tea, coffee, drinks and often main meals. Once contact is made, it also allows the possibility of further repeat business and greater number of parties.

5. **Sales of hotel lawns, Mandapams for marriage, etc.:** With the growing urbanization, changes in the lifestyle of the people particularly in cities, a new demand for space with catering facilities has cropped up particularly for organizing family and social functions such as marriages, birth or death anniversaries, etc. Many South Indian hotels having enough open space, lawns, etc. have wisely jumped upon this new market and they are quite successful. Some hotels in Chennai have permanent structure known as Mandapam for organizing such function and these are rented out on mutually agreed terms for hotel revenues. Other city hotels having no such space, let out their banquet halls, rooftops and other spare space for such programmes.

6. **Sight seeing tours, car rentals:** Many airport hotels, hotels in cities having no good organized public transport system started car-rental services for their guest. This is a quite attractive means of earning revenue as well as extending useful services to the guests. In resort hotels or hotels in tourist places, guests have demanded for sight-seeing arrangements. Hotels in many places render this service on competitive terms. This is also jointly arranged by the hotels with the travel agents or transport operators. In any case, the business of guest transport can be tapped with proper planning for generating additional revenue for hotels.

7. **Recreational facilities of the hotels:** In large good hotels, swimming pools, billiard rooms, health club facilities, etc. are available to the guests. In order to achieve the full use of these facilities and for additional revenues, the facilities are made available to resident public as well on fixed terms and conditions. This arrangement also leads to additional sale of foods and drinks sometimes and also helps in advertising of hotels.

8. **Car-parking:** Car-parking is a big problem now in many cities all over the world.

The hotels having such facilities particularly in midtown areas or within any business district can utilize this facility for generating more business and for extra revenue.

General Profile of Hotel Guest

Unfortunately in hotel business, many hoteliers and the hotel staff do not have a clear cut image or profile of a hotel guest prior to the start of their business and career. The knowledge about the customers and the information regarding the customers of the hotel products help the men in business to render proper service and handle situations with less errors.

In general, people in the hotel environment confront so many men, so many options or so many difficulties, because of human nature. Hotel people face infinite different situations and problems everyday. Variations between the different guests are also wide and cannot be generalised.

Unreasonable guests, short-tempered guests, drunk guests often create problem for the hotel staff. There is a general psychological tendency among some guests to treat hotel staff as their own paid staff or servants. The techniques, odd gestures, lack of mutual respect often create unpleasant misunderstanding between the guests and the service people. The products and services of hotels are very typical and are not like selling soap or toothpaste from a shop. Guests often spend days with the hotel staff with their families also. They come in touch with them personally for many reasons and even to fulfill many of their very private requirements. Thus, the interpersonal relationships, careful and balance understanding are needed.

Behavioural responses away from home, group behaviour in isolation are some of the aspects that should be understood by the hoteliers in dealing with the guests. Many misunderstandings can be avoided by spelling out the hotel policy, and house rules to guest before checking or prior booking by way of appropriate communication.

The limitation of the hotel in respect of general service, food service, water shortages, lack of room services facilities, lack of telephone facilities, etc. should be clearly known to the guests well in advance for avoiding bitterness and mutual distrust. Satisfaction of the guest results from the realisation of his/her expectations. An honest approach to the delivery of the services, sale of products, etc. would yield better results. Guests should not be informed of the services, facilities, products, etc. in an excessive rosy manner to heighten air expectations and later on for frustration and irritations.

Guests in India often have many typical attitudes and habits which must be handled properly for better management of hotels. Indian guests spend comparatively more times in hotel rooms and frequently demand room service facilities and non-specific services as well even in odd hours. Many guests have the habits of entertaining number of friends and relatives in the hotel rooms which are not designed for accommodating so many people to sit down and chit chat. Hotels plan to provide room service to the individual guest, but it becomes a difficult task for them to handle the lunch, dinner, etc. for so many people in different rooms at hours on demand from guests. Frequent lunch/dinner services in the individual rooms make room dirty resulting in unwanted pressure on the hotel staff as well as requisitions for housekeeping materials. These things disturb to a great extent the working schedule of the normal service sequence of hotel and also annoyance to peace loving guests residing together in the hotel. The guests who monopolise the bathroom, hot water supply, public telephone where there are shared facilities inconveniencing the fellow guests, similarly uncontrolled children, in the hotel garden, corridors, public rooms may cause discomfort. Some guests monopolise the facilities without any reason and without being asked for.

Guests, after long railway journeys and due to cancelled or delayed flights, often show great irritations, even for small matters. Guests in group are sometime talking to press their points often together, creating a real difficult situation for the hotel staff to manage. Another very difficult situation becomes cause of grievance to the members in group tour, is that of receiving inferior room compared to a fellow member in spite of paying the same price.

Apart from business interest, the hoteliers must try to know from the complaints the nature of actual shortcomings and may like to improve services on analysing the nature of complaints. It is far better for a hotel to receive complaints than none at all. Each complaint highlights an area of inefficiency about which the manager or proprietor may know nothing. But there are many people who prefer to accept in silence whatever services are offered. Hoteliers sometime adopt some suggestion "form" to find out feedback reactions from guests and carry out corrective follow-up actions.

It is a practice in most hotels to treat regular guests, senior public servants, political executives with some special attention. But this special VIP treatment must be done very carefully without hurting the feelings of other guests. Each and every guest in a hotel like to be treated as a VIP.

Whether a hotel is small or big, sometimes it faces guests who are in the habit of slipping without paying bills. With proper judgement and by taking advance deposits, etc. the chances of loss can be reduced. Chain hotels, hotel association members keep record of black-listed guests for circulation and for references to avoid registering those guests. Payments made by cheques or through credit cards may also be falsely used by some unwanted guests. The overall policy should be that of cheerful, efficient and willing services to the guests. The guest must feel that he/she is getting the value of his/her money while staying at the hotel and having happy experience.

Requirements and Procedures for Application for Star Hotels and Feasibility Determination of Hotels

2

Form of Acceptance of Regulatory Conditions

To
The Director General
Department of Tourism
New Delhi.

Subject: Acceptance of regulatory conditions

Dear Sir,

I have received a copy of the regulatory conditions prescribed by the Department of Tourism for hotels placed on its approved list, and wish to confirm that I have read and understood the same and hereby agree to abide by the same and such other conditions as may be laid down from time to time by the Department of Tourism for approved hotels.

Yours faithfully,
(Name in block letters)

Managing Director/Partner/Proprietor
Name of Hotel

Application Form for Approval of Hotel Project

1. Proposed name of the hotel
2. Name of the promoters (a note giving details of business antecedents may be enclosed)
3. Complete postal address of the promoters.
4. Status of owners/promoters:
   Whether:
   a. Company (if so, a copy of the memorandum and articles of association may be furnished)

or

b. Partnership firm (if so, a copy of partnership deed and certificate of registration under the Partnership Act may be furnished)

or

c. Proprietory concern (given name and address of the proprietor)

5. Location of hotel site along with postal address.

6. Details of the site:

a. Area

b. Title

Whether outright purchase (if so, a copy of the registered sale deed should be furnished)

or

On lease (if so, a copy of the registered lease deed should be furnished)

c. Whether the required land-use permits for the construction of a hotel on it have been obtained (if so, a copy of the certificate from the concerned local authorities should be furnished)

d. Distance from railway station

e. Distance from airport

f. Distance from main shopping centres

7. Details of the hotel project (a copy of the project/feasibility report should also be furnished).

a. Star category planned

b. No. of guest rooms and their area

	No.	Area
Single		
Double		
Suites		
Total		

c. No. of attached bathrooms and their area

d. How many of the bathrooms have bathtubs or the most modern shower chambers

(Give break-up)

e. Details of public areas

	No.	Area of each

i. Lounge/lobby

ii. Restaurants

iii. Bar

iv. Shopping

v. Banquet/conference hall

vi. Health club

vii. Swimming pool

viii. Parking facilities

Note: It may be ensured that areas of guest rooms and attached bathrooms conform to the minimum standards laid down by the Department of Tourism for different star categories of hotels.

f. Blueprints of the sketch plans of the project—a complete set duly signed by the promoter and the architect should be furnished, including/showing among other things, the following:

i. Site plan

ii. Front and side elevations

iii. Floorwise distribution of public rooms/guest rooms and other facilities

iv. Area of guest rooms with dimensions

v. Area of attached baths with dimensions

8. Air-conditioning:

a. Whether all the guest rooms will be air conditioned

b. Whether all the public areas will be air conditioned

c. Give details of the type of air conditioning

9. Approval: Whether the hotel project has been approved/cleared by/under the following agencies/acts wherever applicable:

a. Municipal authorities

b. MRTP Act

c. Urban Land Ceiling Act

d. DGCA

e. Any other local authorities concerned

10. Proposed capital structure:

a. Total estimated cost:

i. Equity

    ii. Loan

    iii. Total

  b. Equity capital so far raised

  c. i. Sources from which loan is proposed to be raised

    ii. Present position of the loan

11. Acceptance of Regulatory Conditions (This should be furnished in the prescribed proforma)

12. Application Fee
(Demand draft for ₹ 13000/- in the case of hotel projets planned for 5-star deluxe categories and for ₹ 8000/- in the case of 3- and 4-star categories and ₹ 5000/- for 1- and 2-star categories).

13. If you are interested/not interested in availing of any or all of the following benefits of the Income Tax Act-61, kindly mention yes/no against each of the following provisions:
Section 80 L
Section 80 H–H
Section 32 (i) (ii a)
Section 32 (i) (v)
Section 33

Signature ....:

Full name and designation of the applicant

....

Place: ....

Date: ....

REGULATORY CONDITIONS FOR APPROVAL OF HOTEL PROJECTS

All hotels approved by the Department of Tourism are required to furnish the following information:

1. The hotel will furnish documents relating to its legal status, i.e. if the company is incorporated under the Companies Act, a copy of its memorandum and articles of association; if it is a partnership firm, a copy of the partnership deed and the certificate of registration under the Partnerships Act; if it is a proprietary concern, name and the address of the proprietor, etc.

2. The hotel will submit the following information to the Additional Director General, Department of Tourism, so as to reach on or before 31st May each year for the proceeding financial year:

a. A bank certificate in regard to foreign exchange deposited by the hotel.

b. Total bed capacity offered by the hotel as under:
   - Single room
   - Double room
   - Suites

c. Number of rooms occupied on a permanent/semipermanent basis by residents/staff/officers, etc.

d. A specimen copy of the current tariff card.

e. List of the names of the following officers with their designation, experience, etc. (departmentwise)
   i. Senior executives
   ii. Junior executives
   iii. Other staff

f. Total number of persons employed indicating separately the number of Indian and foreign staff.

g. Annual report of the hotel and a statement showing the audited balance sheet and profit and loss account; within 4 months of the close of the financial year.

h. Statistical returns in regard to the number of guests, rooms occupancy, income and employment on regular basis as prescribed by the Department of Tourism from time to time. Release of foreign exchange, issue of import licences, grant of approval for fiscal benefits including income tax reliefs, etc. will be cleared only if the concerned hotel has submitted updated statistical returns.

3. The Regional Director/Director/Manager of the Government of India Tourist Offices

of the region and the Director General, Department of Tourism should be kept informed from time to time of facilities introduced or withdrawn and of any additions or alterations made in regard to the bed capacity of the hotels.

4. The hotel tariff should be fixed in consultation with the Department of Tourism should be obtained for any revision of hotel rates. The hotel tariff should be prominently displayed in each room. The card shall also indicate sales tax, service charges, etc.

5. Applications for revision of tariff must be despatched sufficiently in advance so as to reach the Additional Director General (Tourism) latest by 15th of May each year. Applications received after this date shall not be entertained.

6. Normally, no rooms will be let out for purposes other than residential. However, with the prior permission of the Department of Tourism not more than 10% of the rooms in the hotel will be let out to any person or company for residential or commercial purposes.

7. Any licence and/or approval required from the local administration, police or other concerned authorities for the construction/operation of the hotel should be obtained directly by the promoters from the concerned authorities. The approval by this department will not in any way substitute for them. This department's approval will be deemed to have been withdrawn in case of violation of this condition, when brought to its notice.

8. In the event of the promoters making any changes in the plans of the project as submitted earlier, the approval of this department will have to be applied for afresh.

9. In case, the hotel is required to provide guides for tourists, only approved guides of the Department of Tourism should be employed.

10. The hotel should at all times adhere to the high standards of maintenance and services

for which it has been recognised and in all dealings with its guests observe business practices worthly of an establishment of repute.

11. Officers of the Department of Tourism or any other officer deputed by the department to inspect the hotel premises from time to time will be allowed free access with or without prior notice.

12. As a project which has been approved from the point of view of its suitability for foreign tourists, the promoters will be entitled to grant of loan from Central/State Finance Institutions and priority in the procurement of building materials, telephones and telex connections, etc. However, this approval should not in any way be considered as an assurance for the grant of these facilities since this would fall within the jurisdiction of the concerned authorities.

GUIDELINES FOR APPROVAL OF HOTELS AT THE PROJECT/PLANNING STAGE

General: The hotel industry is entitled to various benefits including, among other things, Income Tax concessions under the Income Tax Act and priority consideration of its various requirements such as telephones, telex, ATM, dish antenna, rain water harvesting, solar power system, fire safety equipments, LPG, etc. by the government authorities at municipal, state, union level or a semi- or quasi-government body. To be eligible for these benefits, a hotel has to be approved by the Department of Tourism. Such approval is granted from the point of view of the suitability of a hotel for foreign guest. Approved rates are to be maintained for a certain minimum level of standard of services and amenities. There are six categories of approved hotels ranging from 1- to 5-star deluxe. A special 7-star is also in existence.

Application: The application for approval of a hotel at the project/planning stage should be submitted, in the prescribed form complete in all respects, to the Director General of Tourism, Transport Bhawan, Parliament Street, New Delhi-110 001, in the case of hotel projects planned for the 4, 5 and 5-star deluxe categories, to the Regional Director of the concerned Government of India Tourist Office at Delhi/ Mumbai/Chennai/Kolkata, in the case of 1, 2 and 3-star categories, a copy of the application should be endorsed to the Director/Manager of the nearest Government of India Tourist Office and to the Director of Tourism of the concerned State Government.

Requirement: The various documents and information to be furnished about hotel projects, when applying for this approval, are given in detail in application form. However, the basic requirements are given below and these may be sent along with the application.

   i. A project report establishing the feasibility of the proposed hotel and describing the amenities to be provided at the hotel particularly mentioning any special or distinctive feature and indicating the star category which the establishing has been planned for. The criteria which are applied in determining the star category of a hotel, when it is inspected for classification committee as a functioning unit, are briefly described later in these guidelines.

  ii. The site selected should be suitable for the construction of a hotel intended for use by foreign tourists. Its suitability will be determined after actual inspection by representatives of the department in the case of 4, 5 and 5-star deluxe hotels and in the case of 1, 2 and 3-star categories by representatives of the Regional Director of the concerned department of Government of India Tourist Office and the State Tourism Department, when such aspect as its accessibility from airport/railway station/shopping areas, etc. which would make it a convenient location will be kept in mind, as also the fact that its environs are not crowded, noisy, unhygienic, etc.

  iii. Valid documentry evidence that the site in question is owned/leased by the promoters of the hotel project.

  iv. A certificate from the concerned local authorities that under the prescribed land-use, it is permissible to construct a hotel on it.

  v. Blueprints of the sketch plans of the project (including front and side elevation) indicating the areas with dimensions of the rooms/bathrooms/public rooms, etc. duly signed by the architect and the promoter. The department has prescribed certain minimum areas standards for guest rooms and attached bathrooms and it should be ensured that none of the guest rooms/attached bathrooms falls short of the prescribed minimum carpet area standards which are given in Table 2.1.

  vi. a. Names and business antecedents of the promoters.

     b. Proposed ownerships of structure, giving full details as to whether the new undertaking will be owned by individual (s) or a firm or a company.

     c. Estimated cost of the project and the manner in which it is proposed to raise the funds to meet the cost.

  vii. The department has prescribed regulatory conditions to be abided by promoters of approved hotel projects. The promoters should furnish the acceptance of these regulatory conditions in the form of their acceptance.

CLASSIFICATION/CRITERIA OF STAR HOTELS

Five-star Deluxe Category

This is a qualitative extension of the 5-star category while quantitatively, the basic features are as of the 5-star category. In 5-star deluxe hotel, the all-round standard of service and amenities are of very luxurious and superior quality.

Table 2.1: Minimum areas standards for guestrooms and attached bathrooms

Type of hotel	Star	Single room	Double room	Attached bathrooms
1. Normal hotels	5-star deluxe/ 5-star	180 sq.ft	200 sq. ft	45 sq. ft
	4-star	120 sq. ft (A/C & non-A/C)	140 sq. ft (A/C & non-A/C)	36 sq. ft
	2-star/ 1-star	100 sq. ft (A/C & non-A/C)	120 sq. ft	30 sq. ft
2. Resort hotels	5-star	180 sq. ft	200 sq. ft	45 sq. ft
	4-star 3-star	120 sq. ft	140 sq. ft	36 sq. ft

FIVE-STAR CATEGORY

General Features

The facade, architectural features and general category construction of the building should have the distinctive qualities of a luxury hotel of this category. The locality including the immediate approach and environs should be suitable for a hotel of this category. There should be adequate parking space for cars. The hotel should have at least 25 lettable bedrooms, all with attached bathrooms with long baths or the most modern shower chambers, with 24 hours services of hot and cold running water. All public rooms and private rooms should be fully air-conditioned (except in hill stations where there should be heating arrangement) and should be well appointed with superior quality carpets, curtains, furniture, fittings, etc. of a good standard.

It would be advisable to employ the services of professionally qualified and experienced interior designers of repute for this purpose. There should be an adequate number of efficient lifts in buildings of more than 2-storied including the ground floor with 24 hours service. There should be a well-designed and properly equipped pool (except in hill station). There should be a well-appointed lobby and ladies and gentlemen's cloak room equipped with fitting of the highest standard.

Facilities

There should be a reception, cash and information counter attended by highly qualified, trained and experienced personnel and conference facilities in the form of one each or more of the conference rooms/banquet halls and private dining rooms. There should be a book stall, beauty parlour, barber shop, recognised travel agency; money changing and safe deposit facilities, left luggage room, florist and a shop for toilet requisites and meditations, on the premises. There should be telephones in each room and telephone for the use of guests and visitors and provision for a radio or relayed music in each room. There should be a well-equipped, well-furnished and well-maintained dining room/restaurant on the premises and wherever permissible by law, there should be an elegant well-equipped bar/private room. The pantry and cold storage should be professionally designed to ensure efficiency of operation and should be well equipped.

Services

The hotel should offer both International and Indian cuisines and the food and beverage services should be of the highest standards. There should be professionally qualified, highly trained, experienced, efficient and courteous staff in smart, clean uniforms and the staff coming in contact with guests should possess a good knowledge of foreign languages and staff knowing at least one continental language should be rotated on duty at all times. There should be 24 hours service for reception, information and telephones. There should be provision for reliable laundry and dry cleaning services. Housekeeping at the hotel should be of the highest possible standard and there should be a plentiful supply of all linens, blankets, towels, etc. which should be of the highest quality. Each bedroom should be provided with a vacuum jug / thermos flask with ice cold boiled drinking water except where centrally chilled purified drinking water is provided. There should be a separate restaurant / dining room where facilities for dancing and orchestra are provided.

FOUR-STAR CATEGORY

General Features

The facade, architectural features and general construction of the building should be distinctive and the locality including the immediate approach and the environs should be suitable for a hotel of this category. There should be adequate parking facilities for cars. The hotel should have at least 25 lettable bedrooms, all with attached bathrooms. At least 50% of the bathrooms must have long baths or the most modern shower chamber with 24 hours services of hot and cold running water. All public rooms and private rooms should be fully air-conditioned (except in hill stations where there should be heating arrangements) and should be well furnished with carpets, curtains,

furniture fittings, etc. of a good standard. It would be advisable to employ the services of professionally qualified and experienced interior designers of repute for this purpose. There should be an adequate number of efficient lifts in buildings of more than 2 storied including the ground floor. There should be a well-appointed lobby and ladies and gentlemen's cloak room equipped with fittings of the standard of a hotel of this category.

Facilities

There should be a reception, cash and information counter attended by trained and experienced personnel. There should be a book stall, recognised travel agency, money changing and safe deposit facilities and a left luggage room on the premises. There should be telephone in each room and telephone for the use of guests and visitors and provision for a radio or relayed music in each room. There should be well-equipped, well-furnished and well-maintained dining room / restaurant on the premises and wherever permissible by law, there should an elegant, well-equipped private room. The kitchen, pantry and cold storage should be professionally designed to ensure efficiency of operations and should be well equipped.

Services

The hotel should offer both International and Indian cuisines and food and beverage services should be of the highest standard. There should be professionally qualified, highly trained, experienced, efficient and courteous staff in smart, clean uniforms and the staff coming in contact with guests should understand English. The supervisory and senior staff should possess a good knowledge of foreign languages and staff knowing at least one continental language should be rotated on duty at all times. There should be 24 hours services for reception information and telephones. There should be provision for reliable laundry and dry cleaning services. Housekeeping at the hotel should be of the highest possible standard and there should be of the highest quality available. Similarly, the cutlery and glassware should be of the best quality available. Each bedroom should be provided with a vacuum jug/thermos. Chilled purified drinking water is provided. There should be a special restaurant/dining room where facilities for dancing and orchestra are provided.

THREE-STAR CATEGORY

General Features

The architectural features and general construction of the buildings should be of a very good standard and the locality including the immediate approach and environs should be suitable for a very good hotel, and there should be adequate parking facilities for cars. The hotel should have at least 20 lettable bedrooms, all with attached bathrooms with baths and/or shower and should be modern in design and equipped with fitting of a good standard with hot and cold running water. At least 50% of the rooms should be air-conditioned except in hill stations, where the rooms should have heating arrangements. In all the bedrooms, dining rooms, restaurant and lounge, the furniture and furnishing such as carpets, curtain, etc. should be of a very good standard and design. There should be adequate number of lifts in buildings with more than two-storied including the ground floor. There should be a well-appointed lounge and separate ladies and gentlemen's cloak rooms equipped with fitting of a good standard.

Facilities

There should be a reception and information counter attended by qualified and experienced staff, and a book stall, recognised travel agency, money changing and safe deposit facilities on the premises. There should be a telephone in each room except in seasonal hotels where there should be a call bell in each room and a telephone on each floor for the use of hotel guests and visitors to the hotel. There should be a well-equipped, well-maintained air-conditioned and wherever permissible by law there should be a bar/private room. The kitchen, pantry and cold storage should be clean and organised for orderliness and efficiency.

Services

The hotel should offer a good quality Indian as well as continental cuisine and the food and beverage services should be of a good standard. There should be qualified, trained, experienced, efficient and courteous staff in smart and clean uniforms and the supervisory staff coming in contact with the guests should understand English and the senior staff should possess a good knowledge of English. There should be provision for laundry and dry cleaning service. Housekeeping at the hotel should be of a very good standard and there should be adequate supply of linen, blankets, towels, etc. of good quality. Each bedroom should be provided with a vacuum jug/thermos flask with cold and safe drinking water. The hotel should provide orchestra and ball-room facilities, and should attempt to present specially choreographed Indian dance.

TWO-STAR CATEGORY

General Features

The building should be well constructed and the locality and environs including the approach should be suitable for a good hotel. The hotel should have at least 10 lettable rooms of which at least 75% should have attached bathrooms with showers or a bathroom for every 4 of the remaining rooms. All bedrooms should have modern sanitation and running cold water with an adequate supply of hot water, soap and toilet paper. 25% of the rooms should be air-conditioned except in hill station where there should be heating arrangements in all rooms and all the rooms must be properly ventilated, clean and comfortable, with all the necessary items of furniture. There should be well-furnished lounge.

Facilities

There should be a reception counter with a telephone. There should be telephone or call bell in each room and a telephone on each floor unless each room has a separate telephone. There should be a well-maintained and well-equipped dining room/restaurant, serving good clean wholesome food, and a clean hygienic and well-equipped kitchen and pantry.

Services

There should be experienced, courteous and efficient staff in smart and clean uniforms. The supervisory staff coming in contact with guests should understand English. There should be provision for laundry and dry cleaning services. Housekeeping at the hotel should be of a good standard and clean and good quality linen, blankets, towels, etc. should be provided. Similarly, crockery and glassware should be of a good quality.

ONE-STAR CATEGORY

General Features

The general construction of the building should be good and the locality and environs including immediate approach should be suitable. The hotel should have at least 10 lettable bedrooms with a bathroom for every 4 of the remaining rooms. At least, 25% of the bathrooms should have Western style WCs. All bathrooms should have modern sanitation and running cold water with adequate supply of hot water, soap and

toilet paper. The rooms should be properly ventilated and should have clean and comfortable beds and furniture.

Facilities

There should be a reception counter with telephones and a telephone for the use of guests and visitors. There should be a clean and moderately well-equipped dining room/restaurant serving clean wholesome food and there should be a clean well-equipped kitchen and pantry.

Services

There should be experienced, courteous and efficient staff in smart and clean uniforms and the senior staff coming in contact with guests should possess a working knowledge of English. Housekeeping at the hotel should be of a good standard and clean and good quality linen, blankets, towels, etc. should be supplied. Similarly, crockery, cutlery and glassware should be of a good quality.

FEASIBILITY DETERMINATION OF HOTELS

In determining the feasibility of a hotel, certain major areas are to be considered in particular. These are as under:

- Preparation of feasibility study for the project
- The estimation of the costs of the projects
- Sources of financing the project

Within these, many individual areas are also to be considered for feasibility determination. The feasibility study itself can be broken down into several segments which finally determine the success of the project.

The market survey for tourists arrivals, demands for hotel rooms, sites of the existing hotels, supply position of rooms in future, nature of proposed urban developments/resort development, labour projection, types of consumers, etc. are to be carefully reviewed and assessed.

Apart from the information stated above, the financial projections are most important part of the feasibility study. Projected room demand vis-a-vis estimated at least for five years on competitive basis will determine the anticipated room rates acceptable to future guests. In the financial projections/payroll of the staff, related expenses including employee benefits, price calculations, depreciations, etc. are to be taken into the account.

In a hotel project, the following elements of cost are involved:

- Cost of land
- Cost of construction
- Cost of interest during construction
- Cost of furniture, fixtures and equipment
- Cost of operating equipment
- Cost of inventories
- Cost of pre-opening expenses
- Cost of working capital
- Cost of consultancy
- Cost of payment of interests
- Cost of taxes and other fees
- Cost of legal expenses

In the present state of affairs, to construct hotels on the newly purchased plots in good location is one of the major cost hurdles for small operators. If this figure goes very high, then the project becomes infeasible. While considering the cost of the land for hotel, the developmental cost, if any, including landscape must be considered as part of the overall cost. The cost of construction is the biggest element of cost in any hotel project. The construction cost can be controlled by adopting appropriate contract policy and by wise forecast. In general, per room cost of construction within 5 lacs is reasonable at the present market rate.

There can be various methods of purchase of hotel furniture, fixtures and equipments in an economic way with expert advice from technical people. The furniture, fixture for guests use and in the view of guests should be of acceptable quality befitting for the hotels in question in particular. Out of view furniture and fixtures may not be necessarily of that expensive quality. On an average, a good quality hotel can cover the cost of furniture, fixture, linen, china, silver, etc. within 5 lacs per room basis.

SOURCES OF HOTEL FINANCE

Finances for constructing and starting hotel business are available from government financial institutions under various schemes and on various agreed terms. The portion of promoter's share varies according to the terms and conditions of the financial institution. Apart from these, several tax incentives, pay back relief, etc. are also available to the hoteliers. Hotel tourism has been declared as industry in many states in India for matter of extending financial relief and other incentives as applicable in other traditional industries in the country. Foreign exchange is also available in the country on restricted terms and on the basis of foreign exchange earned by hotels during business. Industrial Development Bank of India, State Financial Corporations, Public Banks, State Development Bank of Tourism, State Department of Industry also provide finance and certain subsidies. Greater reliefs are also available for hoteliers interested in hotel business in hill areas, backward districts, etc. Thus with an appropriate planning, a prospective hotelier can handle his financial requirements. A hotel finance corporation to finance hotel industries has been proposed by the Government of India to help the development of accommodation sector of the tourism business.

Presently, many hoteliers are linking their hotel business with international chain of hotels or with National hotel chains on specific financial and other terms. This is technically known as Hotel Franchise.

General Procedure for Obtaining Loan from State Financial Corporation

Term loans are available for the hotels and motels established or to be established for catering to the needs of tourists as per the norms established by the Department of Tourism. The hotels/motels should have the facilities of boarding, lodging and restaurants, all planned on modern lines. Necessary provisions for car-parking space, stalls for milk and snack bar, open restaurant and availability of fast food, as per the needs of the tourist are considered necessary to serve all classes of tourists visiting the state.

Items Eligible for Assistance

Financial assistance is made available for acquisition of fixed assets such as land, building, furnitures, equipment like air-conditioning plant, refrigerator, water cooler, geyser, tube well, pump set, kitchen equipment, crockery, cutlery, vehicles maintained for the use of tourists, light fittings and fan, etc.

Promoters Contributions

Financial assistance is ordinarily granted on a debt equity ratio of 2:1. Promoters contribution in financing the project in different areas ranging from 12½% (12.5%) to 15½% (15.5%) only, for different categories.

Limit for Sanction

The maximum limit of loan grant by BSFC is ₹ 60 lacs. However, for the purpose of promoting Tourists Infrastructure in the State of Bihar including construction of hotels/motels as well as wayside facility in order to cover the maximum number of locations, the loan amount may vary from ₹ 50,000/to ₹ 5 lacs in most of the cases excluding the major towns where the cost of project may be much higher.

Repayment of Loan

Repayment of loan advanced is normally spread over a period of 8.5 years including 1.5 years moratorium for loans up to ₹ 7.50 lacs. For loans beyond ₹ 7.50 lacs, the spread over of repayment

period is 10 years including 2 to 3 years of moratorium. The principal instalment together with interest is to be paid half yearly.

Rate of Interest

Rate of interest charged on the loans for hotel/motel is 16% and 14.5% in non-backward and specified backward areas respectively on refinance by IDBI with a provision of 2% rebate for timely payment.

How to Apply for Loans?

A set of six application forms can be had from the branch office of BSFC under whose jurisdiction the site of the project falls, on payment of ₹ 15/- per set. The application form duly filled in, has to be submitted to the concerned branch office along with other papers and documents as detailed in the check list of the application form.

Processing fee at the rate of ₹ 100/- and ₹ 50/- per lac of loan is charged in non backward and backward districts for loans up to ₹ 5 lacs. For higher loans the rates are ₹ 150/- and ₹ 75/- per lac up to the maximum limit of ₹ 1500/- and ₹ 750/- respectively. These rates keep changing with government policy decisions and market value.

Subsidy

Central subsidy is available for hotel/motel projects as per the details given below:
 a. A category (no industry districts)—25%
 b. B category districts—15%
 c. C category districts—10%
 d. Other districts—nil

MODEL FORMAT FOR CALCULATING HOTEL PROJECT COST

I. **Land and Building Development:***
 i. Open land 3150 m²
  @ ₹ 1200 to ₹ 1400/-
  per m²   ₹ ....

---

* Figures to be placed based on market value and sites.

ii. Site development of the
above land by site
cleaning, vegetation, etc. ₹ ....

Total ₹ ....

II. Built up Area and Civil Works:

i. **1. Rooms:**

No. of rooms = 60
Average area per room = 20 m²
Average cost of
building a room ₹ ....

2. Layout of rooms:

At ground floor	No room
At 1st floor	8 rooms
At 2nd floor	13 rooms
At 3rd floor	13 rooms
At 4th floor	13 rooms
At 5th floor	13 rooms
Total	**60 rooms**

ii. 2 conference hall each
of 299 m² accommodate
75 persons at the cost rate
of ₹ ....

iii. Restaurant, capacity of
300 persons, in
the area of 500 m² at
an average cost rate of ₹ ....

iv. Banquet hall, capacity of
400 persons, in an area
of 500 m² ₹ ....

v. 10 shops at ground floor,
each of 20 m² ₹ ....

vi. Admn. office, reception
counter, etc. 200 m² ₹ ....

vii. Swimming pool

viii. Parlour, luxury shop,
stores, etc.

ix. Civil works such as
boundary walls, inner and
outer approach roads,
watchman cabin, etc.

Total **(Based on local market)** ₹ ....

III. Plant and Machinery and Equipment:

S.No. Equipment
1. Air-conditioner
2. Elevator
3. Vacuum cleaners and other
cleaning equipment
4. Water coolers
5. Computers
6. Storage equipment
7. Power backup equipment
8. Colour TV/DVD/i-pad
9. Emergency lights/smoke
alarm system/security alarm system
10. Fire fighting equipment
11. Kitchen appliances such as gas,
ranges, microwave ovens,
utensils, mixtures, juicers, etc.
12. Laundry equipment
13. Misc equipment and apparatus

Total ₹ ....

IV. Furniture and Fixtures:

i. Furnitures for rooms ₹ ....
ii. Admn. offices and
reception counter ₹ ....
iii. Conference hall ₹ ....
iv. Restaurant, bar ₹ ....
v. Other misc. ₹ ....

Total ₹ ....

V. Pre-operative Preliminary Expenses:

i. Company formation and
other legal expenses ₹ ....
ii. Consultancy and project
report preparation ₹ ....
iii. Architect's fee ₹ ....
iv. Cost during construction ₹ ....
v. Other misc. expenses ₹ ....

Total ₹ ....

VI. Total Fixed Capital:

i. Land and site development ₹ ....
ii. Building and civil work ₹ ....
iii. Plant and machinery
equipment ₹ ....
iv. Furniture and fixtures ₹ ....
v. Pre-operative and pre-
liminary expenses ₹ ....
vi. Misc. fixed assets ₹ ....

Total ₹ ....

VII. Working Capital Per Month:

A. Staff and labour:

S.No.	Designation	Nos.	Rate of salary per month (₹)	Amount (₹)
1.	Manager	1	₹	₹ ....
2.	Inspection staff	2	₹	₹ ....
3.	Reception and admn. office staff	12	₹	₹ ....
4.	Kitchen staff	10	₹	₹ ....
5.	Attendants	30	₹	₹ ....
6.	Watchman and warden	15	₹	₹ ....
7.	Gardeners	5	₹	₹ ....
8.	Cleaners	5	₹	₹ ....
	Total			₹ ....

25% fringe benefits   G.Total

B. Utilities:
1. Power consumption   ₹ ....
2. Water   ₹ ....
3. Other consumable stores   ₹ ....

Total*   ₹ ....

C. Overheads:
1. Admn. expenses such as postage, stationery printing, telephones, telex, etc.   ₹ ....
2. Repair and maintenance   ₹ ....
3. Sales promotion and sales expenses   ₹ ....
4. Misc. expenses   ₹ ....

Total   ₹ ....

D. Raw material:
Kitchen expenses, eatable reqd. @ ₹ per room per day cost of the above per month   ₹ ....

E. Working capital per month:
i. Salaries and wages   ₹ ....
ii. Utilities   ₹ ....
iii. Overheads   ₹ ....
iv. Raw materials   ₹ ....

Total   ₹ ....

VIII. Total Project Cost:
i. Fixed capital   ₹ ....
ii. Working capital (2 months)   ₹ ....

Total   ₹ ....

IX. Annual Working Capital for the First Year at 50% Occupancy:
1. Salaries and wages   ₹ ....
2. Utilities   ₹ ....
3. Overheads   ₹ ....
4. Raw materials   ₹ ....

Total   ₹ ....

X. Annual Expenditures
i. Working capital   ₹ ....
ii. Interest @ 15% p.a. on total capital investment   ₹ ....
iii. Depreciation:
   a. On building @ 5% p.a.   ₹ ....
   b. On machinery and equipment @ 15% p.a.   ₹ ....
   c. On furniture, etc. @ 20%   ₹ ....

Total   ₹ ....

XI. Annual Receipts:
1. From routes (double bed) @ ₹ 600 each room   ₹ ....
2. Banquet hall @ ₹   ₹ ....
3. Shops office @ ₹ per shop per month   ₹ ....
4. Restaurant @ ₹ per day   ₹ ....
5. Misc. (laundry, swimming pool, parlour, etc.) at an average cost of ₹ per day   ₹ ....

Total*   ₹ ....

Gross profit per year   ₹ ....
1% profit on sales
Rate of return on investment   ₹ ....

*Final figures derived from actuals as per market rates from place to place.

HOTEL TARIFF

Hotel tariff or the room rate is determined by several factors. To maintain services, every hotel needs some kind of investments for wages, electricity, taxes and for the purchase of different provisions. In case of new building, the cost of construction, cost of furnishing, cost of interest on loan, etc. are also to be considered at the time of fixing the tariff. For a new hotel, the return on investment with profit cannot be visible immediately, it will be visible only after it picks up the market.

Hotels, having multiple other services do well compared to the hotels having accommodation services only. Return from the sale of food is good. Hotels having restaurants can expect larger profit out of the food sales particularly that of breakfast and dinner. Hotels in comparatively isolated locations (forest hotels, wayside hotels) have good prospect for food sales. Hotels, thus may fix the tariff as per different plans. There are four different types of plans recognised in the hotel business. These are:

   i. American plan (AP) includes room rate plus all meals.
   ii. Continental plan (CP): Tariff includes room and continental breakfast.
   iii. Modified American plan (MAP): Tariff includes room rate, breakfast and any of the principal meal, i.e. lunch or dinner.
   iv. European plan (EP) includes only room rate.

In India, majority of city hotels (non-star categories) now charge only for room and this charges vary from ₹ 500 to ₹ 2000 per night or per 24 hours of occupation. This wide range of variation in tariff is due to the location, local competition and other services available to the hotels such as attached WC and bath, TV, quality of furnishing, restaurant, bar, etc. In almost all the hotels in the above tariff range, some kind of room service is available. Indian hotel room services can be considered a sort of valet service for the guest. This satisfies the guest as well as the workers engaged for the sevice for the extra over their wages (tips).

Star hotels have to follow certain guidelines for fixing tariff and the maximum limit cannot be exceeded without approval from the government. However, there is upper limit fixed. On the sale of food items or drinks, there is no upper limit. For groups of company's client and even for other guests, hotels are free to negotiate and they can fix tariff on mutually agreed terms. In the trade circle, this is known as discount. Sometimes off-season discount for family groups can be offered by the hotels for greater business and for the promotional purposes.

For large luxury hotels, star hotels, etc. government has fixed some luxury tax (15%), expenditure tax (20%), etc. This affects the hotel tariff but government is getting revenue. However, it must be remembered that hotels need introduction of new facilities, renovation, etc. and for this and for meeting the higher price index of the commodity, there is a need for fixing the tariff for a particular period only. Regular guest must be informed of the changes of hotel tariff to avoid their confusion.

INCENTIVES EXTENDED TO HOTELS AND MOTELS LOCATED WITHIN THE STATE OF WEST BENGAL

Hotels and motels have been recognised to be an important component for the development of tourism in the state and accordingly incentives in different forms are being extended to such units both by the Commerce and Industries Departments and also by Cottage and Small Scale Industries Department of the State Government.

Incentives allowed by the Cottage and Small Scale Industries Department are applicable to units having fixed capital investments in land, building and machinery not exceeding ₹ 20 lacs. The incentives have been specified under notification no. 1949-GOT (SI)/12554/83 dated 22.4.83. The scheme envisaged extension of certain benefits and incentives to Cottage and

Small Scale Industries. Hotels and motels have also been termed 'Industries' for being eligible under the scheme vide notification no. 3354-GOT (SI)/125-119/83 dated 26.9.83. The incentives available under the scheme of S&SSI Department may be summarised as follows:

i. **Subsidy towards consultation service*:**
   a. For consultancy fees up to ₹ 2,000/- – 100% of the fees
   b. For fees up to ₹ 5,000/- –₹ 2000/- + 75% of the balance
   c. For fees up to ₹ 14000/- –₹ 4,250 + 50% of the balance
   d. For fees exceeding ₹ 10,000/- – ₹ 6,750/- +25% of the balance subject to a maximum of ₹ 10,000/-

ii. **Subsidy towards rent on land:** This is applicable in the case of units in occupation of the land allotted by West Bengal Industrial Infrastructure Development Corporation, WBSIC or other development agencies of the state or central government in a backward area.
   a. For the first 2 years —100% of the rent paid by the unit
   b. For the next 3 years — 50% of the rent.

iii. **Subsidy towards rent for sheds:** This is for the units located in the sheds of Industrial Estate run by WBSIC, not applicable to hotels and motels.

iv. **Subsidy on fixed capital investment:** 15% subsidy on fixed capital investment for a new unit being set up in a backward area or an existing unit in such an area going for substantial expansion.

v. **Subsidy on captive power generation set:** Subsidy to the extent of 23% of the capital investment subject to the ceiling of ₹ 1.5 lacs for purchase/installation of a captive power generating set.

vi. **Subsidy on cost of transformer/power line:** 20% subsidy on the cost of drawing HT/LT power line and transformer.

vii. **Subsidy in consumption of power:** New units or the existing units undertaking substantial expansion located in areas outside the areas covered by the Calcutta Electric Supply Corporation will be entitled to a subsidy amounting to 30% of the bill for consumption of power.

viii. **Subsidy on interest on term loan:** Subsidy up to a maximum of ₹ 10,000/- in any particular year, payment of interest on term loan secured from West Bengal Financial Corporation by any unit having a total investment in land, building and machinery not exceeding ₹ 2 lacs and situated in a backward area.

ix. **Subsidy on interest on working capital loan:** 3% subsidy on working capital loans received from banks/financial institutions by units undertaking substantial expansion in a backward area.

x. **Subsidy as rebate on raw material:** This is applicable to artisans and units for production of handicrafts, not applicable to hotel industry.

xi. **Special employment subsidy:** Units located all over the state employing additional person on a regular basis on or after 1.4.82 will receive special employment subsidy to the extent of 15% of the annual wage bill excluding bonus.

xii. **Subsidy on stamp duty and registration fee:** New units or the existing units going in for substantial extension in an area will get subsidy of the entire amount of registration fee and stamp duty paid by it for execution of purchase or lease deeds.

xiii. **Return of octroi/entry tax:** In case of new units in backward areas, the entire amount of octroi duty/entry tax paid by it for a period of 3 years from the date of commencement of production, processing or servicing, will get return of the entire amount of octroi duty/entry tax.

---

* Value charges on periodic notification figures based on available information

xiv. **Return of sales tax as interest free loan:** A new unit will be entitled to return by way of interest free loan of sales tax paid by it for 2 years after availing of the sales tax holiday, as admissible under the statute. For the existing units undertaking substantial production in KMDA area, the period of calculations is 5 years and for units outside KMDA area, the period is 7 years.

All such loans are unsecured and interest free and payable in three equal annual instalments after 10 years from the date of first disbursement of the loan.

xv. Entrepreneurs belonging to ST/SC communities as also those who are physically handicapped will get additional subsidy on all the items at the rate of 50% over the rates admissible to normal categories.

Besides incentives applicable under Incentives Scheme of the Cottage and Small Scale Industries Department for small scale units having capital investment of not more than 20 lacs, the Commerce and Industries Department extends special benefits in the shape of incentives to hotel under West Bengal Incentive Scheme, 1978 as notified vide resolution no. 6501–Ind/PL dated 30.9.78. The incentives applicable under scheme of Commerce and Industries Department may be summarised as follows:

Such incentives are available to new hotel units set up in any area which is termed backward area, i.e. any area of West Bengal excluding the developed areas of KMDA including the area of Nadia district within the KMDA areas.

i. 15% development loan
ii. 15% state investment subsidy
iii. 75% contribution towards the cost of feasibility study
iv. Return of sales tax paid by it at loan
v. Term loan up to limit of ₹ 60 lacs to a single unit eligible for refinance assistance.

INCENTIVES AVAILABLE TO HOTEL INDUSTRIES IN ORISSA

i. **Industrial Co-ordination Bureau:** To assist entrepreneurs in completing the various formalities necessary in setting up a hotel project, the state government has set up a single point contact forum known as Industrial Coordination Bureau. The Bureau's function is to ensure that all applications for power, water, loan assistance, etc. are disposed of within 21 days.

To review the progress of the new project, a high-level Nodal committee headed by the Chief Secretary and consisting of Secretaries of the concerned department has also been set up.

ii. **Foreign investment division:** To attract non-resident Indians to invest in Orissa, a foreign investment division will be set up to give publicity to the various incentives offered by the state government.

iii. **Infrastructure Development Corporation:** Would develop sites, contract industrial sheds, provide water supply, housing facilities for workers to help entrepreneurs set-up industries in the state.

iv. **Preparation of feasibility report:** The state government has agreed to bear the cost of preparation or feasibility reports subject to a maximum of 1% of the fixed assets.

For project feasibility reports prepared by the state government or through them, entrepreneurs are required to pay 25% of the cost as security deposit, which is refunded after the project is implemented. Where entrepreneur obtains the feasibility report through his own source, the actual costs of the feasibility report up to a ceiling of 1% of the fixed assets will be reimbursed the entrepreneur after completion of the project. Further the state government also reimburses the entire cost of preparation of project/feasibility report of the entrepreneur subject to a maximum of 1% of the fixed assets which are less than ₹ 1 crore or ₹ 1 lac plus half per cent of the additional fixed asset beyond ₹ 1 crore subject to a maximum of ₹ 3 lacs.

v. **Capital investment subsidy:** New industrial units and existing units going in for expansion are eligible for 15% subsidy on fixed capital investment subject to maximum of ₹ 15 lacs.

vi. **Octroi:** Machinery and spare parts of new industrial units and existing units going in for expansion are exempt from payment of octroi. Raw material is exempt from octroi from the date the industry goes into period of 5 years production.

vii. **Stamp duty and registration:** Industries are eligible for exemption from payment of stamp duty and registration charges for government land and building.

viii. **Sales tax/VAT:** Exempted from payment of sales tax for purchases of machinery, spare parts and raw materials.

ix. **Water:** Shall be charged at no profit no loss basis.

x. **Land:** To estimate procedural delays, ground rent shall be charged at the uniform concessional rate for government land as given in Table 2.2.

Development cost in case of developed site or area, would be limited to the actuals calculated on no profit no loss basis and would be recoverable in 10 equal instalments. Other states have their own calculations which are more or less in the same pattern.

Table 2.2: Uniform concessional rate for government land			
Areas	*Rate*	*Mode of premium*	*Ground rent payment*
Bhubaneswar Cuttack–Jagatpur Choudwar Paradeep Rourkela Chattarpur Berhampur Gopalpur Barbil Joda and Talcher	₹ 2500 per acre inside the municipal area and within 8 km municipal area	Three equal annual instalments	10% of area rated
All other notified urban areas	₹ 1250 per acre inside the notified areas	Two equal annual instalments	10% of area rated
All other areas per acre	₹ 625/- instalment	One	10% of area rated

Laws and Acts Governing Hotel and Catering Business

Hotels like any other business or industry are within the jurisdiction of the laws of the land. But because of its very different style of business like keeping inmates—domestic and foreign, supply of foods and drinks to the guests, etc. several moral and statutory obligations are required to be followed by the hotels.

In hotels, guests stay on the basis of some unwritten contract, but it is the duty of the hotel-keeper to look after the safety and security of the guests and their properties. Starting from small injuries to even death due to any negligence, the hotelkeeper may be held responsible for the damage and may be convicted. Hotels are often used by anti-social as well and it is also the duty of a good hotelkeeper to keep away from ill reputation which might follow due to the association of anti-social elements staying in the hotel as guests and using the hotel premises as the centre of their activities. It is a very common phenomenon throughout the world to utilise the hotel premises for secret deal, exchange of narcotics, illegal flesh trade, etc. In all these, huge money is also involved. Under the above, the responsibility of the hotelkeeper multiplies a few-fold not only to protect the innocent honest guests but also to keep the business going without legal hustling with the authority and the government.

However, the following laws, acts and licences are directly and indirectly related to the hotel business. Depending upon the location of the hotel, various state laws and acts are binding on the business of hotel.

1. If the hotel is a rented one, then the Tenancy Act is involved in case of disputes.
2. Police licence need to be obtained for business.
3. Municipal licence/trade licence is required within the Kolkata Corporation area.

The following requirements are necessary for obtaining licence for food business in Kolkata city.

  i. Sufficient means of effectual drainage shall be provided.
 ii. An adequate supply of filtered water shall be provided and in no case there shall be any tap for unfiltered water for any domestic or even washing purpose.
iii. The floor shall be properly paved or cemented.
 iv. The walls shall be repaired and lime-washed.
  v. The furnace and the cook room shall be so constructed and ventilated and shall be of such a nature and so used to prevent any nuisance from smoke.

vi. A separate cook room shall be provided and in no case road-side or removable oven shall be allowed.

vii. A proper washing place for cleaning utensils used in preparation and services of food shall be provided; the same being fitted with glazed tiles or properly paved and drained.

viii. A proper receptacle made of galvanised iron for the storage of adequate filtered water for purpose of drinking, cooking and washing utensils shall be provided; the same being fitted with a tight fitting lid or cover at the top with lock and key arrangements and a tap at the bottom for draining and cleaning the residual water which shall be placed on a stand or a platform at least 3 feet above the ground level.

ix. A suitable receptacle for keeping foodstuff in such a manner as to prevent contamination thereof by dust, flies, vermin or any other things likely to affect in such a way as to make it injurious to human health shall be provided.

x. A covered metallic coal reservoir shall be provided.

xi. A covered metallic refuse bin shall be provided.

xii. All cups, saucers, dishes and other utensils and all receptacles and vessels shall be thoroughly scoured and cleansed with running water and later on by hot water before they are used.

xiii. A notice in vernacular prohibiting spitting on wall and floor shall be exhibited and sufficient number of spittens shall be provided which shall be placed conveniently and cleansed and disinfected daily.

xiv. The table used in preparing, keeping or serving food shall be marble topped or zinc plated or some other non-absorbent material.

xv. No person shall be allowed to sleep or keep any bedding and clothing inside a dining room or kitchen.

xvi. The original licence granted by the Corporation and a signboard in front of such premises in a prominent place containing the number granted the name of the keeper or owner, the licence number granted by the corporation and a certified copy of the law properly framed shall be exhibited.

xvii. Utmost cleanliness shall be observed at all times.

xviii. The keeper of any eating house, tea-shop, hotel or boarding house shall not sell or expose for sale or store any unwholesome or adulterated foodstuff within the premises where he carries on business.

4. Hotel stores LPG or may have petrol pumps, etc. the explosive licence is to be obtained for that purpose.

5. Depending upon the gadgets used and depending upon the use of fuels, hotel comes under.

a. Smoke Nuisance Act

b. Pollution Control Act

6. In the course of midnight entertainment programme, cabaret show, etc. violations of the provisions of Immoral Traffic Act may lead to problems and closure of the hotel premises.

7. Hotels employ various categories of staff and as such there are statutory obligations for their benefits and working conditions of the workers. In general, these are looked after and governed by the laws and Acts of the Labour Department of Government of India. The Acts are as follows:

a. Payment of Wages Act

b. Engagement of Child Labour Act

c. Punishment and Dismissal Act
d. Minimum Wages Act
e. Payment of Bonus Act
f. Payment of Gratuity Act
g. Apprenticeship Act
h. Subsistence Allowance Act
i. Terminal Benefits Act
j. Employees' Provident Fund Act
k. Fatal Accident Act
l. Employees' State Insurance Act
m. Workmen's Dispute Act
n. Trade Unions Act
o. Sarai Act
p. Environment Regulation Act
q. Legal Metrology Provision
r. Fire Safety Regulation
s. Police Provisions
t. Pollution Act
u. Food Safety Standards Act 2006

In addition to the above brief list, the employees leave, leave travel concession, overtime, holidays, weekly off, etc. are regulated by set of norms based on rules, acts and laws, etc. But because of social system, weak enforcing authority, the industrial climates even in the 5-star hotel sectors are not free from disputes.

8. Hotels are required to keep profit and loss accounts and other statutory books of accounts as required by the Sales Tax and Income Tax Act for their annual verification, etc. In case of disputes things will have to be settled through relevant Income Tax Act, Sales Tax/VAT (value added tax), etc.

9. Hotels required the supply of electricity and sometimes boilers are installed in hotels. All these require conformity and approval as per the relevant Boiler Act, Electricity Act.

10. Most hotels serve alcoholic beverage made locally or from imported supplies. These alcoholic beverages services are strictly regulated by "Excise laws" and under the regular supervision of "Excise inspectors". Excise licence department's rules vary from state to state as also the excise licence fees, etc. Hotels do require strict compliance of the excise directives and maintenance of liquor sales records. For the violation, strict penalties along-with the suspension or cancellation of licence are imposed.

11. Hotels deal with food. It is a well-known fact that a large number of people suffer from gastrointestinal and bacterial disease due to contaminated food and drinks. For the sake of unhampered reputation and peaceful business, the hotels and catering establishments must be aware of the implications of the sale of adulterated foods or sale of stale foods and foods otherwise unfit for human consumption. Even the drinking water must conform certain standards and then only it becomes fit for drinking and known as "potable water". In order to obtain the details, the hoteliers may contact the local public health authority for guidelines.

Prevention of Food Poisoning

'Prevention is better than cure', it is important that simple precautions are taken to prevent occurrence of food poisoning.

Precautions

i. Do not allow flies to get access to the kitchen. A fly carries with it six million bacteria every time it flies from one place to another.

ii. Hot or damp garbage should not be thrown in dustbin, instead placed in the air-conditioned room (garbage store).

iii. Skins of vegetables, fruits, used tea leaves, etc. should be collected in old newspapers and then kept in waste paper basket.

iv. Do not keep the garbage bin in the kitchen. Keep it a little away.

v. Even food preparation for pets should be kept covered and not exposed.

vi. If it is not possible to clean the dinner plates and vessels immediately after meals, at least pour water on them and keep away from kitchen. Flies are attracted by dumped vessels. The best method is to clean the vessels and plates immediately after meals.

vii. Napkin and cloth used for wiping vessels should be washed daily with soap water, dried and then only used.

viii. Kitchen cupboards and tables should preferably be painted with blue colour. The blue colour keeps flies away from such a coloured furniture.

ix. Provide all kitchen cupboards and windows with fly-proof netting.

x. Do not use the handkerchief used to wipe face or cleaning the nose, while you are working in the kitchen. This will prevent pathogenic bacteria to enter into the kitchen.

xi. Do not use broken or damaged cups or saucers, because dirt accumulates on such damaged articles and gets contaminated with bacteria.

xii. Clean vegetables, fruits, fish and meat before use.

xiii. Wash hands everytime you enter the kitchen.

xiv. Preserve food preparations, raw vegetables or fruits in a freeze.

xv. Use home-made powdered spices.

Hotels and Restaurants

Hoteliers and restaurant owners should in addition to the precautions listed above, take the following steps in their own interest and in the interest of public health.

i. Raw and uncooked food articles, vegetables, etc. should be stored in cupboard provided with fly-proof nettings.

ii. The walls and floors of the kitchen should be smooth, plastered and capable of being washed.

iii. Provide a ceiling to the kitchen. Provide all windows and doors with fly-proof netting and automatic closure system. This will prevent entry of rats, flies, birds, insects, rodents, lizards in the kitchen.

iv. Prepared food should be stored in fly-proof containers.

v. Use only potable water for preparation of articles.

vi. Clean the cooking vessels regularly.

vii. Wash walls, windows, frames of the kitchen with detergent and soap water, use a disinfectant regularly. Similarly, cups and saucers, spoons, cooking vessels, etc. should be cleaned with hot soap water, dried and then used.

viii. Workers should be medically examined before appointment, and regular medical check of the workers should be carried out in every 6 months.

ix. Workers suffering from cough and cold should not be allowed to work in the kitchen.

x. Provide necessary toilet facilities to workers. Ensure that they wash their hands and feet every time they enter the kitchen.

xi. The importance of personal hygiene and cleanliness should be impressed on the workers.

Food industry and trade are regulated basically by the following legislations and orders (Table 3.1).

Rules for Licencing of Food Articles

Under the provisions of the Prevention of Food Adulteration Act, licence for manufacture, sale, stock or distribution of certain food articles is

Table 3.1: Regulatory legislations and orders for food industry and trade	
1. Agricultural Procedure (Grading and Marketing) Act, 1937	Director of Marketing and Inspection, Ministry of Agriculture and Irrigation
2. Fruit Products Order, 1955	Department of Food, Ministry of Food and Civil Supplies
3. Sugar (Control) Order, 1966	Director of Sugar, Ministry of Agriculture and Irrigation
4. a. Vegetables Oil Products (Control) Order, 1947 b. The Solvent Extracted Oil, Deoiled Meal and Edible Oil (Control) Order, 1967 c. Vanaspati Control Order, 1975	Directorate of Vanaspati, Ministry of Civil Supplies and Cooperation
5. Technical Standardisation Committee (TSC), 1914	Army Purchase Organisation, Department of Food
6. Export (Quality Control % Inspection) Act, 1963 and Rules, 1964	Export Inspection Council of India, Ministry of Commerce
7. Indian Standard Institution and ISO-provisions	ISI, Department of Industrial Development, Ministry of Industry and Civil Supplies
8. Meat Food Products Order, 1975	Directorate of Civil Supplies and Cooperation, Ministry of Food and Civil Supplies
9. HACCP Provisions	A global standardisation
10. Food Safety Standards	Act 2006
11. The Standards of Weight and Measure Act, 1976	Department of Civil Supplies and Cooperation, Ministry of Commerce
12. Consumer Protection Act	
13. Import Provisions	Custom Authority

required. Though all food articles have to be manufactured, stocked, sold or distributed in conformity with the provisions of the Prevention of Food Adulteration Act and Rules made thereunder, these required to be sold under a licence and according to the conditions of licence. Thus, for manufacture, stock, distribution or sale of food articles, a valid licence is required. The violation of rules or conditions of licence would be an offence under the Act.

Rules framed by the Government of India and state governments stipulate the conditions of a licence and also specify the conditions of a licence for compliance. For the sake of convenience, it will be helpful to know some of the terms defined under the Maharashtra Prevention of Food Adulteration Rules, 1962.

i. Manufacturer means a person engaged in manufacturing of any article of food for the purpose of sale.

ii. "Wholesale dealer means a person engaged in the business of sale of any article of food to another trader for the purpose of resale". If such wholesale dealer sells to another retailer 500 gm of food article, even then it shall be sale by wholesale.

iii. "Retail dealer means a dealer in any article of food, other than a wholesaler dealer." It means that he does not sell any article of food for resale to another trader.

It is necessary to obtain a licence for the following food articles under the prevention of Food Adulteration Rules, 1955 made by the Central Government.

a. Milk of all classes and nomenclatures.

b. Milk products, such as cream, malai, curd, skimmed milk curd, chenna, skimmed milk chenna, cheese, processed cheese, ice cream, milk ices, condensed milk, sweetened and unsweetened, condensed skimmed milk, sweetened and skimmed milk powder, skimmed milk powder, partly skimmed milk powder, khoa, infant milk food, table butter and desi butter.

c. Edible animal body fats such as beef fat, mutton fat, goat fat and lard.

d. Edible vegetables oils.

e. Edible fats including margarine.

f. Pulses, gram, nuts, starches, sage, suji such as maida, besan and articles made of flour including bakery products.

g. Non-alcoholic beverages such as carbonated water, tea, coffee, cocoa and chicory.

h. Spices and condiments, whole or ground including saffron, curry powder, mustard seeds, asafoetida and compounded asafoetida.

i. Sweetening agents such as sugar, honey, gur or jaggery.

j. Flavouring agents, antioxidants, emulsifying and stablising agents and preservatives permitted for use in food and container and wrappers.

k. Artificial sweeteners.

l. Confectionery, sweetmeats and savoury.

m. Ice candies.

n. Edible gelatin.

o. Molasses.

p. Copra.

q. Meat and meat products, fish and fish products.

r. Silver leaf for human consumption (aluminium leaf not for use).

s. Sweetened ice thread candies and similar products.

t. Sugarcane juice, fresh fruit and sarbats (not covered under the fruit products order).

u. Prepared food and ready-to-serve food.

v. Import and sale, storage of beverages. Central Government rules and regulations are modified in Food Safety Standard Act 2006.

Staff Management in Hotel

Hotel has many different functions to be performed for varieties of people. All hotels thus need suitable manpower in the different departments. The global pattern of staff ratio per room is also not of uniform nature. The ratio between hotel room and staff varies from place to place and from hotel to hotel. On an average, the ratio between room and staff is 1:1 to 1:3. In the Western world, in spite of greater mechanisation and organised management, there has been often shortage of suitably trained manpower in the hotel industry till today. The turnover of the hotel labour is also quite high in the hotel industry in spite of comparatively decent working environment. In India, the profile of hotel staff is little bit typical compared to that of other countries of the West. There are several reasons for this situation. Here we see the first generation hoteliers mostly and also the first generation consumers. Lack of technical and managerial know-how encourages the hoteliers to run the business on the basis of personal design. The hoteliers have their own method of calculating the profit and so long they get that they are happy and do not bother much for employees' benefit, productivity, waste control, quality improvement, marketing, etc. Their attitudes toward changes with time are in general indifferent and slow. But it is well known to the business world that by application

of suitable management techniques, desirable improvement with additional profit can be achieved and for all these it is not always necessary to have investments beyond capacity.

Managing of staff comes under the purview of personnel management. The basic principle of personnel management as applicable in other industry is more or less applicable in the hotel industry as well. All the more in hotels, sales of services are the major activity rather than sales of any tangible products produced from a factory. The organisation in the hotel business by and large depends on the people who are engaged in carrying out the numerous tasks in hotels. The outline of various categories required for managing the different departments of the hotels has been detailed out as model at the end of the chapter dealing with the individual hotel departments.

In a large hotel with clear cut division of work, organisational pattern, etc. the problem of personnel management becomes easier to handle. Negotiations can be achieved at time of disputes and conflicts with the unions which invariably exist in large establishments. However, this must be kept in mind that the so-called trade union activity is not appreciated in hotel business because of its typical nature, odd working hours and involvement of human factor in rendering services to the guests.

Smaller hotels exist in a large number than large hotels all over the world and are relatively free from trade union activity. Although the individual work force of the smaller hotels may become the member of some outside unions or central body as member and those organisations in turn may like to intervene in the matter of disputes with the employer for their member worker.

Sources of Manpower for Hotel Catering Industry

The industrial concept for running hotel catering industry is relatively a new concept among the entrepreneurs. In majority of the places, the functioning in hotels is organised on the basis of domestic concept, i.e. employing a few servants and maids to look after the jobs of washing, cleaning, arranging beds, sweeping, cooking and serving of foods picked up from the local source irrespective of the desirable personality, health condition, education, previous training or concept of the job. Employers often calculate the tips as part of the wages to some workers and negotiate with them accordingly. There are very little avenues for the dedicated workers to go up to secure any senior and responsible positions. Workers frequently change over from organisation to organisation principally for higher pay and even for marginal benefits. One can hardly find workers serving in a small/medium hotel more than 5 or 6 years, in India. For a good management of hotels, this situation should be changed and the employers must prepare themselves to regard the hotel workers with some amount of dignity and respect. Employers should value the need of institutional training and education of the workers side by side with the value of the job or in-house training for suitable manpower in running hotel business. Government of India in collaboration with the various state governments has opened up several hotel catering institutions for training and education of future manpower for hotel catering industry. These institutes impart junior level worker's training,

supervisory level training as well as some kind of managerial training.

Many large chains such as ITDC, Taj, Welcome Group of Hotels keep close touch with these institutions for picking up suitable manpower for their hotels over and above their own training institute.

Small hotels, usually look for multipurpose workers at salaries minimum they can negotiate. These hoteliers sometime pay wages below the government recommended minimum wages and as such these negotiations become a contract of exploitation which frequently does not last long resulting into the fresh procedure of advertisement, selection, wage negotiation, recruitement, and induction into the service, etc. causing service gaps in the business.

The hotels proprietor in the first place must know his manpower requirement. There is no fixed standard nor there is any standardised method to arrive at a general decision regarding the manpower requirement for hotels. This is widely variable because of the nature of operations, places of operation, size of the establishments, nature of management, policy, types of services to be offered, etc. Thus, the hotel and catering industry is extremely diverse in terms of the types of jobs it offers and the nature of the individuals it requires. Occupations range from the unskilled porter to the highly talented manager of an International hotel. However, various occupations in hotel industry can be grouped as under.

1. Managerial occupations
2. Food preparation occupations
3. Food service occupations
4. Bar service occupations
5. Housekeeping occupations
6. Uniformed staff occupations
7. Clerical and office occupations

All these occupations generally come under unskilled, semiskilled, skilled and managerial categories. In general, the higher number of staff employed by the hotel catering industry belong to the unskilled to semiskilled categories. In India, like many other countries, the general feeling of staff in the private hotel industry is that of low prestige and poor pay. Bulk of the unskilled workers in many developed countries comprises women but in India the workers in hotels are largely male workers. In our country, because of disorganised and less mechanised environment, part-time workers cannot function or fit in the day-to-day hotel jobs. Waiters, receptionists, chefs can be grouped as skilled and semiskilled persons of the hotel industry though in most cases their skills are confined to non-managerial skills. It is also difficult to search the managerial skills and acumen among the fresh products from hotel management schools.

The hotel catering industry has been expanding with considerable speed and dimension. With its developments, the conditions of services have changed and are still changing particularly in the developing countries which have relatively new tourists industries. The changes in the industry have altered methods of operations which have in turn changed traditional conditions of employment and working environment. Introduction of power-operated gadget, new sources of cooking fuel, use of packaged items, etc. require greater skill and knowledge for persons handling them. However, despite these changes there is a little doubt that many sectors of the industry remain very traditional in their treatment of manpower. Many establishments have not made any effort to adjust conditions of employment with the demand of time and situations. The reason for this has been particularly due to the availability of manpower (unskilled in particular), and lack of conciousness among customers.

Personnel management is the management of people at work and management of their relationships with the establishments. The following are the main areas for the personnel manager.

1. Manpower recruitment, selection, placement and termination

2. Terms of employment, methods and statements of remuneration
3. Working conditions and service of employees.
4. Formal and informal communication and consultations
5. Negotiation and application of agreement on wages and working conditions.

Manager should not consider the occupation of personnel in isolation from the lives of the individual who work within the firm and the society in which the company operates. All personnel have a responsibility to keep the firm within the laws and within the normally accepted moral standards of the society. Personnel must ensure that the company has an efficient worker's group capable of achieving its objectives. In order to maintain an efficient work force, the manager's duty is to formulate appropriate personnel polices. All oragnisations large and small have some form of personnel policies, which are usually passed on by words of mouth to the employees. Policy can be defined as the predetermined course of action to guide an organisation towards its objectives.

Thus, policy should precede actions and not otherwise. In hotel industry, the clear cut policy in the area of personnel is very important so that they are not burdened with conflicts and constraints in carrying out consistent actions. In service industries the efficient use of staff is imperative to good service and higher returns.

The nature of policy is often influenced due to the factors as under:

i. *The location and size of the operation:* Resort hotels, small seasonal hotels prefer to have part-time, seasonal staff, whereas larger organisation may have more formalised policies to create uniformity in their operation between units.

ii. *The quality and expectation of the workers:* Some establishments decide to recruit only unskilled workers to save on wages, whereas others have policy to engage trained qualified people.

iii. *The type of employee:* Organisations employing outstation workers, part time workers, female workers, must adjust their policies accordingly.

iv. *Government legislations:* This exerts strong influence on the specific character of personnel policies. If legislation dictates requirements, unfair dismissal, minimum wages and other service conditions, the adequate changes in the personnel policies will have to be effected. Many organisations dodge these legislations causing undesirable conflicts with the workers.

Wages and Tips in Hotels

In the hotel industry, the wages of the workers, the working hours of the workers are to be carefully evaluated for good relationship between the fellow workers and between workers and management.

In the absence of any standard or nationally accepted wage policy of the hotel workers in India, certain standard salient points should be carefully considered in the matter of wage determination for the employees.

Most of the industrial disputes are concerned with aspects of pay. A study indicates that 84% of the working days lose in strikes related to pay. Thus the wage aspect is particularly important in this industry because unsocial hours, overtime working, etc. are an accepted practice in hotel industry. Workers' wages can be determined on the following factors:

1. Basic wages are based on negotiations with the employees or from the prescribed scale of pay for the job.
2. Tips which naturally place certain jobs at an advantage, notably waiters, porters, room staff, etc.
3. The system by which tips are pooled and distributed under a point system. The system is open to manipulation and abuse also.
4. Service charge which may be made, usually at the level of 10% is distributed to all staff, but is resented by those who are usually

benefitted from tips who may solicit tips additionally.

5. Commission on sales is a valuable element in the remuneration of many wine waiters, drivers, countries and front office staff who sell local tours, etc.
6. Bonuses may be paid for productivity and merit, but most commonly for long service in view of the problem of labour turnover. This is now paid to all the staff once in a year.
7. Food and lodging may be provided at rates which represent a considerable saving to certain employees, in areas where private accommodation is scarce and expensive such as Mumbai, New Delhi, etc.

In some situations, the basic wage bill form a minor part of the total payments. In developing countries, high-tipping Western guests may double the employees' wage.

A good employer thus, has to analyse the total picture and formulate a wage policy not only to have a satisfied work force but to retain them from employers who often lure them with other incentives, fringe benefits and higher pay. Contemporary pay scales of some different categories of hotel workers are given in Table 4.1.

Duty Hours of the Hotel Workers

It is an accepted phenomenon that hotel workers have unsocial working hours, night duties, odd timing for lunch, dinner, etc. Because of the nature of the business, it has to be managed through proper management by organising the service time schedules, mechanisation, etc. Improvement has been achieved to reduce the odd working hours. In general, there is no global agreement over the working hours in hotel catering industry. ILO published a monograph from which it is seen that the working hours vary widely from country to country and also in the same country. For example, workers work for 10–12 consecutive hours in India, 176 hours in 4 weeks in Japan,

Table 4.1: Contemporary pay scale of some different categories of hotel workers

Designation	Qualification and experience	Pay range/total emoluments
General Manager	Graduate + MBA or Degree/Diploma in hotel management from a recognised institute in India/abroad with a minimum of 10 years experience in a 5-star hotel should have been in a senior position.	₹ 10–15 lacs per annum
Deputy General Manager	Graduate + MBA or Degree/Diploma in hotel management from a recognised institute in India/abroad with minimum of 7 years experience in a 5-star hotel should have been in a senior position.	₹ 6–8 lacs per annum
Restaurant Manager	Degree/Diploma in hotel management from recognised institute with a minimum of 6 years experience in a deluxe restaurant, of which at least 3 years should have been in a senior supervisory position.	₹ 5–8 lacs per annum
Assistant Restaurant Manager	Degree/Diploma in hotel management from a recognised institute with at least 3 years experience in the F & B service on a 4 or 5-star hotel in a senior supervisory capacity. Knowledge of foreign language is desirable.	₹ 50,000 per month
Maitre de'hotel	Degree/Diploma in hotel management from a recognised institute with at least 2 years experience or NCTVT certificate with 5 years experience. Knowledge of a foreign language is desirable.	₹ 10,000–20,000 per month
Chef D'Range	Degree/Diploma in hotel management from a recognised institute or NCTVT certificate or one year craft course in restaurant and counter service from a recognised institute with 3 years relevant experience. Knowledge of a foreign language is desirable.	₹ 8,000–20,000 per month
Demi Chef D'Range	H.S. with NCTVT certificate in the relevant trade with 2 years experience in relevant field.	₹ 8,000–15,000 per month
Bar-man	H.S. with NCTVT certificate or one year craft course in relevant and counter service from a recognised institute with 2 years experience in relevant field.	₹ 10,000–20,000 per month
Commis D'Range	H.S. with NCTVT certificate or one year craft course in the relevant trade.	₹ 8,000–12,000 per month
Executive Chef	Will be responsible for the preparation of continental and Indian cuisine, ordering, menu	₹ 10–20 lacs per annum

(Contd.)

Table 4.1: Contemporary pay scale of some different categories of hotel workers *(Contd.)*

Designation	Qualification and experience	Pay range/total emoluments
	planning, porting control, etc. Preference will be given to Diploma holder having a minimum of 10 years experience. Non-diploma holders should have 15 years experience.	
Sous Chef (Indian)	Minimum of 7 years experience as Assistant Chef with 2 years experience in a similar position or 3 years Diploma in hotel management with 3 years experience in relevant field.	₹ 2–3 lacs per annum
Chef	Minimum of 5 years experience as Chef-de-Partie with 1 year experience in a similar position or 3 years Diploma in hotel management with 2 years experience in relevant field.	₹ 6–10 lacs per annum
Commis Grade-1 (Indian/ tandoori/continental/ bakery confectionery)	H.S. with NCTVT/craft course certificate in relevant trade. Candidates with experience in the relevant field may get preference.	₹ 15,000–25,000 per month
Utility Worker	VIII pass candidates with NCTVT/craft course certificate in cookery/bakery and confectionery/ pantry may be given preference.	₹ 8,000–12,000 per month
Kitchen Steward	Degree/Diploma in hotel management of NCTVT/craft course certificate with 3 years experience in relevant field.	₹ 8,000–12,000 per month
F.O. Manager	Degree/Diploma in hotel management from recognised institute with a minimum of 6 years experience in a 4 or 5-star hotel of which at least 3 years should have been in a senior position in relevant field.	₹ 2–3 lacs per annum
Assistant Manager Front Office	Degree/Diploma in hotel management from a recognised institute with at least 3 years experience in F.O. Dept. in a 4 or 5-star hotel in a senior supervisory capacity.	₹ 2–3 lacs per annum
Front Office Assistant Grade-I	H.S. with 3 years Diploma in hotel management with 2 years experience or graduate with 5 years relevant experience.	Negotiable salary
Front Office Assistant Grade-V	Higher Secondary with NCTVT/craft certificate in the trade of hotel reception and book keeping or 3 years diploma in hotel management or graduate with 2 years experience.	Negotiable salary
Bell Captain	H.S. with 3 years Diploma in hotel management with 2 years experience or graduate with 5 years relevant experience.	Negotiable salary

(Contd.)

Table 4.1: Contemporary pay scale of some different categories of hotel workers *(Contd.)*

Designation	Qualification and experience	Pay range/total emoluments
Porter-cum-page Boy	Matric/H.S. with 5 years relevant experience	Negotiable salary
Doorman	Matric with 5 years relevant experience	Negotiable salary
Public Relation Officer	Graduate or diploma in hotel management with 5 years experience in public relation. Candidates must have pleasing and charming personality. An excellent command over English is essential. Knowledge of a foreign language will be an added qualification.	Negotiable salary
Public Relation Assistant	Graduate from a recognised University with minimum 1 year experience in public relation have pleasing and charming personality and ability to converse fluently in English and Hindi.	Negotiable salary
Telephone Supervisor	Graduate with diploma in PBX/PABX from recognised institute with at least 3 years relevant experience.	Negotiable salary
Telex/Telephone Operator	Graduate with certificate course in telex operation/PBX/PABX from a recognised institute with at least 1 year relevant experience.	Negotiable salary
Sales Manager	Graduate or MBA from a recognised University perferably with 3/4 years experience in a hotel, airline or travel agency. The incumbent must have ability in the preparation of special promotions, advt. concepts and media selection, etc.	₹ 2–4 lacs per annum
Purchase Manager	Graduate preferably with a degree in business management, having 5 years relevant experience in hotel or food processing industry.	₹ 2–4 lacs per annum
Assistant (stores & purchase)	Commerce graduate with one year experience in relevant field.	₹ 20,000–40,000 per month
Storeman	Matric with 5 years relevant experience	₹ 20,000–40,000 pm
Manager Housekeeping	Degree/Diploma in hotel management from a recognised institute with a minimum 6 years experience in a 5-star hotel of which at least 3 years should have been in a senior supervisory position.	Negotiable
Housekeeper Chamber Maid	H.S. with 2 years relevant experience NCTVT certificate holders may get preference.	Negotiable

(Contd.)

Table 4.1: Contemporary pay scale of some different categories of hotel workers *(Contd.)*

Designation	Qualification and experience	Pay range/total emoluments
Maint. Engineer	Degree in electrical/mechanical engineering with 5/7 years experience in repairs and maint. of pumps, water tube boilers, diesel generators, water treatment plants. Preference may be given to those having experience in a 5-star hotel.	₹ 3.5–6 lacs per annum
Technician Grade-II	ITI with licence where needed/requisite trade certificate and 5 years relevant experience.	₹ 15,000–30,000 per month
Security Officer	Graduate, JCOs or equivalent rank with 15 years of service in Army/Navy/Air Force/Police.	₹ 15,000–30,000 per month
	A commissioned officer from the police on deputation is desirable.	₹ 15,000–30,000 per month
Security Guard	S.S.L.C. with 1 year relevant experience	On contract
Personnel Manager	Graduate with 10 years experience. Diploma in personnel management desirable and MBA.	₹ 3.5–6 lacs per annum
Steno-typist	Graduate with 100/40 wpm in shorthand and typing with one year experience.	₹ 30,000–50,000 per month
Clerk-typist	Graduate with typing speed of 40 wpm. Diploma/certificate in secretarial course desirable.	₹ 30,000–50,000 per annum
Accounts Manager	CA or AICWA with a minimum of 2 years experience in commercial accounts. Preference will be given to those having experience in hotel accounting.	₹ 2–4 lacs per annum
Assistant	Commerce graduate with 2 years relevant diploma/certificate in secretarial course desirable.	Negotiable
Assistant (Accounts)/ Night Auditor	Commerce graduate with 2 years relevant experience	Negotiable
Accounts Clerks	Commerce graduate with 2 years relevant experience.	Negotiable
Bill-cum-cash Clerk	Commerce graduate with one year relevant experience. NCTVT certificate holders may get preference.	Negotiable
Life Guard	H.S. with certificate in swimming and knowledge of first aid and life saving services with 5 years relevant experience.	Negotiable

(Contd.)

Table 4.1: Contemporary pay scale of some different categories of hotel workers *(Contd.)*

Designation	Qualification and experience	Pay range/total emoluments
Swimming Pool Attendant/Cleaners	Middle pass with 2 years relevant experience. Relaxable for candidates with more experience.	Negotiable
Garden Supervisor	Diploma in horticulture / agriculture with 2 years experience as garden supervisor.	Negotiable
Gardener	VIII pass with 2 years experience as gardener	On contract
Driver	Matric, clean driving licence with endorsement for light and heavy vehicle and driving experience of 5 years. Motor mechanic course (ITI) desirable.	₹ 10,000–15,000 per month
Training Manager	Diploma in hotel management from a recognised institute having a minimum of 5 years experience in the profession should have at least 1–2 years experience of teaching in a catering institute or industry.	₹ 6–12 lacs per annum

43 hours per week in France, 55 hours per week in Pakistan, etc. The 40 hours a week has become a common practice in many countries. The whole concept of maximum hours of work varies depending upon the following:

- On the general normal daily, weekly hours of work
- On the official status of the establishment
- On the category of the establishment
- On the age of the workers
- On the sex of the workers
- On the occupation of the workers
- On the status of the workers
- On the way the hours of services divided up
- On the form of remuneration
- On the distance between worker's home and place of work
- On the basis of available residential accommodation close to the working place
- On the basis of local labour rules and regulations
- On various non-specified considerations.

Thus, it is seen that hotel managers or proprietors should also formulate and plan hotel jobs to be carried out in the manner to best utilise the working hours and also the utilisation of staff in the so-called off-hours of the employees but otherwise on duty.

SOME EXAMPLES OF TASKS WITHIN VARIOUS HOTEL JOBS

A good personnel deparment must be aware of the various tasks and task elements within a specific hotel job. This is also very important for the matter of selection of right type of employees and also for formulating training methodologies.

Following are some typical tasks which are further broken down into various tasks elements for better understanding of the task elements, required skills, knowledge and attitudes of the employees as guidelines.

1. Job: Preparing for the Guest Arrivals

Task elements:
- Checking correspondences
- Sorting correspondence into alphabetical order

- Preparing rooming lists
- Adjusting for unconfirmed bookings
- Preparing bedroom forms
- Preparing bedroom cards
- Informing other departments
- Modifying of expected VIP arrival
- Allocating rooms
- Making special advance arrangements
- Arranging meeting procedures
- Arranging mail, telegrams/fax/e-mail messages
- Preparing expected arrivals list

Skills, knowledge and Attitudes Required

Ability to:
- Comprehend, read, write, calculate and communicate
- File and retrieve
- Make decisions
- Co-operate with other departments

Knowledge of:
- Legal aspect
- Company policy
- Foreign languages at appropriate level
- Facilities and layout
- Reservation procedures
- Reservation system
- Transport arrangements

Attitudes:
- Accuracy
- Discretion
- Pleasantness

2. Job: Dealing with Arrivals

Task elements:
- Opening and closing vehicle doors
- Assisting passengers
- Greeting
- Opening and closing hotel doors
- Conveying arrivals to reception desk
- Marking luggage for delivery to room
- Storing heavy luggage

Skills, Knowledge and Attitudes Required

Ability to:
- Comprehend, read, write, calculate and communicate
- Carry and move quickly and efficiently
- Deal with large groups

Knowledge of:
- Complimentary salutations
- Layout of hotel and surroundings
- Hotel facilities
- Checking arrival procedures

Attitudes:
- Dexterity
- Willingness

3. Job: Receive Guest

Task elements:
- Greeting guests
- Confirming length of stay
- Registering guests
- Dealing with problems arising
- Allocating rooms
- Explaining hotel facilities
- Writing and handling over bedroom cards
- Handling over mail and messages
- Handling over room keys
- Dealing with group arrivals

Skills, Knowledge and Attitudes Required

Ability to:
- Communicate effectively in the mother tongue in speech and in writing
- Communicate effectively at appropriate level in a foreign language
- Write clearly
- Use judgement in allocating rooms
- Deal with problems
- Discriminate

Knowledge of:
- Legal aspects of registration
- Complimentary exchanges
- Hotel layout and facilities
- Passport formalities

Attitudes:
- Helpfulness
- Discretion
- Accuracy

4. Job: Dealing with Mail

- Receiving incoming mail
- Date and time stamping
- Sorting
- Receiving/recording registered mail
- Distributing
- Dealing with packets and parcels
- Dealing with mail for future guests
- Dealing with mail for departed guests
- Checking and emptying mail boxes
- Checking mail rack
- Dealing with outgoing mail

Skills, Knowledge and Attitudes Required

Ability to:
- Comprehend, read, write, calculate and communicate

Knowledge of:
- Mail delivery systems
- Registered post system
- Layout of the hotel
- Sorting procedures
- Disturbing procedures
- Forwarding procedures
- Postal information

Attitudes:
- Discretion
- Initiative
- Accuracy

5. Job: Cleaning Restaurant Equipment

Task elements:
- Cleaning ashtrays
- Cleaning hotplates
- Cleaning spirit lamps and service and heaters
- Cleaning sideboards
- Polishing cutlery
- Polishing glassware
- Polishing crockery
- Cleaning silver
- Cleaning condiment equipment
- Cleaning wine service equipment
- Cleaning trays
- Cleaning bread baskets
- Cleaning cigar and cigarette service equipment

Skills, Knowledge and Attitudes Required

Ability to:
- Identify restaurant equipment
- Identify various materials of equipment
- Identify various cleaning materials
- Choose appropriate way to polish and clean equipment
- Choose cleaning materials and use them

Knowledge of:
- Effects of various cleaning materials
- Storing equipment and cleaning materials
- Standards of hygiene and safety

Attitudes:
- Care
- Tidiness
- Willingness

6. Job: Preparing Service Tables and Sideboards

Task elements:
- Setting outsideboards and service tables, laying table clothes on service tables
- Equipping sideboards with:
  - Service spoons and forks
  - Dessert spoons and forks
  - Soup, tea and coffee spoons
  - Fish knives and forks
  - Meat knives and forks
  - Side knives
  - Linen
  - Trays and salvers
  - Ashtrays
- Stocking condiment containers
- Placing the condiments on the sideboards
- Stocking bread containers
- Stocking butter containers

Skills, Knowledge and Attitudes Required

Ability to:

- Understand table plan
- Select cloths for service tables and side-boards
- Lay table cloths
- Identify condiments
- Handle condiments and equipment
- Handle bread and butter
- Handle equipment

Knowledge of:

- The arrangement of the equipment condiments and accompaniments on the sideboards and services table
- The characteristics of condiments and accompaniments
- The storage of condiments and accompaniments
- Standards of safety and hygiene
- Establishment policy

Attitudes:

- Accuracy
- Care
- Efficiency

7. Job: Preparing the Room Service Pantry

Task elements:

- Checking the store
- Obtaining supplies
- Storing the supplies including refrigerated goods
- Cleaning resultant equipment
- Cleaning room service trolleys
- Cleaning toasters
- Cleaning coffee machines
- Starting coffee machines

Skills, Knowledge and Attitudes Required

Ability to

- Identify room service equipment
- Write supply order
- Store supplies
- Handle goods and equipment
- Use gueridon trolleys
- Prepare toast
- Prepare coffee, tea and other beverages
- Use room service lifts
- Recognise malfunctions of equipment

Knowledge of:

- Equipment and goods needed in pantry
- Operation of relevant mechanical equipment
- Hygiene and safety lifts
- Departments of the establishment

Attitudes:

- Accuracy
- Care
- Efficiency

Sanitation, Safety and Security in Hotels

Hotels and places, where tourists, stay, eat and have entertainment, need to have a reasonably safe and secured atmosphere. People do not like to suffer while on recreation or on visit to places away from home and in unfamiliar conditions. Injuries may leave the tourist in a very difficult situation apart from physical and mental agonies.

The word sanitation has root in the Latin word 'sanus' meaning sound and healthy. In general, it is found that if the environments within the premises and outside the premises are kept and looked after as per various norms and standards, then sanitation can be achieved to a great extent. Bad sanitation is due to non-observance of right methods of food storage, waste disposal and apathy towards control of insects and rodents. It may be stated that for appropriate procedures adequate knowledge is essential. In India, the toilets, baths, urinals, wash-up areas, in general, are poorly maintained. Special emphasis must be given for the improvement of the above, particularly for hotels, motels, and other tourist places.

SANITATION IN FOOD ESTABLISHMENTS

The essential elements of health protection in food establishments are as follows:

1. Adequate refrigeration equipment and prompt and proper refrigeration (at 70°C) of perishable and prepared foods.
2. Cooking at proper internal temperature of pork (67°C), poultry, and all stuffed meats (74°C); holding of hot foods at 60°C, and thorough reheating (71°C) of refrigerated cooked food before service.
3. Use of wholesome food and food ingredients.
4. Cleanliness and good habits of personnel hygiene in employees, who should be free from any communicable disease or infection transmissible through food or food service; a minimum handling of food.
5. Clean surface for food preparation and adequate and proper equipment that is easily washed and sanitised.
6. Structurally sound, clean facilities in good repair and adequately lighted and ventilated premises that can be properly cleaned.
7. An adequate supply of potable water both hot and cold, detergents and equipment for the cleaning and sanitization of dishes and utensils.
8. Proper storage of refuse and disposal of all liquid and solid wastes.
9. Control of rodents, flies, cockroaches, and other vermin and proper use and storage of pesticides.

Hygiene

All employees should wear clean outer garments, preferably uniforms supplied and cleaned daily by the management. The employees should maintain a high degree of personal cleanliness and observe hygienic practices while at work. Hands should be thoroughly washed after every break in food service operations, particularly after use of the toilet and after the handling of raw foods such as poultry and meat. A conveniently located wash basin with water, soap, and clean towels (in addition to those placed in the toilets) is necessary to facilitate personal hygiene and cleanliness.

Architectural Features

The structural soundness of the building housing the food establishment, the facilities provided, and the layout of equipment are also important for food hygiene. All outside openings should be screened during the fly season with 1.5 mm (16-mesh) screens. The building should be of rodent-proof construction. Walls, floors and ceilings should be easy to clean. Adequate lighting and ventilation are needed in all working areas, storage rooms, passages and toilet rooms. Toilet and hand-washing facilities must be provided for the use of employees. Hot and cold water under pressure and proper sewage or other waste-water disposal system are essential requirement. Advice on the layout and design of new food establishments and the placement of equipment should be obtained from professional designers and health authorities.

Equipment Layouts

These should be planned efficiently as well as for easy cleaning and appropriate servicing. Temperature regulated equipment should properly conform the temperature standards and in general, equipment should be corrosion-resistant and non-toxic.

BASIC PLUMBING PRINCIPLES

While certain details of plumbing installations vary with location, the basic sanitary and safety principles are the same. The essential criteria are as follows:

1. **Potable water supply.** All permanent premises intended for human habitation shall be provided with a supply of potable water. Such a water supply will not be connected to unsafe water source nor will it be subject to the hazards of backflow or back siphonage. Faucets should not be provided on non-potable water lines in areas accessible to the public, but if this is unavoidable, the outlet must be labelled as unsafe drinking and should preferably be operable only by means of a special key.

2. **Adequate water requirements.** Plumbing fixtures, devices, and accessories shall be supplied with water in sufficient volume and at pressures adequate to enable them to function properly and without undue noise under normal conditions of use.

3. **Water conservation.** Plumbing will be designed and adjusted to use the minimum quantity of water consistent with its proper performance and cleaning requirements. Rain water harvesting system may be used, when possible.

4. **Danger of explosion or overheating.** Devices for heating and storing water shall be so designed and installed as to guard against dangers from explosion or over-heating as well as risks of carbon monoxide poisoning and asphyxiation.

5. **Disposal of wastes.** Every building with installed plumbing fixtures will be served by an adequate sewage system.

6. **Plumbing fixture.** Plumbing fixtures shall be made of durable, smooth non-absorbent and corrosion-resistant materials and shall be free from concealed fouling surfaces. All such fixtures shall be protected by an air gap between the water outlet and fixtures overflow rim, or by other approved means,

from the possibility of backflow or back-siphonage.

7. **Drainage system of adequate size.** The drainage system shall be designed, constructed and maintained to prevent undue noise and vibration fouling, deposit of solids, and clogging; it should be so arranged that pipes may be readily cleaned.

8. **Durable materials.** The piping of the plumbing system will be of durable material free from defective workmanship and be designed and constructed to give satisfactory service for a reasonable lifespan.

9. **Liquid sealed traps.** Each fixture directly connected to the drainage system will be equipped with a liquid-seal (non-siphoning) trap to prevent the entry of sewer gas into the building.

10. **Prevention of contamination.** Proper protection shall be provided to prevent the contamination of food, water, and similar materials by backflow of sewage. When necessary, the fixture, devices or appliances shall be connected indirectly (through an air gap) with the building's drainage system.

11. **Lighting and ventilation.** No water closet or similar fixture will be located in a room or compartment that is not properly lighted and ventilated.

12. **Prevention of sewage overflow.** Where a plumbing drainage system is subject to backflow of sewage from the sewer, suitable provision will be made to prevent sewage overflow in the building.

13. **Proper maintenance.** Plumbing systems shall be maintained in a safe and serviceable condition in relation to both mechanical functioning and health.

Cleaning and Sanitisation of Eating and Drinking Equipment

All crockery, glassware, cutlery, and kitchen utensils should be cleaned and sanitized after use. Food preparation and serving equipment should be cleaned and sanitized as needed during the day. Separate arrangements are usually provided for washing and sanitizing glassware and cooking pots.

The use of approved types of automatic machines is recommended wherever possible for washing crockery, glassware, and cutlery. After washing, the items should be rinsed in hot water at 82°C. Handwashing of eating and drinking equipment is acceptable, if all items are thoroughly cleaned with hot water and an effective detergent and then rinsed in hot water at 82°C for at least 30 seconds (2 minutes is recommended). A booster heater in the form of an electric immersion heater or an under-sink gas heater is generally used to keep the water hot, and long-handled baskets are essential for submerging washed dishes and utensils in a separate hot water sink. Immersion in a chlorine solution (or other disinfectant) providing at least 53 mg/l of available chlorine for at least 2 minutes may also be acceptable to the health authorities in place of hot water disinfections. However, chlorine or other chemical disinfections should not be used as a substitute for hot water. Washed and rinsed articles should be left in a rack or on a draining board to drain and air dry. When water at 82°C is used to sanitize equipment after washing, the heat retained is usually enough to produce rapid drying. Dry clothes should not be used because they may cause contamination and are in any case unnecessary, if dishes and utensils are properly cleaned and sanitized in ideal situation.

Protection of Chilled Foods

Refrigeration equipment should be capable of maintaining perishable food at a temperature of 7°C or below. Frozen foods are generally kept at or below −18°C. The refrigerator capacity should be adequate for refrigeration at all times. Cooling of cooked foods at room temperature prior to refrigeration permits the growth and multiplication of bacteria and the production of toxins that can cause food-borne illness. Prepared perishable food should be sliced or cut into small portions, if necessary placed in shallow pans to a depth of 5–8 cm (2–3 in) in refrigerator within half an hour.

Protection of Hot Food

Equipment used for keeping or serving hot food should be capable of maintaining the food at a temperature of at least 60°C. At this temperature, the growth of pathogenic organisms is inhibited and in many cases, the organisms are destroyed.

Catering

When food is prepared for off-the-premises services for consumption, special additional measures are necessary to prevent food contamination and to inhibit the growth of microorganisms. This applies to catering operations for airlines, railways, and bus companies, to group catering as well as to restaurants that use ready prepared foods. The food should at all times be protected from contamination by airborne contaminants, insects, rodents, and from handling during storage, transportation and service.

Special precaution should be taken to keep hot foods hot, and cold foods cold until they are served. If it is impracticable or undesirable to keep prepared foods at or above 60°C, they should be chilled promptly and refrigerated and heated at 70°C just prior to service. Facilities for maintaining proper refrigeration temperatures and for heating foods should be available at the places of service.

Insect and Rodent Control

The proper management of hotels, tourist establishments and recreation areas include effective control of insects and rodents since their presence can reduce the attractiveness of the area. In addition to being a nuisance, many are actual vectors of disease while rodents can also cause economic damage and fire hazards. Many insecticides and rodenticides are available for controlling insects, pests and

rodents but the use of these chemicals must be considered a supplement to basic sanitation and other physical and biological control measures aimed at the elimination or control of breeding areas.

Some basic sanitation measures that are particularly applicable in hotels, motels, eating places, camping sites, and resort areas are as follows:

1. Proper storage, collection, and disposal of refuse, including manure.
2. Elimination or reduction of breeding areas by control of water impoundments, clearing of bush, and use of rodent-proof construction methods for all buildings and other structures.
3. Screening of doors and windows in all places of work, preparation and service areas.
4. Special sanitation precautions for all food storage, preparation and service areas.
5. Pest control operations at regular intervals or as needed.

The success of insect and rodent control measures depends largely on the existence of a basic sanitation and environmental control programme. For example, the draining or filling of mosquito production. Various chemicals can be used as larvicides to destroy the larvae and their breeding habit and adulticides to control the adult mosquitoes and may be in the form of residual sprays of dusts, fogs, or other aerosols such as those used in ultra-low volume applications. The objectives in pest control should be the application of a combination of physical, biochemical, chemical and educational measures to produce the best results with the least use of selective chemical poisons and the minimum hazard to men, domestic animals and desirable wildlife.

Mosquito Control

Control must include attack of both larvae and adults, preference normally being given to the control of larvae. Larvae can be controlled through the following measures:

1. Empty and remove all water containers such as cans, jars, buckets, etc. from the area.
2. Eliminate depressions, mud flats and other water holding areas by draining or filling.
3. Clear of vegetables likely to harbour larvae and if possible, allow water levels to fluctuate to reduce the production of larvae.
4. Treat areas of water with light oil or insecticide against larvae.
5. Introduce top-feeding minnows, goldfish, or similar fish into ornamental pools to consume larvae.
6. Screen or cover cisterns, water tanks, and other permanent water containers.

The residual fumigant dichlorvos is effective against the adult mosquito for periods of 2.5–3.5 months in enclosed spaces. One dichlorvos dispenser per 28 m^3 (1000 ft.^{3}) of space has been recommended but such dispensers should not be permitted in rooms where infants or sick or aged persons are confined or in areas where food is prepared or served.

Fly Control

The primary sources of fly production are garbage and manure. The elimination of these sources is an essential step in the control of flies. Under warm weather conditions, the reproduction cycle from egg to larvae to pupa to adult winged fly requires approximately 1 week. For this reason, garbage collection and manure removal should be carried out twice weekly. Doors and windows should be fitted with 1.5 m (16-mesh) screens and all screen doors should open upwards. Residual sprays, where permitted, will control most species of flies. Walls and vegetation, especially near refuse containers may be sprayed with diazinon, dimethoate, dichlorvos and dichlorvos impregnated baits for effective control of adult flies. In addition, pyrethrum can be used as an indoor space spray for quick knock-down of flies.

Cockroach Control

Cockroaches live and breed in moist dark places behind baseboards, around plumbing, under refrigerators and in cupboards, pantries and kitchens. They are found in piles of debris, rubbish and garbage at outdoors. Cleanliness is the first objective in the elimination of cockroaches. All food-handling areas should be cleaned frequently.

Diazinon, propoxur, dichlorvos, or malathion can be sparyed into places where cockroaches hide or travel. Painting a band of insecticide 10 cm wide around the base of a room has been found to be the most effective in eliminating cockroaches. The band must be continuous to assure contact with the cockroaches as they enter or leave the room. To obtain a quick kill in heavy infestations, the use of aerosol formulations of pyrethrum or dichlorvos to flush the insects from their hiding places is of value.

Bedbug Control

Bedbug infestations can usually be controlled by the application of an insecticide to baseboards and mouldings, wall crevices, bedsheets, springs and mattresses. Residual sprays containing lindane, fenchlorphos or malathion have been found effective. A pyrethrum spary applied to baseboards and other protected places just before the residual spray will cause the bedbugs to migrate and ensure contact with the residual spray. Pyrethrum can also be added to the residual spray. Mattresses should not be soaked with the spray. Infant bedding or cribs should not be treated.

Scorpions, Spiders and Wasps Control

Scorpions, certain spiders such as the black widow and brown spiders, and wasps are dangerous to man. Recognition and avoidance of dangerous species and elimination of their hiding and resting places are the best protective measures. Chemical control of scorpions can be obtained by spraying their hiding or nesting places with carbery (1–2%), chlordane (2%) or dieldrin (0.5%), malathion (2–3%). Nests of wasps yellow-jackets and hornets can be treated with water-based sprays containing propoxure (0.5%), carbaryl (2%), 1 diazinon (0.5%) or malathion (2%).

Rat Control

Domestic rats and mice live in close proximity to many, being found in living quarters, kitchens, storerooms, outbuildings and animal quarters. In addition to their disease transmission potential, rats can cause substantial structural damage and consume and contaminate large amount of foodstuffs.

A rat consumes about 8 kg (17 Ib) of food (including garbage) yearly and can produce 4 or 5 liters a year.

Rat control should start with a survey to determine the source of the rats and the conditions that encourage the infestation. This is followed by a programme to: (1) kill the rats by poisoning; (2) remove their sources of food and water; (3) eliminate their harbourages and make them ratproof and (4) educate and obtain the cooperation of the people affected. If the food supply is removed first, and if this is done effectively, the rats will migrate to other areas, making their poisoning more difficult. Trapping is of limited value, since it eliminates only a small proportion of the rat population. These measures by themselves are usually inadequate, unless they are supported at all times by proper food storage and the collection, storage and disposal of refuse. Continuous surveillance should be maintained and places where rodents have been gnawing to gain entry to a building should be flashed with metal; doors are particularly vulnerable to rodent attack. Materials stored in the open, in sheds or in buildings should be stacked at least 30 cm (1ft) above the ground or floor.

The use of poisons for rodents is a secondary control measures. Anticoagulant poisons are preferred because of their low levels of toxicity for men and domestic animals; they include coumafurl, diphacinone, pindone and warfarin. While the relative degree of hazard for men varies according to the poisoning of the poison employed. Extreme care should be taken in distributing and placing all poison baits. Every possible precaution should be taken to prevent risks to man and animals, particularly children and domestic pets, and the contamination of food. The rodent proofing of structures, elimination of food, water, and harbourage for rodents, and maintenance of proper sanitation should eliminate rats and there should be no need to use poisons for rodent control. However, these control measures are rarely carried out with complete effectiveness and continual surveillance is necessary.

Extreme care should be taken in the transportation, storage and use of insecticides and rodenticides to prevent health and environmental problems arising from their improper use. New insecticide formulations and rat poisons are continually being developed. The chemical compounds mentioned in this chapter as being suitable for pest control, are judged to be the best available. The situation may change, but the pesticides mentioned will probably continue to be produced and used for sometime to come.

Sanitation Aspects of Swimming Pools

Many different types of swimming pools are found in recreational areas. The designs and operational requirements vary with the type of pool and are discussed briefly here. New pools generally incorporate filtration, recirculation and chlorination. Guidance should be obtained on the design and operational requirements of swimming pools and plans should be approved by the health authorities before construction begins and before any equipment is purchased. The following basic criteria should be met in the design and operation of pools for public use.

1. The pool should be properly located to reduce air-borne contamination by dust,

algal spores, leaves, etc. The location should not encourage non-swimmers to congregate near the pool. The area around the pool should be drained and fanced.

2. A supply of approved water must be available for filling and regulating the level of the pool. There should be no direct connection between the drinking water system and the pool water system.

3. The pool should have a capacity adequate for the expected use by bathers, swimmers, etc.

4. Approved materials should be used in the construction.

5. The design should not include features that could create accident hazards, e.g. sloping walls, inadequate depths of water for diving, excessively steep bottom slopes in the bathing area, and inadequate walkways or decks around the pool.

6. Provision should be made for continuous purification of the water in the pool. Where the water is recirculated, purification can be achieved by a turnover rate of 4 times per 24 hours with filtration and the use of a disinfectant such as chlorine to provide a bactericidal residual at all times.

7. Surveillance should be maintained to prevent bathers with communicable disease, open wounds, infected sores, or skin disease from using the pool.

8. There should be continuous supervision of pool used by trained lifeguards and operating personnel.

9. The pool and its related facilities, particularly the recirculation and disinfection equipment, should be properly maintained. Warm water showers can reduce the amount of pollution introduced by bathers.

10. Regular bacteriological and chemical sampling of the pool water should be carried out during heavy use. Daily testing for free available residual chlorine and of the pH is required before and during use of the pool.

11. Rules and regulations governing the use of the pool should be pasted in a conspicuous place for the information of pool users.

Standards for the guidance of swimming pool operators are discussed below. Pool owners and operators should adhere to established criteria and standards of this type as a protection against legal claims that might arise. (In some countries, standards and permits are issued for operation of swimming pool.)

Swimming Pool Operation

The sanitary quality of swimming pool water is determined by certain bacteriological, chemical and physical tests. Some of the important tests and the standards used are described in American Public Health Association's publication. Briefly, the standards are as follows:

• pH	7.2–8.2
• Alkalinity	At least 50 mg/l
• Clarity	A 15 cm (6 in) black disc. on a white field should be readily visible at the deepest point.
• Plate count	Not more than 15% of samples over a considerable period of time should contain more than 200 bacteria per ml
• Coliform organisms (dischlorinated sample of water)	Not more than 15% of samples over a considerable period of time should be positive (confirmed test) in any of five 10-ml portions or show more than 1.0 coliform organism per 50 ml in membrane filter test

The singlemost important factor in controlling the sanitary quality of swimming pool water is the maintenance of an adequate concentration of a satisfactory disinfectant in the water at all times, when the pool is in use. Chlorine, bromine, iodine, chlorinated cyanurates, ozone and ultraviolet lamps are also used but have not been widely adopted. Iodine has been used to a limited degree is reported to be more stable than chlorine in outdoor pools.

Safety

Safety consideration is very vital not only for the guests but for the welfare of the hotel staff also. The safe atmosphere free from possible accidental hazards not only provides peace of mind but also assures the operators not to worry about possible claims and compensations in lieu of damages to lives and properties of the guests. Some major safety precautions, applicable to hotel business in particular, are discussed on the following heads:

- Safe clothing
- Safe storing
- Safe floors
- Safe doors and drawers
- Safe with containers
- Fire safety
- Safe handling of food preparation equipment
- Safe handling of machines
- Safe handling of dishes
- Safe handling of knives
- Safe handling of insecticides and pesticides.

"Prevention is better than cure" and the person incharge of a kitchen should foresee the possible causes of accident and eliminate them.

Safety instructions should be pasted and the attention of the kitchen staff directed to them.

The phrase *"accidents are costly"* is true, if you think of the pain, the suffering, permanent injuries or even death they can cause.

Accidents are caused by not knowing the right way to do things, or by deliberately or thoughtlessly doing things the wrong way. Most accidents are caused because of excessive haste: Walk—don't ever run or slide.

Conditions within the work environment affect the safety of staff. A happy working environment which creates among staff an interest, satisfaction and contentment with work contributes much, not only to improve job performance, but also to reduce accident rate.

External environment influences the work performance. Illness at home, financial problems, etc. can cause absentmindedness which may lead to several problems such as fail to use a kitchen cloth when picking up a hot cooking pot. Similar faults can occur as a result of poor health.

Alcohol and drugs have serious effects upon the safety of the worker.

A serious view should be taken of staff who misbehave or who are involved in general horseplay within the kitchen, such action may lead to serious accidents.

Safety Precautions

Safety rules should cover personnel, equipment and premises from the following aspects.

Safe Clothing

- Ensure that protective clothing is worn.
- Safe shoes with closed toes.
- Sensible heels provide balance.
- Do not wear loose clothing, you may easily get caught.

Safe Storing

- When opening boxes, remove nails. Do not bend them down.
- Store heavy materials on bottom shelves, medium weight next above, light weight on top.
- Food containers should always be covered except when in the actual use.
- While opening anything, keep away from food containers, they might catch splinters, bits of paper wrapping, etc.
- Get rid of dirt, trash and grease to reduce fire hazards. Use ladders, not boxes and chairs to get things from high shelves. Avoid loosing your balance. Store full containers below eye level.
- Do not overload trolleys. Do not carry bulky objects too big for you to see over or around.

Safe Floors

- Keep floors in good repair, dry and clean.
- Clean up spillage promptly.
- Tiled floors may be slippery when weather is humid, be careful to avoid falls.

- Never leave utensils on the floor, someone might trip over them
- Walk—do not run or slide.

Safe Doors and Drawers

Be careful in closing drawers, they might pinch fingers and hand. Open and close doors by handles.

Safety with Containers

- Do not overflow containers.
- Place food scraps in protected sanitary containers.
- Keep hands out of mechanized garbage disposal machines.

Fire Safety

- Smoke only in designated areas.
- Report any fire immediately.
- Know where the fire extinguishers are located and how each should be used.
- Know the fire exits.
- Follow the fire exits.
- Have fire doors, exits, staircases clear of equipment.
- Do not let grease accumulate on grill canopies and filters.
- Point out the location of switches to shut off electricity supply.

Safe Handling of Food Preparation Equipment

- Use only dry cloth, towels, to handle cooking utensils.
- Lift edge over cover on side of pot away from you first, so that steam does not blast into your face.
- Do not peep into open steam kettles.
- Keep handles of pans away from the stove and out of the side so that they would not be brushed off.
- Get help in moving hot, heavy containers.
- Keep oven doors closed and out of aisle, when not in use.
- Ventilate a gas oven several minutes before lighting. Strikes matches away from clothing. Open gas gradually.

- Do not clean ovens and stoves before they are cool.
- Protect food from foreign substances.
- Avoid overfilling containers with hot liquids or foods.
- Warn service people of hot dishes.

Safe Handling of Machines

- Ensure that machines are kept in good working order and are operated correctly.
- Never sue any machines you have not been trained to use.
- Put plug into "off" position before cleaning or adjusting the machine.
- Check all switches.
- Do not start a mixing machines until the bowl or the kettle is locked.
- Always use the proper tool for pushing food into the grinder.
- Particular care must be exercised in cleaning the slicing machine. Pull the plug, turn the gauge to zero, do not touch the edge of the cutting blade, clean the blade from the centre out, while cleaning hold a protective cloth in the other hand to use in rotating the blade.

Safe Handling of Dishes

- Take care in handling dishes and glasses.
- Sweep up large pieces of broken glass with broom; use dampened paper towel to pick up silvers.
- Put broken glass or china in a special container.
- Chipped or cracked glassware should be discarded.
- If you suspect broken glass in soapy water, drain water first.
- Do not use cups to hold disinfectants and solvents.

Safe Handling of Knives

- Use knives correctly and store them correctly.

- Cut away from your body, and away from fellow workers.
- When drying a knife, keep sharp edge away from your body.
- Use cutting boards—never a knife edge against metal.
- Keep all knives in proper storage places, when not in use.
- Do not leave knives anywhere they cannot be seen (sink).
- A sharp knife is safer than a dull one.
- Sharpen knives properly. Remove any additional steel burns. Never reach for a failing knife.
- Use the knife for the use for which it is intended.
- Be careful when handling knives, pick them up by handles, not by blades.
- Knives should be carried with the blade point downwards.
- Never bone frozen meat, because knife would slip too easily.

Safe Handling of Insecticides and Pesticides

Because of the dangers involved, safety precautions for the use, storage and disposal of pesticides and other hazardous materials are listed below. They should be carefully observed.

1. Use a selective chemical that has the least effect on non-target species.
2. Treat only the area affected.
3. Take care to avoid the contamination of food and drinking water (for animals as well as men), streams and lakes and inhibited areas.
4. Time the treatments to coincide with the presence of the pests.
5. Use the most suitable chemicals with the minimum amounts needed to achieve the desired result.
6. Store chemicals in properly labelled containers out to reach of children and animals and away from food. Supplies should be kept in a separate locked building and away from housing areas, food, animal feeds, water supplies, children and irresponsible persons and above the highest possible flood level. Do not transport chemicals in vehicles used for carrying people, food, animals or animal feed.
7. Follow the directions on the label exactly in preparing chemicals and use the proper equipment, when applying them.
8. Avoid inhalation of dusts and fumes and contacts with the skin, personnel should wear protective clothing and headgear, and change their clothing and wash thoroughly with soap and water after applying pesticides.
9. Work in well-ventilated areas. In confined areas, wear an approved type of respirator. Wear a respirator for outdoor spraying or dusting organic phosphorus compounds.
10. Do not spray on a windy day. Protect guests from accidental poisoning by pesticides.
11. Dispose of used or leaking pesticide containers immediately by burial to a depth of at least 45 cm (18") in an isolated marked area, downhill and at least 60 m (200 ft) away from any water sources and 1–2 m above the highest groundwater level. Do not bury containers in sandy soil.
12. Never transfer pesticides to unlabelled or mislabelled containers. Keep in clearly labelled containers.
13. Pesticides are toxic and hazardous; use with extreme caution. Security in hotel business covers many things and depends upon the social, political and other considerations. The mode of security in hotels has to adopt appropriate methods. There are two major aspects of security. One for the protection of the guest. Second is to protect the hotel premises, its properties and records.

For guest protection major points should be taken care of are:

1. Responsibility begins at the time of registration. Once the guest is registered, the

hotel necessarily is concerned with the protection. The hotel staff simultaneously need to realise that it must also be concerned with protection.

2. The issue of guest security, including the guest's property, is one of the most difficult and delicate problems confronting hoteliers throughout the world. The difficulty is largely due to the fact that most incidents would have been avoided, if the guests themselves were not so careless. The delicacy of the matter revolves around the question of how one educates guests on the subject of self-protection without frightening them to the point where they avoid a particular property altogether.

Tent cards mention the availability of safe deposit boxes. Most guests ignore them. The answer to the question of guest education seems to lie with a combination of both verbal and written suggestions. For example, at registration time, front desk personnel should ask specifically, if guests would like to avail themselves of the safe-deposit-boxes. A written message would urge them (tent card in the guest room) not to leave valuables lying in drawers or on table tops, but rather to secure them.

3. An overwhelming majority of front desk personnel will make keys available upon request and without question. In most cases, one simply needs to walk to the desk to ask, may I have the key 926? Rarely will that person be asked for a name to check against the information rack and to verify registration before the key is handed over.

4. A far more suitable, but not less important consideration involves control over information regarding the rooms to which guests have been assigned. The ease with which room assignment data can be obtained frequently has been used to advantage by persons intent upon every form of mischief ranging from bombings, robberies and assaults to celebrities. Concerned hoteliers should instruct both, switch board and front desk personnel that room assignments are not given out upon inquiry. All telephone calls for guests simply need to be put through to them, and messages can be taken in their absence. Such steps are designed to help protect guests and their property. However, for the optimum effect, other security factors such as patrols, employees trainings must be considered. Nowadays metal detectors, explosive detectors are used in 5-star hotels.

Security of guest's automobiles must also be considered (including contents). Adequate lighting in the parking lot and area septation by patrolling are helpful measures.

For hotels, own security consideration should be securing the perimeter, i.e. perimeter security.

A. PERIMETER SECURITY

Entrances: The best way to provide this type of perimeter protection is to lock the door. Either using a key, also involving a person, or an electromechanical lock, controlled and activated at the front desk. The outside should be well illuminated. Nowadays CCTV is widely used for security purposes.

- This would be for the main door. One of the things to be considered by management is the period, if any, during which the main entrance can be secured.
- Two or possibly three other entrances still require attention in so far as perimeter protection is concerned:
  a. The receive entrance
  b. Employees' entrance
  c. Entrances from an outdoor swimming pool or car park
- **The receiving door:** Should be heavy duty steel or aluminium, overhead or side coiling type, approved as a fire door. A window-type vision panel and pass door may be included.

The receiving door should be opened only when necessary, preferably during predetermined hours.

- **The employees' entrance:** If it is possible to secure the main entrance during certain prescribed hours, it is equally possible to close the employees' entrance. The periods will be determined by the time of shift changes. This should also be a fire door with steel frame, easily observed by the timekeeper/security guard.

- **Other doors:** If there is a door, the sole purpose of which is to provide direct access between a swimming pool and/or a parking lot and the building, it would be closed and locked at all times, if activity is minimal. The hardware should be the same as that used on the emergency exit.

- **Light:** It is one of the least expensive but most effective deterrants to the commission of a wide variety of crimes.

B. SITES OF INTERNAL DESIGN

- **Security/timekeepers office:** Should enable them to see clearly and easily every person entering and leaving via employees/receiving entrance. If the time clock and time card racks are not located in his office, they should be placed where he can easily see them. The office itself should be large enough to accommodate facilities for the safe storage of parcels brought to work by employees. The room should also be assigned as the hotel security office.

- **Receiving clerk—cost controller:** These offices should be adjacent to the receiving platform. The receiving clerk should be located as close as possible to the receiving platform.

- Store rooms should be placed near the receiving area, foodstuff-dry store, general store, etc.

- Laundry, uniform issue and housekeeping operations should be in adjacent space.

- **Personnel office:** Should have easy access to the employees entrance, for would-be employees as well as those already employed. The corridor leading from the entrance to the offices should be easily observable by the timekeeper/entrances security guard.

- **Lobby:** In planning lobby designs, every possible effort should be made to avoid having the front desk cashier near an exterior door or near a stairwell. By the same token, the front desk should be so situated that duty personnel have a good view of the lobby generally, and an unobstructed view of both, the hotel main entrance and the passenger elevator bays. The space allocated for safe deposit boxes whether for guest or hotel use, may be incorporated with the front desk-cashier station, or it should be adjacent to and observable from that position. Nowadays small safe boxes are provided in individual rooms.

- **Telephone operating room:** Should not be near the stair. From an operational point of view, it is a sensitive activity requiring some degree of protection.

- The executives offices should be accessible, but not to the extent that needless traffic or disruption is encouraged.

- **Elevators:** In designing new facilities, it is best to avoid combining pool and service lifts. Otherwise, there will be virtually uncontrolled access to the entire house, especially between the hours of 11.00 p.m. and 7.00 a.m. when service is minimal, if not non-existent.

C. DOORS AND LOCKERS

Wood doors –	generally office rooms.
Steel doors –	store rooms, F and B lockers, walk-in refrigerators. Doors leading to head cashier's offices to telephone operation room
Fire doors –	must satisfy local requirements and acts, if any.

Electromechanical locks for these and for the main door. Pad locks for refrigerated units.

Time recording locks on store rooms, if available.

All types of stores, linen closets, housekeeping supply rooms, general stores, etc. should be locked at all times, except when appropriate staff are physically present.

D. STORAGE AND PROTECTION OF VALUABLES

- Safe deposit boxes are useful for the storage of guests' valuables. They also can be used by the hotel staff for the safe keeping of cashier's boxes and of certain select keys.
- Cash, other negotiables, and important records be stored in secured facility.

Other important records, such as personnel files, corporate records, insurance policies, accounts receivable and payable, or contracts, the same degree of protection should be given. They should not be available for unauthorised persons. Standard metal-like cabinets secured at the end of the working day are adequate.

There are other fields such as administrative, store, purchase and engineering and transport departments, where adequate security measures are to be taken to protect the loss and pilferage of properties in particular and to guard things from possible sabotage during the courses of strike, etc.

Hotels having outdoor garden chairs, decorative light fittings, etc. should accordingly arrange adequate security measures outside the buildings as well.

Key Control in Hotels

In hotels, guest rooms, entrances, doors to the various other rooms need locking system for security purposes. Age-old process is to lock the rooms with good quality locks, latches and by similar other arrangements.

In a very sophisticated hotels, electronic door locks are now being used in many countries. The system is based on electronically-linked computer located in a central place usually in the reception department. An electronic key looks like a piece of plastic coated card. Imprinted on the key are a number of notches making it useful for number of terms with different combinations. Electronic keys are lighter and easy to store and handle. Housekeeping staff are usually responsible for key control. Otherwise, the job is looked after by the security department staff or by staff deputed for the purpose by the management according to the hotel's policy.

In Western type hotels, the following key systems are in use.

1. Grand Master Key

Usually kept by the duty officer or by the housekeeping manager. It works on every lock in the building—internal as well as external.

2. Master Key

This key works on any internal door.

3. Sub-master Key

This is for a particular floor or for a section. It is kept by the floor housekeeper or by person responsible for the cleaning, etc. of the floor.

4. Room Key

This is given to the guest when he checks in and is taken back, when he checks out. It is usually attached to a long tag on which the room number is engraved. Sometime hotel's name, address and logo are also engraved or written. The purpose is for easy location and prevent it from easily lost during use.

All keys should be stored out of general view of the public. A record should be maintained each time after issue and return from the authorised staff for security purposes. It is also advisable to limit the number of unlocked entrances and exits. Never lend out room keys or master keys.

There should not be any hesitation to question suspicious looking persons in the premises. Housekeeping staff should undertake regular patrols in the premises. Housekeeping staff should undertake regular patrols around the building in and out. In many good hotels in India comprised key cards have been used, walkie-talkie, advance mobile monitoring and CCTVs are also widely used nowadays for guest's and property securities.

Front Office
(Guest Reception Department)

The activities in different parts of the hotel building are broadly classified into two areas, i.e. front office and the back office. In the front office, guests are in touch with the hotel staff directly soon after the entry and functions are visible to the outsiders. Back office activities are not easily seen by the guests but are felt only.

Reception department is the most important in the front office area, and the reception department differs from one hotel to the other. Guests visiting any hotel invariably have to approach the reception desk for information, assistance and answers to their problems and queries. In a small hotel, the reception practically manages the hotel activities. Receptionists in a small hotel will have to act as secretary to the proprietor as well. Reception is the eye and ear of the hotel establishment.

GENERAL METHODS OF HOTEL RESERVATION

Reservation through Telephones

It is quick, most people can have phone facilities these days. It also gives the receptionist the opportunity to clarify any necessary points about payments, arrival time and so on.

Reservation through Telex (fax, e-mail)

The telex combines the speed of the telephone with the performance of a letter. Most larger hotels now have a telex in the reservation department. There is less opportunity for misunderstanding because of telex. Another important advantage of the telex in reservation department is that a message can still be sent even though there is no one on duty at the other end. This is particularly important for hotels with an international clientele. A guest may book from Australia or America without having to check time to ensure that someone will be available to take the reservation. Equally, the hotel can fax or e-mail back a confirmation at anytime it wishes.

Reservation through Letters (Old System)

Hotels at holiday resorts sell much of their rooms by letters. A letter of reservation is also useful because the customer can explain the hotelier, when he will be arriving and any special request he may have. If the guest wishes to charge the account to his company then this can be mentioned in the letter. The hotel in turn can verify, if necessary.

Reservation through Personal Contact

Here there is a direct face-to-face contact between the customer and the receptionist.

Return bookings are frequently made in this way as a guest departs at the end of his stay. The receptionist has the opportunity to find out the maximum information and can answer any queries the guest have. At times, the receptionist may also be able to show the guest the room type and utilise some sales techniques to the potential customers.

Recordings the Reservation

Record work should be out of the sight of guest and the reception desk should look neat, clean and tidy.

Reservation Form

Telephone and personal bookings are normally noted on a reservation form. The use of a form for this purpose has many benefits:
- It acts as a check list to ensure that all the relevant information is obtained.
- It is helpful to tell the guest certain things about price, check in time, etc.
- It can be easily compiled and stored.

Some hotels combine the reservation form with the Registration Card on the other side so that all the relevant information is available together.

Confirming Reservations

Hotels in India usually confirm the reservation, if some advances are taken against booking. Otherwise, only large hotels confirm by sending letters, mails, telegram, telex, fax and e-mail.

Confirmation by Letters

As individual letters of confirmation become more expensive, some hotels use a standard letter of confirmation to guest booking accommodation. With the use of window envelopes, these can cut down clerical time considerably.

Cancellation Procedure

If a guest cancels the booking, then the reservation procedure has to be reversed; the booking is crossed through in the diary, the chart entry is erased. The hotel may ask the guest for loss, if

RESERVATION FORM

Name .... Mr		Arrival date ....
Mrs		am/pm ....
Miss		Days of stay ....
Address		
....		Departure date .... time ....
....		
Telephone, if any		No. of persons ....
Single	Double	
Twin	Suite	Rate ....
Remarks ....

Signature of the hotel staff
Date ....

the guest cancels the booking after contracting but the hotel must make every attempt to sell the room pomptly among the waitlisted guests or even to chance guests, if available. Apart from the above broad procedure, hotels formulate some policies to organise the total guest arrivals, last minute cancellations, VIP booking, etc. These days many hotels have to handle room reservation for guests from delayed or cancelled flights in odd hours with short notice. Hotel also devices own policy for 'Group bookings' by the tour operators on their mutually agreed terms and conditions.

Registration

There is a legal obligation in some countries for a hotel to obtain, and keep for 12 months, certain information about every person who stays there. The basic requirement is full name and nationality. If the guest is from overseas, then they have to fill in some additional form.

In addition to this legal minimum, hotel requests further information from guests sometimes, who stay with them. A home address and signature are asked for in all hotels. Others take the opportunity to find out more about their

HOTEL
SAMRAT INTERNATIONAL
Frazer Road, Patna-800 001

Full name *(Please print last name first)*	Date arrived Time
Complete Home Address	PASSPORT Date of birth .... Number .... Date issued .... Place of issue ....
Nationality	Purpose of visit .... No. of persons ....
Date of Departure	Probable destination and address
Date of arrival in India	Certificate of Registration Number .... Date .... Issued of ....
Duration of stay in India	Signature ....
Employed in India Yes/No	Room ....
Name and address of organisation	Rate ....
Payment will be made by	Receptionist's Signature ....
Cash .... voucher .... Cheque .... or	

customers by asking information such as purpose of visit, occupation, proposed method of payment and other details. These requests are for administrative purposes to ensure the smooth efficient running of the operation and marketing—where the hotel takes the opportunity to find out more about its customers' habits.

Guest Register

The age-old method of checking in guests is to use a register. This is a bound book ruled into column which the guest fills out on arrival. It is ideal for smaller hotels where guests arrive individually. A register provides a permanent record of guests staying in the hotel.

Disadvantages of Book Registration

If more than one guest comes to check in, their is long waiting. In the case of a group, this time could be considerable. Also the receptionist is unable to process registration information whilst a guest is checking in, so administrative delays could occur in notifying other departments and opening the bill. In this method, the guests find the opportunity to find out information about other people staying at the hotel causing disturbance to the privacy. To overcome this problem, separate registration cards are now widely used all over the world. These cards are recorded and kept properly then the procedure is quick and efficient.

Checking of the Recorded Information

The receptionist should always check the registration card or registration book once the guest has checked into and make sure that the card has been completed correctly and if there is a query, the receptionist can politely ask the guest for clarification. The receptionist can then inform the guest of the room number and the room rate. However, a receptionist must see the following carefully before allotment of room to the guest.

a. That the registration details are correct and legible.
b. That the details of the bookings have not changed.
c. That the guest knows the room rate and what it includes.
d. Whether there is any letter or message for the guest.

REGISTRATION CARD FORMAT

Full name.....................................	Other names ....
Home address	Date ....
Phone no., if any	Nationality ....
Arriving from	Going to ....
For overseas visitors only	Place of issue ....

Passport no. ....
Next destination ....

Signature of the receptionist

e. That the room is clean and ready in all respects.

f. That the guest has no bad records and is not blacklisted.

It is often noticed that guests are allocated the room on the basis of vacancy information only without ascertaining the actual 'readiness' of the rooms. This happens particularly in hotels where there is a little time between guest departures and guest arrivals. In such cases, the receptionist must tactfully handle guests without annoyance to them to allow time to the housekeeping department to make room ready. But the guests who have booked their hotels in advance, must not be kept waiting for their rooms to become ready under any circumstances. A careful and vigilant receptionist must take suitable decisions. It is also important to tackle things at the reception, when a guest desires to overstay and the hotel is otherwise booked.

Room Position

A prime need for every hotel reception is an accurate, up-to-date knowledge of the state of every room in the hotel. Hotel room may be in one of the stages as under:

a. Occupied

b. Vacant but not ready

c. Vacant and ready

d. Under renovation/repair (not fit for occupation).

e. Vacant but needs urgent attention for fault rectification

f. Vacant and ready but not occupied, are to be "now show"

g. Occupied but needs attention for some fault.

A room status system must show these positions for handling guest reservation properly and to organise the quantum of saleable rooms.

Guest Arrivals without Prior Reservation

A guest who comes at the hotel without a prior booking is often referred to as a chance guest.

Transit hotels located close to stations, airports, seaports will receive the bulk of their guests as chance arrivals. The receptionist has practically no information about the guests and their backgrounds. In this situation, special procedures are adopted to handle their bookings.

Chance arrivals with substantial amounts of luggage are unlikely to be able to leave the hotel without paying. An increasing trend, however, is carrying of small amounts of luggage which means the guest may be able to leave unnoticed. In registering the guest, the receptionist first checks whether they have luggage. If they have, then the registration is processed in the normal way and the registration card is marked 'chance'.

If there is a little luggage, then the receptionist has to ensure that the guest will not leave without first clearing his or her bill. This can be done either by taking cash deposit from the guest, or alternatively by taking an imprint of any credit card that the guest may have. It is important that in accepting chance bookings and taking deposits, the receptionist does not suggest to the guest that the hotel thinks he/she may be dishonest, or not willing to pay. Chance guests are often asked to pay cash for all purpose while they are in the hotel, or alternatively a special checks may be kept on the size of their bill so that if the account exceeds some figures, the guest is contacted and asked to pay up to that date, by doing this potential losses from chance guests are minimised.

Room Allocation

When the guest arrives, he will be able to use his room as quickly as possible. If he arrives at unscheduled time, it is unlikely that the room will be ready unless it is vacant from the previous night. In smaller hotels, allocation of rooms is normally done at the time of booking. Larger hotels with a greater choice of rooms often do not allocate until the guest actually arrives and then place the guest in the room. VIP's and guests with special requirements may have rooms pre-allocated to them and a note may be placed in the reception area to ensure that they only go to those particular rooms. In allocating rooms, the receptionist should satisfy the guests as much as possible. Even in large modern hotels not every room is exactly the same, some may have better views than others and certain rooms may be particularly noisy due to their closeness to the lift or to a service area.

Arrival List

In large hotels, this list will be useful to both the hall porter and the telephone operator. The porter or enquiry desk will have to check, if there are any message or letter for guests arriving and the telephone operator answer enquiries from people about the arrival of particular guests. The receptionist desk will be able to use the alphabetical list to locate guests quickly in the diary.

Department Notification

Shifting from one room to another requires an individual notification, because the records of each department need to be updated as soon as possible. A format of notification regarding change of rooms is shown in the following:

GUEST MOVEMENT NOTIFICATION FORMAT

Name ....

Old room ....

New room ....

Distribution ....

Bill office ....

Cashier ....

Porter ....

Signature of the Receptionist

Date ....

An alphabetical guest list is usually prepared each evening by the reception department which is known as 'House list'. This is then distributed throughout the hotel, though some departments may only check it occasionally. The telephone department, porter's desk and reception will need to refer to it constantly. A list of guests in room number order is only kept at the reception through the room board, and anyone wishing to know who is in a particular room would have to check with the reception desk.

Morning Call/Bed Tea/Newspaper, etc.

The reception department may keep a sheet at the front desk which records the exact time at which guests wish to be called in the morning (wake up call). Increasing use is being made of semi- or automatic equipment in this area to relieve the pressure on staff during the morning peak hours. Some hotels install alarm clocks in guest rooms along with tea-making equipment. Breakfast order forms are also placed in the room for the guest to complete and hang outside the door at night for timely service at the morning hours. Nowadays breakfast buffet is layed.

Guest History Board

Luxury hotels have already used guest history cards to record detail of each individual stay by guests and information on their personal likes and dislikes. This can be simplified by the use of a modified computer system. This allows for more information for better personalised service and attention to guests' needs.

General Information

It is usually the duty of the reception department in most places to pass an information about the place and other details of conferences, meetings, etc. which are normally being conducted in hotel conference room or other suitable location.

Information Regarding Medical Attention

At time, the hotel reception has to handle the urgent medical attention for the sick guests. This is done through the hotel's registered medical doctor or through hospital or nursing home services.

GENERAL SEQUENCE OF RECEPTION TASKS

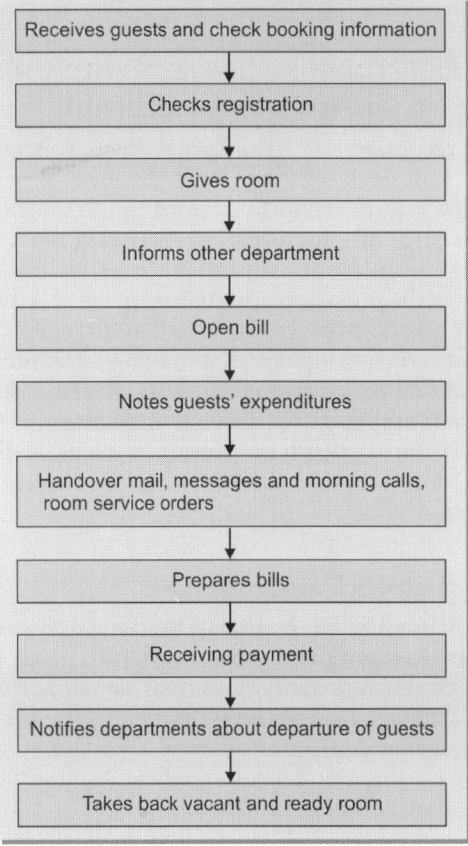

Receives guests and check booking information

↓

Checks registration

↓

Gives room

↓

Informs other department

↓

Open bill

↓

Notes guests' expenditures

↓

Handover mail, messages and morning calls, room service orders

↓

Prepares bills

↓

Receiving payment

↓

Notifies departments about departure of guests

↓

Takes back vacant and ready room

Departure

As the guest leaves there are a number of tasks that have to be completed by receptionist. Once the bill has been paid, the cashier will pass the registration card back to the reception, or send a notification where separate departments exist. The receptionist should then remove the guest name from the room status system and mark the room as vacant but not ready. Notification of the departments is necessary so that they may up-to-date their house list. The housekeeper will be able to assign a maid to clean the room. When the room has been cleaned, the housekeeping department will return it to reception and then it will be possible to re-let the room. Early departments and extensions of stay are notified to departments separately to ensure that they are not overlooked.

Mode of Receiving Payment from Hotel Guests

Hotel guests usually settle bills at the time of leaving the hotel and this procedure should require shortest possible time for guest convenience. Depending upon the types of hotel and depending upon the agreed terms and conditions with the guests, the hoteliers arrange to collect the payment of bills from customers. Universally, normal practice is to collect the payments by cash only.

However, there are different ways of collecting bills.

Cheques

Care should be taken as to the credibility of the persons tendering the cheque. Signature verification, outstation clearance charges, etc. are to be looked into. There is also a possibility of delay because of delayed clearance by banks. Draft is rather safer method than cheque because the clearance is assured regarding the sum for which draft is made.

Through Traveller's Cheque

This method has been gaining popularity in the country as well as among the travelling public. Because it is always hazardous to carry a large sum of money during travelling or in some unknown places away from home. These cheques are issued by State Bank of India and other banks on payment of cash to the bank with a commission by the purchasers. Traveller's cheques are also available in dollors for travelling outside the country on prior sanction of foreign exchange from Reserve Bank of India. Because of traveller's cheque, bank can verify the signature of the holders of traveller's cheques already exist over the cheque documents made before the bank. These are available for specific values hence, calculations will be required for settling the bills and handing over the cheques to the bank for deposit in the account of the hotel.

Through Travel Agent's Voucher

The people who travel with the arrangement of travel agents on agreed terms pay their dues to the travel agents and the travel agents in turn issue coupons or vouchers to the travellers for use as cash in specified hotels and similar other establishments.

Through Credit Advice

Many hotels allow their guests to sign the bills at the time of departure and arrange for sending all the bills to the person concerned or to the company at suitable time or at time as previous contract. This facility can be extended to restricted guests having established credibility. On the other hand, with desirable customers, one can have greater business because it is believed that in view of credit facility guests spend greater amount of money.

Through Credit Cards

The use of this system of payment is very limited in our country and widely used in foreign countries and in large hotels in India also. The credit card issuing companies/banks remain responsible for all bills signed by the customers on the strength of the credit card.

By way of Foreign Currency

Foreigners in India and non-resident Indians are required to use foreign currency for payment in India. Not all the hotels are also allowed by the government to accept foreign currency, only approved hotels by the government can receive foreign currency. Hotels permitted to accept foreign exchange must submit the details of foreign exchange received from guests to the authority and should have money changing facilities and proper day-to-day exchange rate information. The most popular foreign currency internationally accepted and widely used in the travel market is the American dollar. Hotel cashier must have proper knowledge to identify the foreigners and understand the exchange formalities and foreign currencies.

Foreign currencies of some countries	
Country	*Currency*
Australia	Dollar
Austria	Schilling
Baharin	Dinar
Canada	Dollar
Denmark	Krone
Euro countries	Euro
West Germany	Mark
Holland	Guilder
France	Franc
Finland	Mark
Hong Kong	Dollar
Iraq	Dinar
Italy	Lira
Japan	Yen
Kuwait	Dinar
Malaysia	Ringitt
New Zealand	Dollar
Norway	Krone
Saudi Arabia	Riyal
Spain	Paseta
UK	Pound
Sweden	Krone
USA	Dollar*

*Exchange rates vary from day-to-day basis.

Whatever may be the term of payments, the hotels need to record properly the various bills from the guests and income received there. For satisfactory service, all guest bills should be kept up-to-date so that no delay is caused to the customer at the time of payment. This method also ensures that all the dues are recorded properly for recovery.

Tabular Ledger is the most common method of recording all the dues of the guests in hotels. The customer's bill is normally prepared in duplicate. The extra copy is kept for hotel record and accounts. Recently in many hotels, machine billing has been introduced and bills are prepared automatically and kept up-to-date. Electronic machine computers are also gradually finding place in the front office billing section.

Lobby Manager/Public Relation Officer

In a very large hotel to handle huge number of guests at a time, there is a person in a position known as lobby manager who controls and looks after the team of people for the service of hotel guests at the time of entrance and departure. Guests' requirements at the hotel lobby are also looked after by these persons. PRO is another decorative post in some big hotels. They are useful for the maintenance of rapport with the regular visitors and with VIPs and sometimes with the press. The post of PRO is also helpful, provided capable person is appointed. In general, the front office staff particularly the receptionist must tune his or her personality not only to perform the routine tasks of the reception job but also to handle people of different mood, culture, civilisation, language and behaviour. Thus, the quality of the receptionist should be such as to handle the guests in happy state of mind even in the difficult situation. The receptionist quality lies in the word of 'PERSONALITY' itself as drawn by:

P	–	Pleasantness
E	–	Eagerness to serve
R	–	Respect for job and people
S	–	Sense of responsibility
O	–	Orderly and methodical work
N	–	Neatness
A	–	Accuracy in performance
L	–	Loyal
I	–	Intelligence
T	–	Tactfulness
Y	–	Yearning for success

Useful Reference Materials for Reception Department

From extensive survey and research, it has been noted that some useful books printed sources of information connected to the local tourist places, etc. are useful for receptionist to satisfy the guests' queries. These are as follow:

- Telephone directory
- Local road map
- All India Railway time table
- Location and tariff of important local hotels
- Dictionary—English-Hindi in particular
- Lists of local tourist places
- Lists of car-rental companies
- Lists of travel agents with their addresses and telephone numbers, etc.
- Address of Embassies and Consulates, wherever applicable.

Communication in Hotels

In general, the communication indicates passing of messages either oral or written. Messages are also passed through equipment. Here, stress is being on the written communication. These are required for internal staff as well as for clients. Hospitality business faces varied situations and types of people for the sake of communication. For all occasions and whatever may be the reason, proper decorum and politeness must be ensured. There should be right choice of words and phrases while drafting written communication. All letters must be addressed properly as per accepted rules, grammar, correctness of words are also to be carefully checked. Reception departments usually act as the hotel's office for the issue of various communications. All inward and outward communications should be properly filled for reference and for prompt reply or other actions in time. A prompt and decent communication creates reputation for hotels and bring business.

Following are some forms of addresses while writing letters.

Letter to men can be addressed as follows: Mr. Saha, Mr. R. Saha or Mr. Robindra Saha. If the courtesy title Esq. is used, the surname must be preceded by a first name or initials, and any letter must be put after the Esq. e.g. Robindra Saha Esq. M.A., young boys can be addressed as Master. The plural form Messrs is only used with the names of business firms which contain name, e.g. Messrs, Pal and Sons.

Unmarried woman and young girl can be addressed as Miss. Married women are often identified by their husband's first name or initial, e.g. Mrs Shayamali Saha, but it is increasingly common for them to appear as in Mrs. Mira Saha, which is also the usual form for a widow. It is possible to use Ms. instead of Miss or Mrs.

Professional titles are used instead of Mr. etc. as in Dr. A. Sardar, The Rev. Simon Qifford. First names are always used with the title Sir as in Sir Arjun Prasad. Orders, decorations, degrees, qualifications and letters denoting professions appear in that orders. Degrees start with the lowest but orders start with the highest, e.g. Lt General A. Sethna, PVSM, AVSM. Orders and decorations are usually included in addresses, but qualifications, etc. are only used where appropriate, when writing to a person in his official capacity.

A list of some ceremonious forms of address follow at the end of this article.

Postal Address

In India, the recommended form of postal address has the Post Town in capital letters, followed by the country in small letters, followed by the postcode (where applicable), e.g.:

Mr. Rajesh Nandy
Dr. D N Road
Daryaganj, New Delhi
(Post Code)

Address of a Letter

The writer's address should appear at the top right-hand corner with the underneath. The name and address of the intended recipient should come below the date, on the left-hand side of the page.

Beginnings and Endings

These depend on the degree of formality required. The most commonly used forms are as follows:

Very formal	
Sir,	I am, sir, or
Gentlemen,	I remain, sir
Madam,	Yours faithfully
Formal	
Dear Sir (s)	Yours faithfully
Dear Madam,	
Yours, truly	
When correspondent is known	
Dear Mr.	Yours sincerly
(Mrs. etc)	Yours truly
between friends	
Dear	Yours ever
My dear	Yours affectionately

Postscript

This is abbreviated to PS (not P.S). An additional postscript is labelled PPS.

CEREMONIOUS FORMS OF ADDRESS

The Queen

Address – The queen's Most Excellent Majesty. Begin Madam or May it please Yopus Masty. Refer to as Your Majesty and I have the honour to remain, your Majesty faithfully subject.

Member of Parliament

Address according to rank, with the additions of MP begin according to rank.

Secretary of State

Address H.M Principal Secretary of State for (Department). Begin Sir, end I am, Sir, Yours faithfully.

Ambassador

Address His Excellency (rank) H.B.B.'s Ambassador. Begin Sir, My lord, etc. according to rank. Refer to as your Excellency, end I am, etc. (according to rank), Yours faithfully.

Consul-General

Address (name) Esq. J.B.M'd Consul-General, Consul, Vice Consul, etc. Begin Sir, end I am, Sir, Yours faithfully.

Mayor

Address (for certain cities) The right workshipful the Mayor of Begin (Your Lordship), Sir (or Madam), end I am, Sir (or Madam), Yours faithfully.

RECEPTION OFFICE EQUIPMENT

Type machine, billing machine, etc. are in use for long in hotel reception departments. Telephones, PBX, telex, intercom systems are also very common. With the development of electronics, a wide range of changes are now noticed in many sophisticated establishments with great advantages.

Instead of manual type writers, people can have electronic typewriters with additional advantages and for more decent typing. Even the old round dial telephones have been replaced by the push button ones. Hotels now have facilities of Fax machine, EPABX and photocopiers, computers with a lot of advanced communication systems.

Fax

The fax machine, or facsimile machine, has completely revolutionised inter-office communication. Instant overseas communication is now possible in a matter of minutes over the telephone lines. Fax is much better than the telex, and cheaper. Firstly, there is no deposit or waiting periods as there is for a telex. Secondly, an A4 normal letterhead size sheet would take a maximum of minute to transit over a fax line under the worst of conditions at a rate of ₹ 60 per minute. The same document would be transmitted in a minimum time of eight minutes over a telex at the rate of ₹ 24 per minute. Comparative cost: ₹ 60 against ₹ 192 (rates are variable).

But the efficiency of the fax machines is interlinked with that of reliable telephonic systems. The amount of fax machines being purchased is pretty high. Basically, a fax machine works on the same principle of a photocopying machine. A photoelectric eye scans material to be transmitted under ultraviolet which is then reflected into a photoconductor which is electronically sensitive. The photoconductor converts the scanned characters, pictures, shapes, designs, etc. into digital impulses. These impulses are transmitted through the telephones to a similar machine at the other end of the line and the whole process takes place in reverse. Photo scanner flashes over the thermal paper and in doing so generates heat. This heat reacts with the toner on the thermal paper which is sensitive to heat and the document is reproduced. This is being increasingly replaced by e-mail system and by the latest mobile system.

DTP

Good looking letters? That's what Desk Top Publishing (DTP) systems are used predominantly by typesetters and the printing industry in general—they are being used increasingly in day-to-day office communications. This includes not only letters but also reports, research papers and company profiles.

A DM is, in essence, a system of software designed to be used on a personal computer. The PC is connected to a compatible laser writer which prints inputs on paper through a printing mechanism controlled by lasers.

DTPs actually increase readability and accessibility. For instance, the use of the Aldus, the page make-up and lackage/graphic software that come along with the Apple Mac DTP could turn a dull report into easy reading material. One could introduce lively graphics and discover a series of options in page layout designs without using the discover of a series of layout artists. The potential of neat written communication is thus maximised.

EPABX

Almost all offices with over 20 minutes have one or more of these. EPABX stands for Electronic Phone Automatic Branch Exchange. The EPABX is the intercom system combined with the outside line. This system immediately dispenses with the telephone operator. Incoming calls can be answered by anyone and channeled through the person can verbally communicate with each other within the office without leaving their seats.

While the efficiency of, and demand for, automated office equipment is high, there is a hitch in the supply side. Of all the machines mentioned, the only one manufactured in India utilizing indigenous technology is the EPABX system developed by the Center for Development of Telematics (C-DoT).

Photocopiers

The photocopier facilitates swifter communication. If, for instance, a company receives an order, or any communication which has to be examined by more than one person at once, there is no need to type out a dozen copies. Just use the easy-to-handle office photocopier which will make all the copies you need at the press of a button, besides which it also offers enlargement and reduction facilities.

Similarly, official presentations need to be typed only once, conserving time and energy. On good paper, the copies will look as good as the original. The newer machines have security features that allow the machines to make one extra copy of any document copied. This extra copy is then deposited in a locked clipboard under the machine. The clipboard could be opened at the end of the day by authorised personnel who will then know exactly which documents have been copied. This guards against confidential correspondence being illegally copied and smuggled out of an office without anyone being the wisher.

Computer

The computer division of HCL, for example, accounts for 80% of its business. Other companies manufacturing computers with foreign chip include Wipro, HCL, IBM and Zenith. The chip is an integral part of the computer.

It is because of the Indian dependence on imported computer chips that the price of computers is steep. Firstly, there is the cost of imports. And then every fluctuation in the dollar-rupee exchange rate affects the price of computers, and the rate continues to rise unfavourably for the rupee. Many new suitable hotel related softwares are now installed. Credit card swipe machines are also installed now in many hotels.

The International Hotel Telegraphic Code (Old Practice)

There is an international code for reserving accommodation, used by hotels throughout the world. Its use saves money for the sender as one word takes the place of several. Also, possible confusion can be avoided and language difficulties overcome. Nowadays, fax, e-mail, scanning, etc. are in use.

Code regarding hotel rooms, etc.

Code	Description of the codes
LBA	1 room with 1 bed
ALDUA	1 room with 1 large bed
ARAB	1 room with 1 bed
ABEC	1 room with 3 beds
BELAB	2 rooms with 1 bed each
BIRAC	2 rooms with 2 plus 1 beds, i.e. 3 beds
BONAD	2 rooms with 2 beds each
CIROC	3 rooms with 1 bed each
CARID	3 rooms with 2 plus 1 beds, i.e. 3 beds
CALDE	3 rooms with 2 plus 1 beds, i.e. 5 beds
CADUF	3 rooms with 2 plus 1 beds
DANID	4 rooms with 1 bed each
DIROH	4 rooms with 2 beds each
EMBLE	5 rooms with 2 beds each
ERCAJ	5 rooms with 2 rooms 2 beds each
FELAF	6 rooms with 2 beds each
FERAL	6 rooms with 2 beds each

Code regarding general amenities

Code	Description of the codes
KIND	Child's bed
SAL	Sitting room
BAT	Private bathroom
SERV	Servant's room
BELVU	Room with good view
INTER	Room facing courtyard
TRANQ	Room very quiet
ORDIN	Room without running water
BEST	Quality of rooms, very good
BON	Quality of rooms, good
PLAIN	Quality of rooms, simple
BOX	Box for 1 motorcar
CARAX	Ordinary garage for 1 motorcar

Code regarding stay

Code	Description of the codes
PASS	Length of stay, 1 night
STOP	Length of stay, several days
d.	Arrival procedure
AERO	Meet at terminal from airport
AEROZ	Meet at terminal from airport
QUAI	Meet at dockside
TRAIN	Meet at station

Code regarding arrival time

Code	Description of the codes			
	Morning	Afternoon	Evening	Night
Sunday	POBAB	POLYP	RABAL	RANUV
Monday	POCUN	POMEL	RACEX	RAPIN
Tuesday	PODYL	PONOW	RADOK	RAQAT
Wednesday	POGOK	POPUF	RAFYG	RATYZ
Thursday	POHIX	PORIK	RAGUB	RAVUP
Friday	POJAN	POSEV	RAHIV	RAWOW
Saturday	POKUZ	POVAH	RAJOD	RAXAB
POWYZ	This morning			
POZUM	This afternoon			
RAMYK	This evening			
RAZEM	Tonight			
ANUL	Cancel room			

Front Office Staff

As mentioned earlier, the front office staff are vital in the sense that they are required to handle all the formalities of reservation, registration, departures, etc. of the guest right from the time guest steps in the hotel. They are also required to handle the guest complaints, public relation and liaison works with other departments of the hotels.

In very large hotels, the staff distribution for the front office job may be described in the following pattern.

Orders come from the top to downwards and the accountability and reporting moves upwards. Front office manager reports to the general manager or proprietor-cum-manager of the hotel, whichever is applicable.

In small hotels, the above elaborate organisation does not exist. The receptionist or the supervisor in the reception counter often performs multiple functions within the counter in his or her specified working hours. A model organisation for the front office may be chalked out as under:

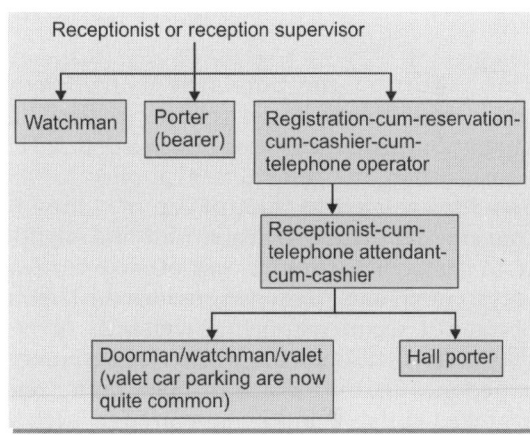

Housekeeping Department of the Hotel

The quality of the hotels as well offices, restaurants, motels, hostels, etc. depends on the quality and efficiency of the housekeeping. The housekeeping is a general term applied for the activities related to the upkeep of things in proper order in the premises inside and outside with sense of aesthetics and other technical ways. Good housekeeping provides the feeling of comfort, security, appeal as well as dignity to the guests and users of the facility. It is a common experience that if a place is looked after and arranged suitably and if there are facilities to throw the empty cigarette in boxes, then people hardly wish to disturb the area and tries to keeping the place in order. In Kolkata, Indian Railways is now operating country's first underground railway and because of the co-operation of users and careful observation and maintenance by the railway—the quality of maintenance of the stations is unique. Adequate sensitive observation, power to locate the disorderly things, dust, dirt, stains, etc. and inherent desire to make things orderly are basic human attitudes required to achieve success in housekeeping.

Description of Housekeeping Service

Areas in Hotels

Bedrooms and toilets (attached or separate) are the most important job sites for the housekeeping staff in any hotel. Then comes other public areas, if allotted to the housekeeping department. Otherwise, in small hotels, cleaning and maintenance of reception and restaurant departments are done by the sectional staff.

Hotel Bedrooms

Standard hotels have more or less uniform pattern of arranging the rooms with single, double (suitable for two) and twin beds (two single size beds) with comfortable mattresses made up of various materials. These days, synthetic materials are being used in many places. Apart from elasticity, these materials cause discomfort in rooms having no air-conditions in summer times. Average height of a bed is 2 ft. from the floor. Standard length of the single bed should be 6 ft. 3 inches × 3 ft and the double bed 6 ft. 3 inches in length and 5 ft. in width. In case of small hotel having no arrangements for air-conditioning and mosquito control, beds must be provided with suitable arrangement for use of mosquito nets.

Beds may have spring base or flat wooden base. In western countries, many choices of beds and bedding materials are available for hotel industry. But in India, synthetic elastic materials are largely used over hard surface of the wooden beds. Hotel's beds are now additionally decorated in rooms with wide decorative hardboard, these can be treated as 'bed top decorative' matching with the decor lights. Small side tables are also provided with the beds for water, telephone, etc. Hotel's bedrooms also have other kinds of furniture. These are usually 2 low chairs or sofas, one tea table, dressing table-cum-writing table with drawers and one chair, mirror and the wardrobe. In some places, bedrooms also have luggage racks. Depending upon the type of hotel policy and based on the investment, the quality of the furniture varies. Presently, television sets, mini bars are provided in many places and for these adequate space and furniture are also needed. Bedrooms are often carpeted wall to wall or partially. Bedrooms may or may not have balconies. There are curtains usually for the windows.

Toilets

In most places, these are attached with bedrooms. Present day toilets provide W.C. (Western style), wash basin combined with granite or marble slab to act as basin table with mirror preferably on the right side of the toilet entrance door and the shower-cum-bath on the left. In some places, only shower cubicle is provided. In good hotels, the bath area be so designed and shower cubicles so isolated with curtains, etc. that there is no wetting of the bathroom floor after use. Bottle opener, towel hanger, candle holders, dustbins, sanitary bins are provided in bathrooms. Adequate lighting and slip-proof flooring are also must in the bathrooms. Indians are in the habit of washing their clothes with bathroom. So wherever possible self-washing arrangements may be provided in order to keep the bathrooms clean or the garments may be collected by hotel staff for washing apparently free of cost. The actual cost of washing with labour, etc. may be invisibly added to the tariff of the hotel without any hint to the guest. The washing service again may be considered as one of the additional service to the guests. However, appropriate management, manpower and timely delivery

system are required to organise the so-called free of charge laundry service to the guest, particularly in smaller hotels having local clients.

METHODS OF CLEANING AND ARRANGING HOTEL BEDROOMS AND TOILETS

As indicated earlier, the hotel bedrooms have bed as well as other furniture and fixtures. These are to be cleaned and arranged daily with replacement of guest stationeries, water tumblers, soap, towels, bedsheets. Wherever flower is given, this needs replacement as well as fresh arrangement. In fact, there is routine repetition of jobs for arranging and cleaning the rooms even when guests continue to stay more than 24 hours. Basic principles of room cleaning and arranging beds are described here.

The cleaning procedure usually starts in the morning after 10 am (normal time to go to the office) with the general exception that guests will be out of the rooms and it is a convenient time to clean and arrange the rooms. After opening the doors and windows for airing the rooms, the used linen of beds and bath are to be taken out for replacement. Guests cloth, reading articles, shaving articles, etc. if any in the room are to be cleaned and arranged. The room carpet and other furnitures are to be dusted and cleaned first before making the bed. The water in water flask is to be replaced and fault in any switches or on other items are to be reported for prompt repair. The windows are to be again closed and door locked. The total appearance of the room should be as fresh as at the time of checking in. Hotel beds are usually provided with the following linen bedsheets.

1. Blanket (in winter and in AC room)—extras may be provided on request
2. Night spread — 1 (under the blanket)
3. Bed cover — 1 (of suitable design)
4. Pillow cover — 2 for 2 thinner pillow or 1 for 1 standard pillow
5. Bedsheet — 1 for one bed

Hotel must keep adequate number of linen in stock (at least 3 sets for each bed).

In hotel where 24 hours laundry facility is not available, 5 sets may be required for undisturbed operations.

Apart from the linen, in good hotels, laundry instruction cards, TV cards, room service menu and order cards, guest's writing pad, envelop, match box, etc. are provided in the room. These things should be kept in order and with fresh supplies whenever necessary so that guests need not have the chance for complaints. The hotel staff should be adequately trained or there should be trained staff having knowledge of housekeeping skills.

Special attention should be paid to clean hotel bathrooms. Presently in most places, attached bath with Western fittings are used. If the bathrooms are not airy, well vantilated and properly cleaned, then the very purpose of attached bath is defeated. Hotel bathrooms are sometimes provided with some amenities such as toilet papers, face papers, match boxes, candles, towels, shower cap, shampoo, sachets, etc. In course of cleaning and arranging bathrooms, adequate care should be taken to replace and arrange these things regularly.

Cleaning staff may be taught the following for proper cleaning of the toilets. Used linen from bathrooms are to be removed as also the waste materials such as empty match boxes, used tissue papers, empty drink bottles, etc. Ceiling, walls, light shades are to be cleaned. W.C. should be washed and dry and properly flushed. Before leaving the toilets, the floor, basin base and mirrors are to be cleaned and dried. Bathrooms should be supplied with fresh towels everyday.

Bath towel	–	2	(for use of two persons)
Face towel	–	2	(for use of two persons)
Hand towel	–	2	(for use of two persons)

Soap, shampoo, other toiletries according to the policy of the hotels are to be provided. Housekeeping also take care of the linen given to a room, particularly at the time of departure of the guests. In case of any missing articles or guest items found must be brought to the notice of the managerial staff.

In many small or large hotels, a further cleaning of rooms takes place before guests retire for the night. This may be carried out on request of the guests or as a policy of the hotels and with the consent of the guests. This is in fact a repetition of the morning service and arranging of the bed in particular, guests often use the carpeted floor, bed, etc. as additional seats for their friends and business associates and rooms are often littered with chicken bones, paper pieces and stain due to alcohol and coffee, etc. Hotels need to provide extra housekeeping services sometimes in odd hours and at the call of the guests becasue of such activities in the room. This also limits the life of furniture, fixtures of a room as well and it is difficult to provide desired level of clean and timely disciplined service from the staff.

Guest Vigilence

Varieties of people come to the hotels for varieties of purposes. Thus, it is very important that some kind of vigilance over the guest is necessary. At the same time for special guests, VIP guests, etc. privacy must also be provided. These are actually carried out by the housekeeping staff. Housekeeping staff keep an eye over the suspicious movements of guests. Guests luggage volume, luggage movements are watched and reported to the superiors in case of suspicion. Under no circumstances there should be a feeling among the guests that they are being watched or spied and the privacy disturbed. The vigilance is for notorious guests for the security of good guests.

Public Areas

Areas not confined in rooms and unattached toilets, balconies are known as public areas. Depending upon the size of the property, public areas include terraces, corridors, elevator, lounge, convention rooms, lobbies, restaurants, bars, general offices, reception areas, carpeted areas and all other areas not specifically defined. Outside walls and outer perimeters of the hotel also need upkeep on appropriate intervals. For the quality of hotel, only clean rooms and toilets are not enough. The hotel proprietor must attach equal importance to the total housekeeping of the hotels both inside and outside. Many 5-star hotels have gardens, lawns and huge other areas which require expert maintenance and upkeep. Sometimes hotel staff get very short interval between parties to organise housekeeping and this matter must be taken into account while accepting party bookings for the sake of good arrangement and maintenance of the reputation.

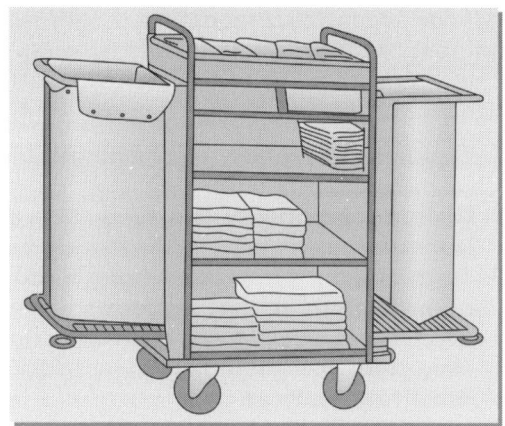

Fig. 7.1: Housekeeping trolley

Tools and Equipment for Housekeeping Operation

Like any other job, the housekeeping jobs also need some specific tools and equipment. Depending upon the investment, availability and requirements, the type of mechanical or fixed ladders, vacuum cleaners, laundry machines, sewing machines, electrical mops, electric brushes of different types, polishes of different types, cleaning chemicals and solutions of different types are used for housekeeping. There are number of products now available in the country. For brass items—brasso, for silver items silvo, for wood mansion—polish, chromium polishes for metal fittings, safe vacuum for carpet freshness and odonil, etc. For room and toilet freshness, room fresheners are used. Harpic, sunny fresh are used for WC cleaning. Dettol, savlon are used for cleaning mouthpieces of telephones.

Housekeeping Trolley or Maid's Cart (Fig. 7.1)

This is particularly must for methodical housekeeping in hotel rooms. These trolleys are located in each floor at a suitable place already designed and contain the following.

2 bags—one for garbage and one for dirty linen. Cleaning items and polishes, brushes for room and WC and other brushes feather duster

and mopes, guest stationery items for room and toiletry, glasses, bulbs, etc. are taken in the trolley. Information cards for the use of guests are carried in the trolley.

Trolley also contains all the fresh linen for replacement and change in the rooms.

Where there is no prior design to place the housekeeping trolley, suitable other arrangement should be made or the trolley function may be carried out through other alternative ways—using sweepers kit, linen kit, etc. and suitably locating them. In fact, the housekeeping trolley (HKT) is a mobile housekeeping store as well as collecting vehicle for used and dirty items from rooms.

Linen and Uniform Rooms

A well-designed and furnished space is necessary for a good housekeeping department. In a very large hotel, the housekeeping views the requirements and services to be offered. The housekeeping department of large hotels must have place for fixing laundry equipment, flower arrangement room, tailoring room, upholstery repair room, etc. There should be well-defined adequate space and counters for storage of supplies and exchange of soiled and fresh linen and uniforms. However, in smaller places, at least one adequate size room fixed with racks and front counter with cupboards is necessary to function as a linen room. Basic functions of the linen room are as follows:

1. Maintain the laundry of restaurant, bed-rooms and staff uniform.
2. Counting groupwise and send them for laundry.
3. To receive the clean linen from laundry, count them and arrange properly and issue.
4. Receive and issue the dirty and clean linen from floorwise preferably. This work is usually done twice a day.

Where there is no arrangement of in-house laundry, outside firm is fixed for washing the hotel's linen as well as that of the guest's garments.

It is very important to take care of guest's garments against loss or damage and also for timely delivery. Staff uniforms are also generally supplied by the hotels. Cotton uniforms are issued for one year and terry-cotton materials are for two years. Uniforms should be exchanged every alternate day. Record of staff uniform for different departments may be maintained with appropriate symbols such as 'K' for kitchen– 'R' for restaurant, etc. Kitchen uniforms are then further marked for individual staff. Linen keeper is the incharge of the linen rooms—he/she maintains the records of incoming as well as outgoing linen and also other official records of incoming as well. Linen inventory should be taken for verifications and every three months total position of the linen and its status should be taken into account. The condemned linen may be used for duster, etc. Because of its nature of operations, it is seen that housekeeping department is very vulnerable to pilferage. Thus, special care should be taken for the outgoing goods. It is for this reason, only entrance-cum-exit is provided in the linen room.

Room for Flower Arrangement

In order to provide beauty and aesthetics, there is nothing to beat fresh and colourful flowers.

In good hotels, there is a separate section under housekeeping for daily arrangement of fresh flowers for reception desk, banquet hall, con-ference rooms, restaurant, etc. Sometimes, guest rooms are also provided with flowers in flower vases. There are many detailed tech-niques for arranging and choosing flowers for various occasions. These must be followed at the time of flower arrangement. The arrange-ment should not be monotonous. It should be variable with matching contrast and befitting for the occasions. Placement is also important and should not create disturbance to the guests. On top table for conference, etc. the faces of speakers should not be covered due to any tall arrangement. The base of the vases should be firm and should not easily tilt due to small movements. Bad smelling flowers or foliage must be avoided as well as the materials which are not fresh should also be avoided. Timely replacement of dried or otherwise non-attrac-tive flowers and foliage should be promptly carried out.

General Techniques for Housekeeping Operation

Because of changes of the present day lifestyle, the hotels keeping has also undergone changes. The housekeeping job is no longer simple cleaning of the rooms. In good hotels, the housekeeping department has to keep link with the reception for the arrival and departure records, with the maintenance department for repairs, etc. Apart from these two departments, it has to keep in touch with food and beverage department, stores department and personnel department. The housekeeping department's activities are generated from the housekeeping desk or housekeeping office.

Housekeeping office co-ordinates the various housekeeping tasks through the staff allotted specific duties and maintains the various records and registers.

It maintains the log books of work, supply and receipt register, memo books, cleaning schedules, etc.

cleaning of some areas are given in Table 7.1. It helps to advice the grooming of staff and provides appropriate training and knowledge for performance of the tasks. The housekeeping department should be aware of latest knowledge of cleaning appliances, chemicals and use of fire fighting equipment and practice.

Stain carpets, bed sheets, and other surfaces are practically a big nuisance to be handled by housekeeping staff. Some details of stain removing methods are also discussed in Table 7.2.

In summary, it may be said that trade of a housekeeping in a hotel is that of a housekeeping a house in a much more bigger way.

Stain Removal

Stain is a mark left on linen by the contact and absorption of some foreign substances. Some stains are easily removed by ordinary methods. But there are some stains which need special treatment. This entirely depends on the nature of the stain. Staff, therefore, must be familiar with the appearance of many of the common stains such as mud, ink, rust, blood, urine, semen, turmeric, etc. Some common stains that appear on hotel linens and their methods of removal are discussed in Table 7.2.

Table 7.1: Some general procedure for daily cleaning	
Daily cleaning	*Methods of cleaning*
1. Toilet	All litter is to be removed after emptying the sanibins. WC is to be washed, dried and floor mopped.
2. Windows and walls	Dust and dirts be removed, metal fillings and handles in particular be polished and cleaned.
3. Bed	Should be rearranged with dusting of head and foot boards. May be covered with bed covers.
4. Room floors	Must be swept, vacuum cleaned and naked floors may be damp mopped.
5. Curtains	Should be checked for dust and neatness.
6. Furniture	Be dusted and stains should be removed.

It maintains and prepares the occupancy reports at least at three intervals:

at 9 am — 4 pm — 10 pm

It plans daily, weekly, monthly cleaning schedule. Some general procedure for daily

Table 7.2: Some common stains on hotel linens and their methods of removal			
Stain	*Condition*	*White cotton and linen*	*Colour cotton and linen*
Butter (grease and colouring)	Fresh	Wash with warm soapy solution.	Same as cotton
Ketchup (kathha beetle leaf spots)	Dry	Apply diluted potassium permanganate solution, then sodium bisulphite, wash. Treat with solvent sodium.	Same as cotton
Curry (grease & haldi)		1. Wash with soap and water. 2. Bleach in sunlight and air.	1. Treat with solvent soap 2. Fast colours to bleach in sunlight and air.
Dye/semen		1. Steep in water. 2. Wash with soap and water.	1,2,3 same as cotton 4. Treat with alcohol, ammonia and dilute acid.

(Contd.)

Table 7.2: Some common stains on hotel linens and their methods of removal *(Contd.)*

Stain	Condition	White cotton and linen	Colour cotton and linen
		3. Steep in dilute alkali or dilute acid 4. Treat with alcohol ammonia and dilute acetic acid. 5. Steep in cold solution of bleaching powder (1-2 pints of water) 6. Bleech with distilled water.	5. For fast colour—Bleach with bleaching powder solution or quick treatment of javelle water.
Egg	Fresh dry	Wash in cold water and then in warm water and soap. Apply salt and pour warm water through	Same as cotton Soak in salt solution until stain is removed.
Grease, oil and ghee	Fresh dry	Wash with hot water and soap Treat with a grease solvent and wash with hot water and soap	Same as white cotton Same as white cotton
Haldi		Refer to curry stain for treatment	
Henna (mhendi)		Dip in warm milk for half an hour, then wash with soap	
Ice-cream and chocolate	Fresh	1. Wash in cold water and soap 2. Steep in warm borax solution 3. Sponge with petrol or carbon tetrachloride	Same as white cotton
	Dry	Treat with alternate application of dilute potassium permanganate solution and oxalic acid.	Same as white cotton
Ink (black and blue)	Fresh	Rub the stain with a cut tomato, wash; rub salt, wash. Repeat the process till stain is removed.	Same as cotton
Marking ink (This stain is very difficult to remove)		Steep alternatively in dilute iodine solution and dilute odium thiosulphate solution or potassium cyanide	Same as cotton

(Contd.)

Table 7.2: Some common stains on hotel linens and their methods of removal *(Contd.)*

Stain	Condition	White cotton and linen	Colour cotton and linen
Ball point ink		Swab with methylated spirit using a pad of blotting paper below.	Same as cotton
Iron rust		Steep in oxalic acid solution and then rinse with dilute borax solution steep in solution of salt and lemon	Same as for white cotton
Lipstick		Steep in methylated spirit and wash with solvent soap Moisten and soften by working glycerine into the stain. Leave for a short while, rinse and then wash with surf or soap.	Same as for white cotton
Medicine (may be a mixture of metallic substances, fruits and alcohol). Therefore, suitable treatment for all of the above must be tried.		Sponge with benzine or carbon tetrachloride wash.	
Mud		Allow to dry and brush it off. Wash with soap and water. If persistant, treat with solution of potassium permanganate and oxalic acid.	Same as for white cotton
Nail varnish		Apply amylacetate (this has smell like bananas) to the stained areas with a cotton wool pad. This must not be used on any acetate rayon fabric.	
Oil, paint and varnish		1. Steep in turpentine, wash with solvent soap. 2. Steep in alcohol, wash with solvent soap. 3. Sponge with equal parts of alcohol and benzine.	Steep in kerosene or turpentine. Wash with solvent soap.
Perspiration		1. Steep in cold water 2. Steep in dilute ammonia solution	For fast colours, use the same treatment as for coloured cotton.

(Contd.)

Stain	Condition	White cotton and linen	Colour cotton and linen
		3. Wet the stain and place it in the sun for bleaching. The fabric must be kept wet until the stain is removed. 4. Bleach with distilled water.	For non-fast colours, steep in dilute ammonia then treat it with dilute hydrogen peroxide solution of sodium byphosulphite.
Perfume		1. Treat with ethyl alcohol 2. Bleach with hydrogen peroxide	Same as for white cotton. Steam the stained portion.
Rain water		1. Steam the stained portion 2. Sponge with dilute acetic acid solution.	
Shoe polish		1. Scrape off the stain, if dry. Apply a little grease. Wash with hot water and soap. 2. Steep in turpentine, wash with solvent soap.	Steep in turpentine, wash with solvent soap.
Urine stains		Apply ethyl alcohol and allow to evaporate. Then apply chloroform and allow to evaporate.	Same as for white cotton.

Table 7.2: Some common stains on hotel linens and their methods of removal *(Contd.)*

Dye stains may be acidic or alkaline and so the nature of the stain is ascertained before a specific removing agent is used.

Mineral stains, such as iron, black ink, and certain medicines, acid reagents to act on the metal and then by an alkaline solution to neutralise the acid agent and act on the dye.

Neither perspiration nor such marks fall into any of the above groups. Perspiration has no protein component and cannot, therefore, fall under the group of animal fabrics. It cannot obviously fall under the vegetable group, even though it is acidic.

Scorch is brown stain caused by a very hot iron and is in a class by itself.

Grass stains come under vegetable groups but a different method is used for removing the green colouring matter (chlorophyl).

Stain removing must be carried out with care and in such a manner as to restore the garment to its original appearance and texture.

General Methods

1. Remove the stains when fresh, as then they are easy to remove with simple methods.
2. Study the nature and texture of the fabric, specially when chemical reagent and bleaches are to be used, as these have injurious effects on wool, silk and synthetic fabrics. When chemical reagents are used and specially on animal fabrics, they must be in dilute solutions, several applications of weak solution or an undiluted reagent. If bleaching has to be done, only hydrogen peroxide in dilute solution (1 teaspoon to

1 pint) is used for silk and wool, and for rayons nothing but sodium perflorate. The fabric must be rinsed in cold water several times after the above treatment.

3. Treat known stains with specific reagents.
4. Unknown should be treated with simple methods such as steeping in cold or hot water or washing with soap. Then use mild reagents and follow with strong ones. If the stain still persists resort to bleaching only when all other treatments fail.

   The fabric should be in contact with the reagent only until the stain is removed. The fabric then should be rinsed in water several times to remove the reagent which if allowed to dry in the fabric, may damage it.

5. All acid reagents should be neutralised with an alkaline rinse and vice versa.

If a stain is removed by the sponging method, sponge the stain with the solution, working in a circular movement starting from the outer edge of the stain to its centre.

Removal of Stain from Carpets

Stains or spots on carpeting of four types:

a. Water soluble
b. Oil soluble
c. Combination of both, such as food, etc.
d. Colour stains such as dyes.

Normal stain problems faced in a hotel and their removal procedures are shown in Table 7.3.

Cleaning of Glass (Fig. 7.2)

Equipment

- Delwin-window cleaning tool
- Cleaning mixture (There are many glass cleaning mixture already commerically prepared)
- A lint-free cloth.

How?

There are several methods of cleaning glass depending on size.

Table 7.3: Different types of stain and their removal procedure

Types of stain	Removal procedure
1. Alcohol, candy (sugar)	Detergent-blot-citric acid-blot
2. Blood, tomato sauce, dyes soft drinks, vomit	detergent-blot-ammonia-blot citric acid-blot (Note: red dye in bleed)
3. Butter	Solvent-blot-detergent-blot-ammonia water-blot-ammonia-water-blot
4. Candle wax, chewing gum	Solvent-blot
5. Coffee, tea, earth, urine	Detergent-blot-citric acid-blot
6. Cosmetics, ink, shoe polish	Paint, oil and grease remove-blot-solvent-blot-detergent-blot-ammonia blot-citric acid-blot
7. Nail polish	Non-oily nail polish remover-blot-solvent-blot
8. Cigarette burn	Clip off burned tips with small scissors

- A small amount of reagent used should first be tested in an inconspicuous part of the carpet to see if it will damage carpet fibre or dye.
- Remove residue with a dull knife
- Remember, identifying the stain is 90% of the solutions of the problem.

Handwashing

- Dampen the cloth with solutions and wipe pane from side to side covering total area
- Dry off with clean dry cloth using the same stroke
- Wipe any spillages immediately.

Squeegee Washing

- Use Delkleen 'Delwin'
- Wash glass with even strokes from top to bottom. Squeegees off in horizontal strokes at 60° angle, keeping edge of the blade with absorbent cloth after each stroke.

- Carefully clean and wipe bottom edge. 'Delwin' has a telescopic handle to help you reach glasses at considerable height.

Frequency

As needed.

Safety

- Do not use powder, paste or abrasive the cleaning agent on glass.
- Do not climb onto window edges above ground level.
- Always wipe spillage from surroundings woodwork as this may permanently stain.
- Treated or painted glass such as 2-way mirrors should be cleaned as specified by the manufacturer, otherwise mirror coating will lift easily, if incorrect solutions are used.
- Take extra care when cleaning windows in carpeted areas. Put protective cover on floor.
- Paint spots can be easily removed with a window scraper.

Cleaning of Curtains

Equipment

Vacuum cleaner, Comvac fitted with long extension pipe and upholstery brush (Fig. 7.4).

How?

- Vacuum or dust mop top of pelmet.
- Vacuum or dust mop total curtain from the top to bottom.
- Check for heavy soiling and refer to supervisor, if further action such as laundering or dry cleaning is required.

Frequency

- Depending on local conditions, but usually weekly.

Safety

- Check condition of curtains before vacuuming.

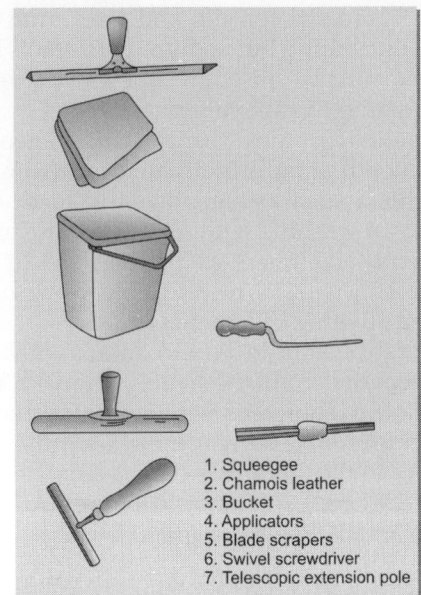

1. Squeegee
2. Chamois leather
3. Bucket
4. Applicators
5. Blade scrapers
6. Swivel screwdriver
7. Telescopic extension pole

Fig. 7.2: Window cleaning set and attachments

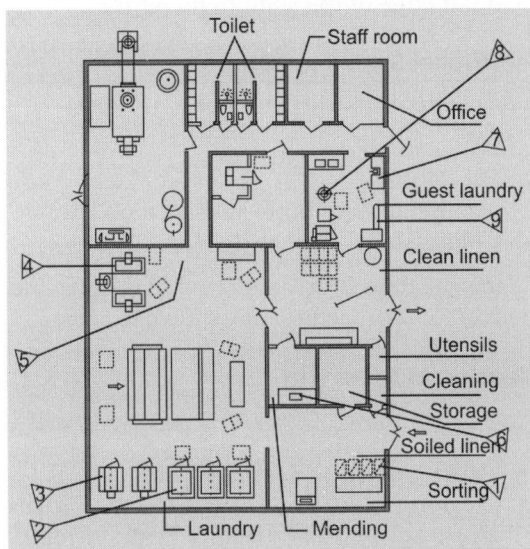

Fig. 7.3: Model layout of a hotel laundry

1. Sorting trolley	6. Sewing machine
2. Washer-extractor	7. Work table
3. Tumbler drier	8. Hydro extractor
4. Laundry press	9. Ironing table
5. Garment rack	

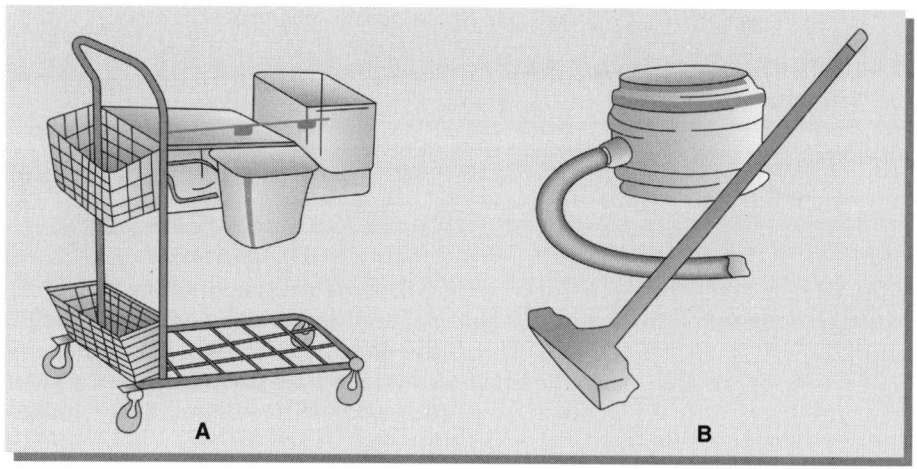

Fig. 7.4: A. Cleaning trolley, B. Vacuum cleaner

- Do not brush dust from the top of pelmet to other areas.
- Take care that very fine curtains are not sucked into vacuum.

Care of Equipment

- Empty vacuum cleaner container.
- Replace all equipment in store.

Cloths used for Cleaning

Cloth		Use
1. Duster	(a)	Collecting dust
	(b)	Rubbing surfaces up to a shine
2. Rag		Applying polish or strong cleaning agent
3. Cloth	(a)	Damp dusting all surfaces above floor
	(b)	Removing marks from surfaces above floor
	(c)	Daily cleaning of sanitary fittings

Contd.

Cloth		Use
4. Floor cloth		Used to wipe up spills from floors
5. Scrim		Use to wipe up windows, mirrors, etc.
6. Chamois leather	(a)	When wet, used on windows and mirrors
	(b)	When dry, used to polish up metals

Staffing Pattern of the Housekeeping Department

In general, three categories of staff are required in hotels:

Managerial category
Supervisory category
Unskilled or semiskilled category

Depending upon the policy, size of the establishments, nature of the service and location, etc. the staffing pattern particularly that of managerial and supervisory category varies. In India, more of unskilled workmen are found in hotels.

Flowchart 7.1: Organisation of housekeeping department in a hotel

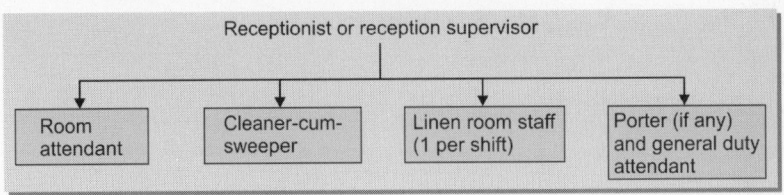

In a moderately big hotel, the organisation of the housekeeping department may be as given in Flowchart 7.1.

Floor supervisor for one shift or on the basis of 1:25 rooms for day shift and 1:50 during the night shift.

The room attendant for every 10 to 12 rooms depending upon the types and facilities. Work distribution if followed on the basis of 8 hourly shift, then adequate increase in staff will be necessary to maintain the work schedule.

Food and Beverage Department of Hotels

The size type, equipment, methods of operation of food and beverage departments of the hotels vary according to the types of hotels. In general, the food and beverage departments of the majority of the establishments in our country are lacking in technological improvements and have been functioning in a primitive way particularly in the areas behind bars and dining halls. The most profitable area in hotel other than rooms is the food and beverage sales. These are sold not only to the resident guests but also to the outsider as well. Hotels having no food and beverage department, however, exist in many places. Similarly, there are several food and beverage outlets exist having no provisions for accommodation.

Numerous details are involved in the whole operations involving hot and cold food preparation, storage and services. In this department, careful expert handling from place to place and during different hours of the day are required. Food and beverage are sometimes handled separately in some establishments but in some places these are handled in the place of the dining area. Food and beverage are also served off the premises on order and in places away from the usual dining or service areas, e.g. in rooms, in poolside, on rooftop and conference halls, etc. So for all these, one has to plan in advance based on the policy of the establishments, as to which way things are to be organised.

The important technical details for standardised food and beverage preparation follow in the subsequent sections.

FOOD PREPARATION (COOKING AND BAKING)

This involves art and skill of the persons incharge of preparation in addition to the proper supply of good quality food ingredients. Any good cooking would be spoiled, if proper quality of ingredients are not available.

EQUIPMENT OF THE KITCHEN

While planning the menu, it is important to see that the kitchen is well equipped so as to cope up with preparation of the various dishes. Care should be taken to see that the method of cooking is not repeated, otherwise certain equipment would be overloaded.

Basically, the preparation is centered around the 'menu' and the menu is planned based on many factors as detailed in the chapter.

Barring a few large hotels, in general, the menu in India is rather restricted to some typical Indian dishes, such as pulao, damalu, dal, meat and chicken cooked in ordinary way or in tandoor. Very rarely one can find egg or fish items. Hotel business, in India, is greatly influenced by the Europeans due to their long stay with us and recently the American influences are in view. Occasionally, we find limited Chinese items such as, chowmein, American chopsoy, fried rice, chillichicken, etc. in the menu of the contemporary eating places located in cities in particular. Local varieties, varieties from other states are also now appearing in the menu of a reasonably good eating places. The overall picture is that though we have not attained the culinary excellence of the foreign cuisine, we wish to market them according to the demand. Our customers are also not very much aware of the culinary excellence and service style to press for quality preparation and service by hoteliers.

In Western countries, the beverage services are equally important to food services, if not more. In India, we hardly have any organised beverage services except some bars dealing only with beers and spirits of limited brands. Wine services, up-keep of cellers, cocktail services are practically not handled by majority of hotels in our country. Hence, it is not necessary to go into the details of their technicalities except the things of practical importance in the hotelkeeping of a particular country.

PREPARATION TECHNIQUES

For any food preparation, appropriate tools are necessary. These are again planned as per cooking methods to be incorporated. Many vegetables and fruits do not require any cooking but these are to be peeled, cleaned and cut before serving as raw dishes ingredients such as salt, sugar or combination of several things, known as dressings, are added. These dressings are very important for raw fruits and vegetables to be consumed as salads and similar dishes.

PREPARATION OF INGREDIENTS (MIS-EN-PLACE)

Foods which are to be cooked require some amount of pre-preparation. Following are some of them.

Washing

This is done to remove surface dirt. Wash vegetables, meat and fish in cold water. If they are soaked for a long period or washed after cutting, there is a greater loss of water-soluble minerals and vitamins.

Peeling and Scrapping

Spoilt, soiled and inedible portions are removed. Skin of vegetables such as potatoes, carrots and fruits is removed by either peeling or scrapping. While peeling, remove as little of the fleshy part as possible.

Cutting

Reducing to small parts by means of a knife or chopper. When the reduction is done by a chopping knife or a food chopper, it is known as chopping. Cutting into even-sized cubes is called dicing. Cutting into very fine pieces is mincing. Shredding is cutting into fine long pieces with a knife or shredder. Slicing is also cutting into thin long pieces, but these are not as fine as in shredder.

Grating

Reducing to fine particles by rubbing over a rough sharp surface or grater.

Grinding

Reducing to small fragments by crushing in a grinding machine or grinding stone.

Mashing

This is a method of breaking up soft foods such as cooked potatoes or vegetables.

Sieving

Passing through mesh to remove impurities, to breakdown to even portions.

Milling

Used for cereals and legumes to remove husks, etc.

Steeping

Extracting, colouring and flavouring by allowing ingredients to stand in water generally at a temperature just below boiling point.

Emulsification

Dispersing one liquid in another in whch it is insoluble, e.g. oil and yolk of egg in mayonnaise.

Evaporation

Removal of excess moisture by heating.

METHODS OF MIXING FOODS

Beating

This method can be used with mixture of liquids. This should be done carefully with the aim of enclosing air. This is known as whipping also as in beating of eggs.

Blending

Mixing two or more ingredients thoroughly.

Creaming

Softening of fat by friction with a wooden spoon, generally followed by gradual incorporation of sugar as in cake making.

Folding

Mixing mixture by lifting and folding motion. The edge of a spoon or hand is used and the mixture is lifted, turned completely and gently replaced.

Kneading

Manipulating by alternating pressure with folding and stretching. The food is pressed with the knuckles. The dough is brought from the outside of the basin to the centre. This ensures a thorough distribution of ingredients, e.g. bread dough, chapati dough, etc.

Rubbing

Rubbing fat into flour using the tips of the fingers and thumb and lifting the hand out of the basin as in the case of shortcrust pastry. Rub until the mixture looks like breadcrumbs.

Rolling

Rolling butter or fat in a soft dough, e.g. puff pastry.

Pressing

This is done to shape foods such as cutlets and sometimes as a method of subdivision to separate liquids from solids by weights or mechanical pressure as for panir.

Stirring

Mixing food with a suitable tool, for example, spoon by a circular motion in contact with the pan. Generally, this is a gentle movement but changed to suit different dishes, as when used to prevent sticking or burning in halwas and toffees.

METHODS OF COOKING FOODS

Food can be cooked in many ways. The brief methods are described below.

Steaming

Cooking is done by moist heat (vapours). There are two types of steaming—indirect steaming where food is sealed with cloth or aluminium foil and placed in a container which is immersed in another container which generates steam from boiling water or from a steamer, e.g. steam pudding. In direct steaming, food items are in direct contact with the vapours.

Boiling

Food items are cooked in boiling water (100ºC). Green vegetables are put into the boiling water and root vegetables are put in cold water and then boiled, e.g. boiled potatoes, boiled green peas, etc.

Roasting

Food is cooked in direct contact with heat. Fat is basted to moisten and soften the meat. There are three major methods of roasting.

1. Pot roasting: Quality meals are trussed to retain their shape and placed in a pot which has crossed rods within to prevent the meat from stricking to the bottom. The meat is basted with fat. This is sealed and heated from below on a slow fire. Root vegetables may be added later for flavour. After the meat is cooked, stock may be added to the liquid inside to make a sauce. Otherwise, the natural liquid formed called 'jus Roti' may act as the gravy.

2. Oven roasting: The meat is basted and roasted in a tray in the oven at temperature of 300ºF. The meat is constantly basted and turned round for even cooking and colour.

3. Tandoor roasting: An Indian concept where meat is marinated with spices and curd and skewered on rods which are placed into mud ovens which is heated from within.

Poaching

Food items are cooked in shallow water. The water never boils but simmers, that is, it is kept below boiling point, e.g. poached eggs, poached fish, etc.

Grilling

The fastest method of cooking expansive meat cuts done on hot grid iron with heat coming form top or below. Meat is marinated before grilling and never picked while cooking as the juice flow out.

Frying

This method of cooking uses fat as a cooking media. There are three types of frying:

i. Saute—Done on slow fire and used for tender items.
ii. Shallow frying—Very little fat used but cooking is done fully.
iii. Deep frying—Done in hot oil or fat, the food is submerged in the oil and cooked.

Baking

The method by which cakes, pies, biscuits are cooked in dry radient heat at different temperatures in an air oven.

Broiling

It is a dry method of cooking by direct heat either from above or below. It can be done on grids or pans where food is cooked uncovered. It is used as a method of preserving food.

Smoking

Food is preserved with the help of smoke from wooden shavings and sawdust, in a close room, e.g. smoked salmon, smoked ham, etc.

Stewing

Very slow method of cooking in a utensils with a closed lid where tough meats and joint are cooked in water to softer them. Herbs and spices are added for flavour and the juice is served as gravy. It is cooked on low fire or in an oven at a low temperature, e.g. mutton stew or Irish stew, etc.

Braising

It is a combination of roasting and stewing. Meat is first browned to seal off the pores so as to retain the juices. The meat is then placed on a bed of vegetables, herbs, bacon, ham, etc. in a casserole. The casserole is sealed with a lid to prevent evaporation and then placed in an oven to cook.

Pressure Cooking and use of Pressure Cooker

The very first step is to know the correct way to fit the lid into the cooker body and how to remove it.

The following steps should be performed for correct fitting of the lid into the cooking body:

1. If gasket (rubber ring) is not properly fitted into curl (groove around the lid's rim), make sure it is properly fitted.
2. Place lid on cooker body so lid handle and body handle are together.
   (Note: Do not force lid into cooker body)
3. Turn lid handle so that it is at a right angle to body handle.
4. See that arrow so that it is at a right angle.
5. Slide the lid slightly away from the body handle and tilt that portion of the lid that has the arrow on it into the mouth of the pressure cooker.

6. Insert lid under rim of the cooker body.
7. Place the lid handle bar on top of the pivot which rests on the body handle. Adjust the lid bar on the pivot until the gasket (rubber ring) on the lid rests comfortably in direct contact with the underneath of the rim of the body of the pressure cooker.
8. Gently squeeze lid and body handles together.
9. Fasten locking loop to catch on end of the main handle bracket.
10. If necessary, to ensure lid is properly seated, press lid and adjust.

Tables 8.1–8.3 give cooking timings for various food items.

The following steps should be performed for the correct removal of lid from pressure cooker:

1. Gently squeeze lid and body handles together.
2. Unfasten locking loop from end of main handles bracket.
3. Tilt the lid down slightly into the mouth of the cooker.

Table 8.1: Cooking timings for cereals and pulses						
Cereals	*Quantity (gm)*	*Quantity of water (ml)*	*Time for cooker to come to full cooking pressure (minutes)*	*Cooking time to medium heat (minutes)*	*Total time (minutes)*	*Remarks (preferably for best cooking)*
Rice (Basmati)	250	250	5	3	8	Soak for 1/2 hour
Tuvar dal	250	500	7	3	10	(dal with- out
Lentil	250	500	7	2	9	gravy)
Whole green Gram	250	500	7	5	12	
White beans	250	500	7	15	22	
Whole black gram	250	900	13	55	68	
Spaghetti	85	500	3	2	5	

Table 8.2: Cooking timings for vegetables

Cereals	Quantity (gm)	Quantity of water (ml)	Time for cooker to come to full cooking pressure (minutes)	Cooking time to medium heat (minutes)	Total time (minutes)	Remarks (preferably for best cooking)
Medium size	500	300	6	5	11	Open immediately
Diced carrots	500	20	3	2	5	Open immediately
Shredded cabbage	500	No water	3	1	4	Open immediately
Cauliflowers	500	20	3	1	4	Open immediately
Whole capsicum	500	20	3	1	4	Open immediately
Diced French beans	500	30	4	2	6	Open immediately
Whole slit tinda	500	30	4	3	7	Open immediately
Diced turnip	500	30	3	3	6	Allow to cool gradually

4. Move the lid handle bar towards the right-hand side.
5. As the lid handle bar approaches 90º right angle position, gently tilt up the position of the lid away from the body handle.
6. Remove the lid out of the mouth of the pressure cooker.

In India, the cooking method is largely based on application of heat in oil medium, i.e. deep fat frying or shallow fat frying. Tandoor is popular in hotels for making nan, tandoori chicken, tandoori paneer, etc. The important fats and oils that are used in hotels are:

i. Vanaspati
ii. Mustard oil
iii. Groundnut oil
iv. Til oil
v. Ghee and butter
vi. Soya oil/olive oil (extra virgin).

Care must be taken about the quantity of fat because these are expensive but easily spoiled. Repetition of used oil should be avoided. In hotels tinned and bottled items are often used. The food and beverage department should see that these items are genuine and they are stored in accordance to the direction. The best way is to use natural colours and pickle, etc. which can be made in the hotel under some expert supervision. Sauces, fruit juices, etc. if prepared in the

Table 8.3: Cooking timings for meet, fish and poultry

Meet fish poultry	Qty in (gm)	Qty of water (ml)	Time for full cooking (minutes)	Cooking time at medium heat (minutes)	Total time (minutes)	Remarks
Mutton	500	75	7	10	17	Allow to cool gradually
Mutton chap	500	75	7	8	15	Allow to cool gradually
Park loin	500	75	7	8	15	Open immediately
Shoulder mineed meet	500	50	5	5	10	Allow to cool gradually
Fish	500	100	4	2	6	Open immediately
Cut chicken	1000	75	7	10	17	Open immediately
Liver	500	75	7	8	15	Allow to cool gradually

hotels, must be properly stored and checked before offering to any guest.

Hand Tools for Cooking

These vary from place to place and from country to country. Cooking is done in India in degchi, kadhai and slicer (perforated as well as non-perforated). Chopping board, grinding stone, knives, kettle, pudding moulds, choppers, scrumps, peelers, mashers, etc. are common equipment in Indian kitchens (Fig. 8.1).

Some Chinese cooking utensils and hand tools are shown in Fig. 8.2.

Traditional Western Cooking Utensils (Fig. 8.3)

1. Double boiler
2. Saucepan
3. Fry pan
4. kettle (Fig. 8.4)
5. Wire whisk
6. Mixing bowl
7. Roast pan
8. Casserole
9. Spoon (wood and metal)
10. Rolling pin
11. Flour shifter
12. Cook's knife (8"–10" blade)
13. Chopping board
14. Grater
15. Grinder
16. Colander
17. Metal turner

Some other modern kitchen equipment is shown in Figs 8.5–8.7.

Kitchen Knife: Its Care and Use (Fig. 8.8)

Knife is the most important tool used in all types of kitchen throughout the world. Without real good knife and without the skill of its use, the kitchen jobs cannot be performed.

In Indian kitchens indigenous cutting tools are still in use instead of modern knives. These cutting tools are known as 'Da', 'Hasua','Bathi', etc. Meat and chicken are usually purchased as pieces made in accordance to the local styles. 'Bathi' is used with sitting posture and to hold the vegetables and fish, etc. 'Da' with various types and shapes of cutting surfaces are somehow the Indian version of the knives.

Modern knives for cookery are improved versions of old kitchen cutting tools. These are now available in various shapes, sizes, weight and length, etc. and are used for multiple or specific purposes. Accordingly, these are also named chef's knife, Chinese chopper, chopper, Japanese knife, butcher's knife, cheese knife, meat curving knife, vegetables curving knife, etc.

These days knives are made up of stainless steel mostly. These are long-lasting and suitable for cutting acidic fruits and vegetables. The knives having carbon steel blades sharpen easily but need frequent cleaning and sharpening.

Knives are sharpened on surfaces such as stone, leather, wood, etc. Newly developed metal with diamond-imbedded surfaces developed in the USA are long-lasting and very effective for quick sharpening.

The use of carborandum or emory (India stone) for sharpening is quite common

Fig. 8.2: Important Chinese cooking utensils

1. Chopper	6. Chinese wok
2. Chopping block	7. Flat spoon
3. Pickle pot	8. Frying pan
4. Strainer	9. Round ladle
5. Chopping board	10. Round spoon

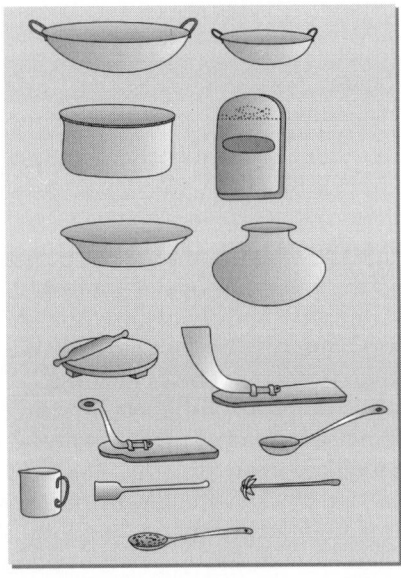

Fig. 8.1: Common Indian cooking utensils

1. Large karahi	6. Indian handi	11. Cholni
2. Small karahi	7. Chakki	12. Kalchul
3. Degchi	8. Hansua	13. Dalghotni
4. Grinding stone	9. Khurni	14. Jhanjhri
5. Gamla	10. Mug	

Fig. 8.3: Traditional Western cooking utensils

1. Saucepan 2. Stock pot 3. Roasting pan

throughout the world. The sharpening stones of 8″ × 2″ × 1″ size may be purchased from hardware store. It has two surfaces—one coarse and another fine. The stone surfaces should be oiled before sharpening the knife over its surface.

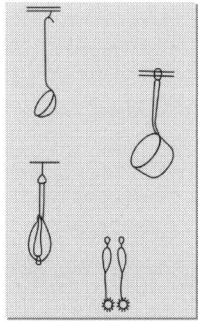

Fig. 8.4: Kettle

1. Wire skimmer
2. Wire chip basket
3. Wire whisks
4. Spiral whisks

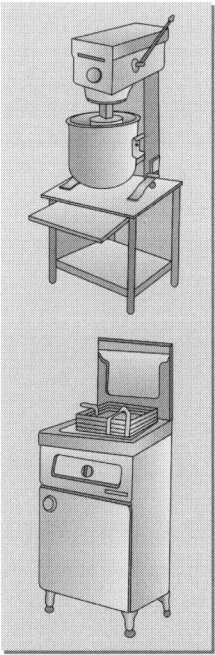

Fig. 8.5: Kitchen equipment

1. Kitchen mixture and grinder   2. Deep fat fryer

Fig. 8.6: Modern kitchen equipment

1. Sink unit   2. Kitchen shelf   3. Potato peeler

The sharpening style varies from person to person, but the following techniques can be of help for the business. The oiled stone should be placed on a steady surface at a comfortable height (for standing operation). The edge of the knife is then placed against the surface of the stone at a small angle for back and front movements or for small circular movements as shown in Fig. 8.9. When the blade is at one end of the stone, it is then either drawn in front or pushed back by turning the blade (Fig. 8.9). For large knife, two hands should be dried before keeping them safely to prevent accidental cuts and injuries. Knives having carbon steel blades may be occasionally rubbed with vegetable oil.

Cutting of Vegetable, Chicken and Fish

Not all vegetables and fishes are used in restaurants as in domestic kitchens. Only limited types of fishes and vegetables are considered for use in commercial eating places.

Vegetables such as potato, lettuce, cauliflower, cabbage, tomato, capsicum, beans, cucumber, onions, onion stalks, green chilli,

1

2

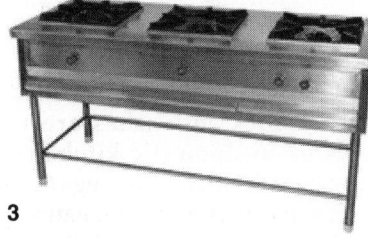

3

Fig. 8.7: Griller and cooking range

1. Griller   2. Cooking range   3. Cooking range

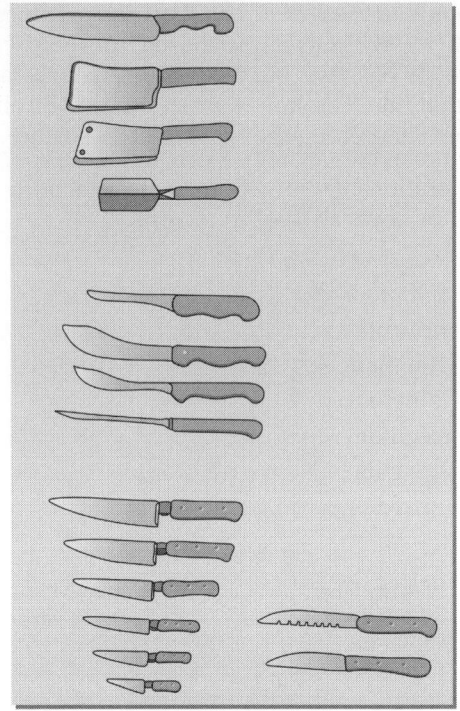

Fig. 8.8: Different sizes and shapes of cutting knives

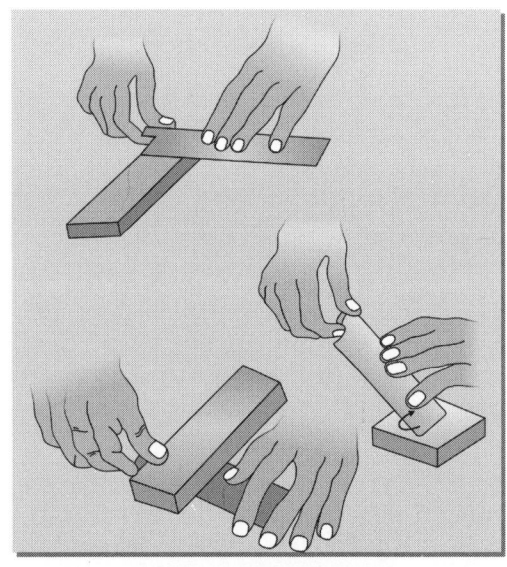

Fig. 8.9: Knife sharpener

ginger are most common items requiring peeling and cutting in different styles for use in catering establishments. Knives are used for "cutting", "chopping" and "slicing". The hold of knife and vegetables are shown in Figs 8.10 to 8.13. Typical vegetables cuts are to be learnt for use in specific preparations. Following cuts of vegetables are used by chefs all over the world:

- Round or oval cuts
- Half moon cuts
- Dice cuts (cubes)
- Thin matchstick-like cuts (julienne cut)
- Chinese rolling cuts
- Irregular cuts (Paysane cut)
- Slice cuts (very thin slice)
- Minced cuts (finely chopped)

Production of all these cuts needs skill and practice of the staff in the kitchen. Table 8.4 gives assessment of good quality of fruits and vegetables for use in hotels.

Cutting of Fishes

Both scaled fishes and fishes without scales are used in hotels. Rohu, Katla, Bhetki, Hilsa, Sole are common scaled fishes used.

Heads and tails are removed after scaling and are cut into round shapes. Hilsas and big variety of Rohu, etc. are sometimes separated into dorsal and ventral portions and then cut into smaller pieces. Arh, Pomphret, Silon, Boari are scale less fishes used commonly in catering establishments. These are cleaned and cuts in rounds (Fig. 8.14).

Fish fillets are cuts usually from Bhetki or Arh fishes. Very thin fillets are cut for fish roll and other similar preparations.

Cutting of Chicken

Depending upon the sizes, the chickens are cut into 6, 8 or 12 pieces as shown in Fig. 8.15. For the sake of uniformity and price many eating establishments use live birds having weight

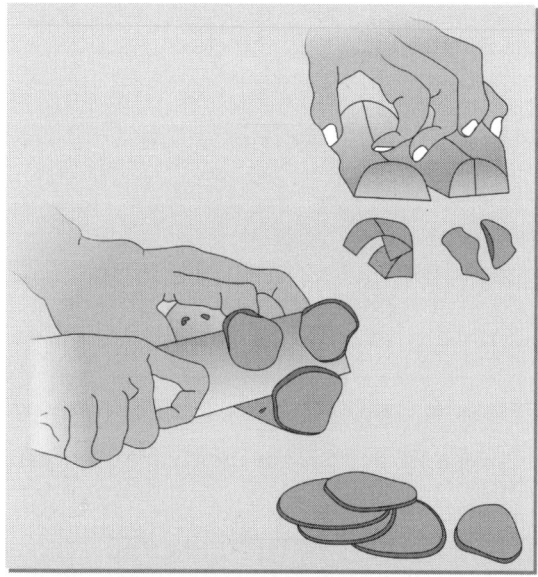

Fig. 8.10: Cutting potatoes

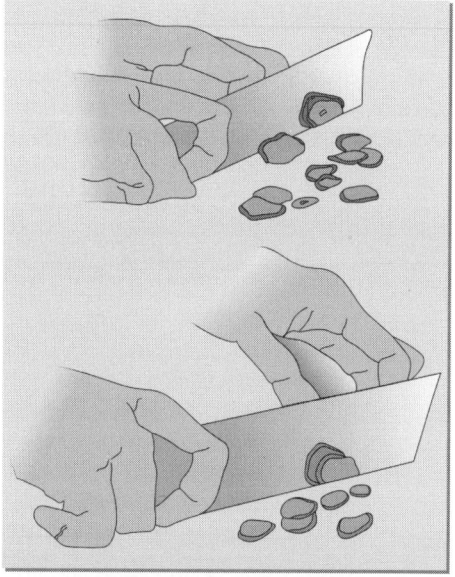

Fig. 8.11: Chopping radishes

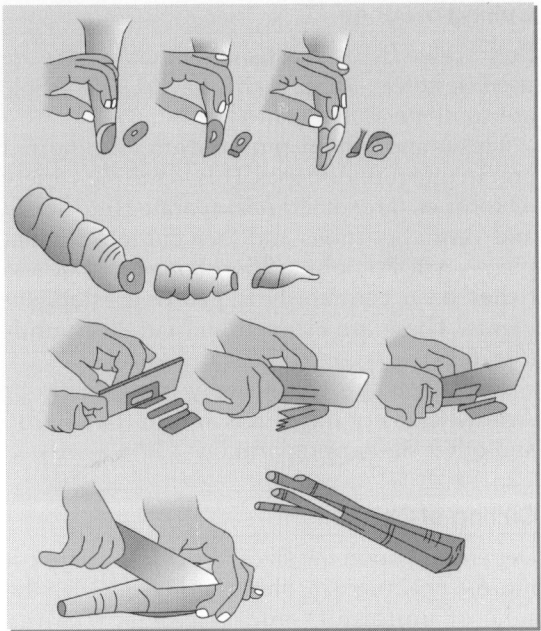

Fig. 8.12: Cutting of carrots

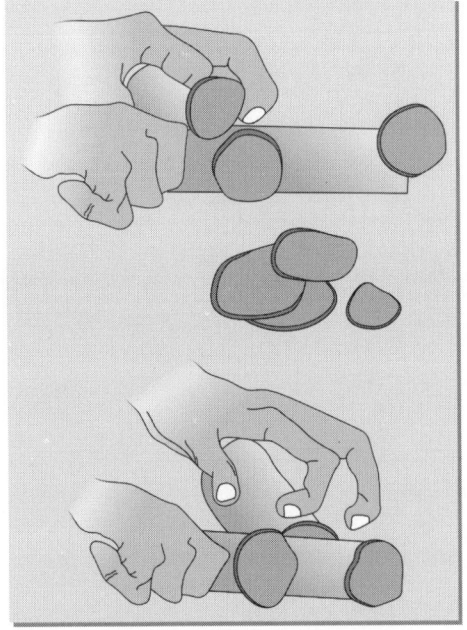

Fig. 8.13: Chopping potatoes

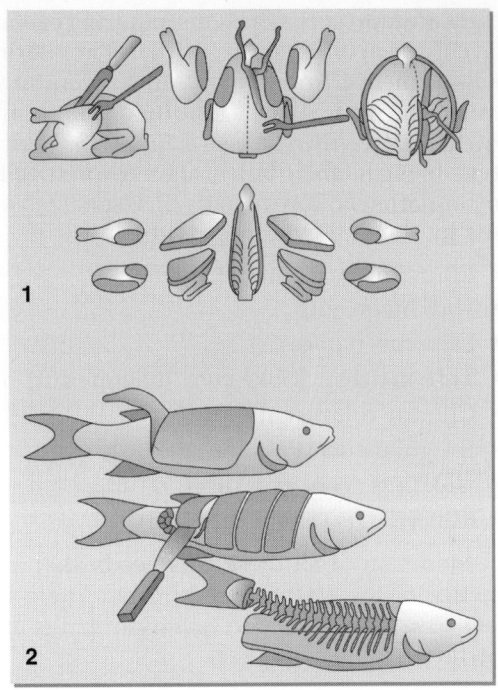

Fig. 8.14: 1. Cutting of chickens, 2. Cutting of centrally boned fishes

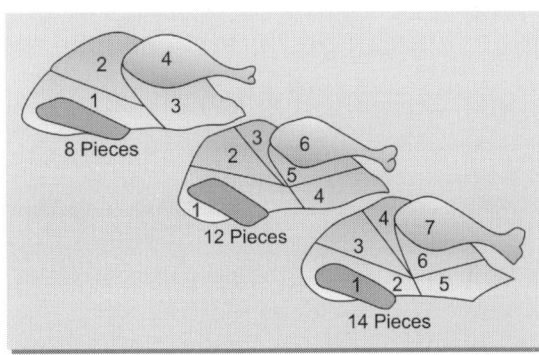

Fig. 8.15: Example showing cutting lines of chicken

between 500 and 600 gm and cut into four parts consisting two portions of legs and two portions of wings with breast. These small birds are also known as "hotel size" birds in the trade. Chicken flesh are also obtained free from bone for certain special bone less preparations.

Cutting of Meat

In India meat is commonly the goat meat. Apart from goat's flesh, lamb, beef, pork are also used and usually cut in accordance to the market style. In big hotels, there is a larger room where cutting of meat, etc. is done. Smaller establishments obtain the supply through the supplier. Meat cuts in our country are not of any uniform pattern, thus it is difficult to maintain quality and portion size in meat dishes. Minced meat or keema can be obtained from the butcher's stall or made in the kitchen. Botis are special cuts used for kababs and biryani.

Table 8.4: Assessment of good quality fruits and vegetables for use in hotels

Fruits	Signs of good quality
Apple	Firm; good colour; peel not shriveled
Apricots	Fairly firm; golden-yellow colour; peel not shriveled
Banana	Plump, well filled for use uncooked; yellow peel flecked with brown, for cooking use, yellow peel with slightly green top.
Grapefruit	Well shaped; unblemished firm; heavy for size; thin skins preferable
Grapes	Fresh appearance; plump; firmly attached to the stem; soft to touch.
Lemons	Waxy skins; heavy for size; moderate firmness.
Melon	Dent free; fragrant free and free from visula defects.
Orange	Firm; heavy for size; moderate firmness
Peaches	Fragrant; plump; smooth skin with no blemishes
Pear	Firm or fairly firm; well shaped; fragrant
Pineapple	Soft to touch; golden yellow; test for ripeness; pull a leaf from top; if easily removed fruit is ripe.
Plum	Fresh looking, plump.

Vegetables	Signs of good quality
Asparagus	Straight; fresh green stalks; heavy for size; crisp
Beans-green	Bright colour; firm pods which snap when broken
Beet	Uniform in size; dark red colour; leaves not to large
Cabbage	Closely packed leaves; only a slight odour
Carrots	Firm; free from decay or cracks clean
Cauliflower	Head firmly packed; white in colour; outer leave green
Celery	Thick; crisp stems free from spots; fresh-looking leaves
Cucumber	Crisp; solid; deep green; long straight without tapering ends.
Eggplant	Firm; fairly smooth; well shaped; glossy purple colour.
Onion dry	Round; crackly skin; no green streaks or sprouts
Peas, green	Young; tender; fresh pods; well filled fresh peas; crush easily
Capsicum	Firm; Fresh; without spoiled surfaces
Potato	Firm; well shaped; shallow eyes in sprourts
Tomato, red	Rich red; fragment; solid, smooth
Green	Fresh crisp leaves flat or crinkle; deep green colour.

General Methods of Food Storage in Hotels

Most of the catering establishments have to depend upon purchases made in bulk which are to be appropriately stored at least for a few days till fresh supplies reach the establishment.

The volumes of materials as well as policy of the establishment are important factors in determining the storage duration of the food materials. Presently many food items are available in packed form which also require appropriate storage facilities at standardised temperature.

There are basically two different types of storages, i.e. dry storage for rice, wheat, pulses, etc. This kind of storage needs appropriate ventilation and humidity control. The refrigerated storage is necessary for fruits, vegetables, meat, fish, etc. It is not possible to have cold storage or cold room in most of the smaller establishments. As a result, in smaller establishments, deep fridge of various capacities and refrigerators are used for storing food materials. The following are the ideal temperatures in which the foodstuff can safely be stored:

• Maximum acceptable temperature for storage of all perishable foods	9–10ºC
• Fruits (except bananas), vegetables and other perishable products	6–7ºC
• Milk products	6–8ºC
• Meat, chicken	5–6ºC
• Fish, prawn, etc.	0–1ºC
• Frozen foods	– 15–17ºC

In Indian context, it is always advisable to depend minimum on the cold storage because of non-standard thermal condition. It is also advisable to periodically check the quality of foodstuff in the refrigerator before using it in the kitchen. In many places, dal, gravies and other cooked items are also dumped in refrigerator without having considerations for appropriate containers and appropriate storing method. Gravies, dal, etc. are highly sensitive

for damage due to bacterial and fungal growth. Under any circumstance, care should be taken to store the food items for only minimum periods as far as possible and there should be routine inspection as to the the state of food in the storage unit. Storage containers, refrigerators and deep freezer unit should be periodically cleaned.

DESCRIPTION OF SPICES AND HERBS USED IN COOKERY

Spices

Spices and condiments both serve a common purpose, i.e. they add flavour to the food we eat. Although they have food value, they serve the purpose of stimulating the appetite.

Essential Qualities of Spices

With the exception of salt, which is a mineral, all spices and condiments are obtained from plants or vegetable substances, the majority of which grow best in tropical countries. The aromatic and flavouring characteristics of all spices and most condiments are attributed to the presence of very minute quantities of chemical substances found in the volatile oils which the plants contain. The spices that have been exposed to the atmosphere over a prolonged period of time will lose their essential to the atmosphere and thus their aromatic and flavouring properties.

1. **All spices (*Pimento officinalis*):** The spice is variously known as 'all spice'. The nature of all spices is given to it because its flavour and aroma resemble a mixture of cloves, nutmeg and cinnamon.
2. **Aniseed (*Pimpinalla anisum*).**
3. **Capsicum (*Capsicum*):** The plants of the genus capsicum have many varieties which are widely distributed throughout the world, and they produce scarlet, yellow and green fruit pods of various sizes. The

large long pods being known as capsicum or sweet peppers and the smaller ones chillies. The smaller pods being much hotter than the large one. Both types are used in the manufacture of pickles and the large ripe pods (capsicums or sweet peppers) are used fresh or canned for culinary purposes, either stuffed as a vegetable, as garnish or as part of an Hors-de' ouvre.

4. **Caraway seeds:** These are the fried, ripe seeds of an umbelliferous plant Carum Carvi, a herb that is cultivated extensively in the UK and other European countries.

5. **Cardamoms:** The chief sources of supply are from India and Sri lanka, where the plant is also found growing wild.

6. **Cayenne pepper:** The hottest of all the peppers. It is prepared from the dried red, fully ripened berries of one of the many types of capsicum plants. There are hundred of varieties in different parts of the world.

7. **Chillies:** Chillies are also used in the manufacture of pickles and certain pungent sauces like piri-piri sauce. Hotness is measured by "scovil" unit developed by M/s Park Davis.

8. **Cinnamon:** The best cinnamon is light-yellow in colour and no thicker than thick pepper. It is gathered in May and again in November, and is allowed to ferment slightly before processing in order to develop the warm, sweet taste and pleasant, fragrant odour for which it is famous.

9. **Cloves:** These are the dried, unopened flower-buds of all tall, evergreen tree *Eugenia Caryophyllata* which grows in most tropical countries, particularly Indonesia, the West Indies, Sri Lanka, India, Africa and Brazil.

10. **Coriander (*Coriandrum sativum*):** These seeds have aromatic qualities similar to those of caraway seeds. They have a fragrant smell and sweet pleasant taste.

11. **Cumin (*Cuminum cyminum*):** The dried fruit of an umbelliferous annual plant and closely related to caraway. It is used for the same purpose but not as widely.

12. **Curry powder:** This condiment is a mixture of various spices and aromatic herbs and its ingredient vary considerably, depending upon the manufacture. The main ingredients are ginger, cayenne pepper and turmeric and among the others are included cinnamon, nutmeg, mace, cloves, tamarins, lemon grass, lime juice, salt cardamom, coriander, mango and black pepper in varying proportions.

13. **Ginger:** Ginger is an aromatic and stimulating spice with important digestive properties. It is obtained from the underground stems or rhizomes of a plant that grows to a height of about three feet. These rhizomes are scalded with boiling water and then dried and stored at which stage they are known as black ginger. Sometimes they are scrapped, washed and dried in the sun, after which they are called white ginger.

14. **Mace:** The kernel of the fruit produces nutmeg and this is covered by a bright crimsion aril called mace.

15. **MSG (monosodium glutamate):** This is not a spice but a widely used chemical food additive commonly known as the fourth condiment, and sold under various names. A white crystalline, soluble substance, similar in appearance to course salt. It is a product of comparatively recent discovery and is, as yet, in more common use in food factories than in kitchens, commonly known as 'azinomoto'.

16. **Mustard:** The mustard commonly used in commercial catering is really a mixture of the ground seeds of two distinctly different plants, namely black mustard (*Brassica niger*) and white mustard (*Brassica albe*), both of which are members of the cabbage family (*Brassica*).

17. **Nutmeg:** This is kernel of the fruit of the myristica tree.

18. **Paprika:** This is a species of capsicum and is known as *Capsicum amuum*.

19. **Pimiento:** This is a species of capsicum known as pimiento or Spanish red pepper,

which is not the same species as is dried and ground to provide Cayenne pepper. The seeds are removed from the fleshy, ripe, red pods of the pimiento.

20. **Poppy used:** Unlike the poppy of the far eastern countries (apaver somniferum), our garden poppy contains no trace of opium. The seeds of the poppy contain a high percentage of very palatable edible oil and that is why these are used in the making of a special type of bread.

21. **Salt (sodium chloride):** This is the only condiment in regular use in the kitchen which is not a vegetable substance.

    a. **Table salt:** The type of salt usually sold and used as table salt contains a small proportion of a chemical substance, usually either calcium phosphate or magnesium carbonate which ensures that its free running properties are retained particularly during rainy season.

    b. **Iodised salt:** When potassium iodide or iodate is added, the salt is known as iodised salt, a free-running salt with medicinal properties. Preventive nutrients against goitre.

22. **Saffron:** A highly-flavoured spice produced from the dried stigma of a species of Crocus called *Crocus sativas*.

23. **Tabasco:** A liquid condiment known by the trade name of 'Tabasco' is manufactured from a mixture of the hottest peppers obtainable, and is marketed in a special type of bottle which dispenses the sauce a drop at a time.

24. **Turmeric (*Curcuma inga*):** An eastern plant closely related to ginger, which yields a spice of a bright yellow colour and pleasant aroma.

25. **Vanilla:** The fruit of a tropical climbing orchid (Vanilla planifolia) native to Asia and America. It is now cultivated mainly in the East and West Indies.

26. **Charmagaj:** Dried seeds of fruits of melon family.

27. **Mixed spices:** Nowadays many companies have started marketing dried spices, to be used in various preparations such as amabar, meat, chola, etc. These are essentially trade mixtures of common Indian spices, used for curry. Paste form of curry spices are also available.

28. **Indian garam masala:** It is a mixture of clove, cinnamon and cardamom.

Herbs

Unlike spices, most herbs are easily cultivated and may be successfully grown in the garden with the minimum of attention.

1. **Bayleaf (*Cerasus laurocerasus*):** The leaf of an evergreen shrub known as the cherry laurel or green bay tree. Its flavour is very strong and must be used in small quantities, otherwise the flavour of the dish to which it is added may be spoiled.

2. **Bouquet garni:** The indispensible 'faggot' of herbs is used in the kitchen for flavouring soups, sauces, stews and braisings and consisting of a bayleaf, a few parsley-stalks and a sparing or pinch of thyre. Often with the addition of a few crushed pepper corns all tried up with white cotton.

3. **Celery seed:** The dried seed of the celery plant (*Apium graveolens*) is used to impart the refreshing flavour of celery to a dish, when fresh celery is not available. Used largely in soups, sauces, tomato-juice, cocktails, etc.

4. **Fennel (*Faeniculum vulgare*):** Related to and similar in appearance to celery is an important ingredient of the soup Bortsch.

5. **Garlic (*Allium sativum*):** A small bulbous-rooted plant related to the onion, with extremely powerful aromatic and flavouring properties. Garlic should be used in extreme moderation.

6. **Horseradish (*Cobhelearia armoracia*):** A very pungent root and very easy to cultivate, horseradish is usually made into sauces, creams or butter and used as one of

the most common accompaniments for roast beef or grilled beef steaks.

7. **Mint:** A very useful herb, the kind used in the kitchen for making mint sauce and for adding to new potatoes, green peas, etc.

8. **Coriander leaves:** Widely used in Indian kitchen.

9. **Onion leaves:** Used as herb also in rice and vegetable preparations. In addition to the above, there are many well-known herbs used in many countries. They are Basil, Cheruil, Chives, Dil, Juniper, Thyme, etc. These are rarely used in Indian hotels.

10. **Parsely (*Petroselimum sativum*):** A commonly used umbelliferous plant easily grown in the herb-garden. The variety is easily chopped. It is indispensable in the kitchen, not only for its excellent flavouring properties but also as a garnish either chopped or in springs.

11. **Shallot (*Allium ascalnicum*):** A plant closely related to garlic, with bulbous-root very similar in form but much milder in flavour. It is very widely used in the kitchen particularly in the making of sauces.

COMPARISON OF COOKING FUELS

Many factors need to be taken into consideration in the comparison of fuels, e.g. the cheapest fuel to buy may not be the cheapest to burn. When comparing electricity with coal, the initial cost of electricity will be much higher, but when considering coal, one has to think of the storage space required, the cost of labour to move it, the cost of labour to clean the dirt it causes, etc.

A list of advantages and disadvantages of each fuel helps to make comparisons.

Gas Cooking

Advantages

1. Convenient, labour saving
2. Free from smoke and dirt

3. Easily controlled with immediate full heat and the flames are visible
4. Special utensils are not required.

Disadvantages

1. Some heat is lost into the kitchen
2. Regular cleaning is necessary for efficiency
3. Storage required

Electricity Cooking

Advantages

1. Clean to use and maintain
2. Easily control and labour saving
3. A good working atmosphere for kitchen staff as no oxygen to burn electricity
4. Little heat is lost
5. No fuel storage is required

Disadvantages

1. Time needed to heat up
2. High cost of installation

Steam Cooking

Advantages

1. Good heat for boiling liquids
2. Low maintenance costs

Disadvantages

1. Methods of cookings are limited
2. High initial cost of installation

Solid Fuel Cooking

Advantage

Low maintenance costs

Disadvantages

1. Cannot meet all cooking requirements
2. Storage of fuel
3. Dirt and dust from fuel
4. Labour costs to move fuel
5. Difficulty of control of heat
6. Pollution results

Oil Cooking

Advantages

1. Clean and convenient
2. Labour saving

Disadvantages

1. Need for large storage tanks
2. Source of supply may be affected

The Storage Space Required for some Fuels

- Coal per tonne 50 sq. ft. storage space
- Coke per tonne 75 sq. ft. storage space
- LPG cylinders 4 sq. ft. per cylinder space

Electricity do not require storage space; this advantage is paid for by higher initial cost.

Disinfectants for Use in Kitchen

In pursuing the goal of clean kitchen and equipment, the chef or the caterer and his staff will depend on new and traditional cleaning aids and methods. Hot soup and water and the scrubbing brush will go far in ensuring cleanliness of utensils and apparatus but is often necessary to consider the use of chemical disinfectants. Hot water (above 80°C) is very effective sterilising agent in locations where it can easily be used. Steam cleaning and sterilisation of floors using commerically available units are increasingly adopted in catering establishments.

Chemical disinfectants should have the following properties:

- Act rapidly on as many types of organisms as possible.
- Have an effective degree of penetration (this will vary according to surface tension)
- Be active and efficient in low concentration because of the cost factor.
- Be active in the presence of organic matter.
- Be stable for storage purposes.
- Be of a price permitting reasonable use.

Types of Disinfectant

Types of chemical disinfectant commonly encountered in catering establishments are as follows:

1. **Oxidising agents**. Some disinfectants destroy becteria by oxidising them and are also able to combat spores. This type is effective but they are unable and hence storage problems arise. Their effectiveness is inhibited also by the presence of organic matter as is found in the solid debris left in washing up soild. Disinfectants of this type include sodium hypochloride, potassium permanganate, hydrogen peroxide and halogens (e.g. chlorine in drinking water).
2. **Derivatives of coal tar.** These are effective disinfectants which are reasonably pleasant to use. They include carbolic acid, lysol and some alcohols.
3. **The quarternary ammonium compounds.** There has been a considerable development in the marketing of this type of disinfectant which is used in modern detergents which also emulsify grease.

Effectiveness of Disinfectant

The effectiveness of disinfectant varies and may be improved by:

1. Heat, for example, hot lysol is much more effective than cold.
2. By lowering the surface tension of whatever is to be disinfected and this can be achieved by using detergent either before hand or mixed with the disinfectant. By emulsifying the grease, it affords the disinfectant an opportunity to reach its objective and to work. Thus, it is advisable to use a disinfectant following a cleaning operation with a detergent to ensure that it works at the maximum efficiency.

Similarly, the efficiency of disinfectant is impaired by the presence of organic matter as found in washing-up water and which can include food soil, fragments of cloth such as wool, cotton or silk, mucus, pus, flesh fragments, blood or wood. These act as barriers and making difficult for the chemical to reach and destroy the bacteria.

Personal Hygiene

The following factors which have been concerned with the food itself, its protection against dirt, insects, vermin and the importance of having clean premises, equipment and the like, are clearly of great importance. Equally clearly they depend to a large extent on the constant interest and vigilance of the human being working in the kitchen. The chef, the caterer and their staff of cooks and kitchen hands must be concerned to see that all the measures to promote hygiene are observed effectively.

Yet, perhaps the most important form of precaution is that in which the operator renders himself safe by personal measures of cleanliness. Contamination is so often caused by human agency that it would not be exaggerating to say that the human being is the greatest potential danger in the kitchen.

There is, however, another aspect of personal hygiene which is important. This aspect is the comfort and well-being of the individual at work. It is always an added point to stress that many of the measures of hygiene and cleanliness which protect the customer and others, also promote health and a sense of well-being in the person practising them.

The type of dress to be worn and the measures to be taken in keeping it clean and in good order have already been dealt with. It is not required to be stressed further that work in many sections of the kitchen induce perspiration, the gathering of cooking odours (fat frying, for example) on the person and that the daily bath or shower is doubly necessary in the case of the kitchen worker as is the daily change of underclothes.

Care of the feet can make a vast difference to the efficiency and contentment of the kitchen worker. Apart from wearing properly fitting shoes maintained decently and socks can cause foot discomfort and damage just as ill-fitting shoes. They should be changed at least once a day and whilst regular employees have found it advisable to soften the feet by prolonged soaking.

Although the cook wears a white cap, the hair preferably should be kept short and regularly washed. Care of the mouth and teeth is also vital to the health and well-being of the cook. Some mouth infections are highly contagious and expert advice should be sought, if there is any puffiness or soreness of the gums or a tendency for the gum to bleed. Whilst it may not be necessary to remind adult staff of ordinary mouth hygiene rules, young workers and apprentices should certainly be made aware of the importance of regularly cleaning the teeth after meals and on retiring at night.

In regard to the maintenance of health generally, it is certainly worth stressing again that whilst the cook must taste frequently for seasoning, that he must guard strictly against packing food and eating except at proper meal times. A great deal of indigestion and more serious stomach troubles have undoubtedly been caused by failure to take meals at proper time and eating on duty in a hurried way. Whilst the cook must be temperate in eating, he must also be temperate in drinking. Overindulgence in both food and drink is usually accompanied by reduced vigilance in other directions including the proper maintenance of good standards of hygiene.

Staff should constantly be reminded about the importance of clean personal habits. These include, particularly, washing the hands after visiting the toilet. Such reminder should not be merely verbal but supported by notices (in or near appropriate places) and even better, by bold slogans or posters.

Final thoughts on the subject of hygiene in the kitchen in the hotel and catering industry should certainly not be one of the mere concern with meeting statutory requirement alone. It is of great social importance that all employees in the industry, particularly employees such as chefs, caterers and others in executive positions, should develop a professional conscience and a professional code in ensuring clean food and clean practices. This should go further than the meeting of minimum legal requirements. Tables 8.5–8.8 give floor area and electrical equipment requirements for hotel kitchens.

The approach to hygiene by the chef and his staff must be interesting and positive. The chef must try to convey both to his apprentices and older workers that hygiene in the kitchen is not a matter of observing regulations but a vital part of culinary aesthetics, health and happiness.

Table 8.5: Approximate floor area requirements for kitchen

Number of meals per day	Approximate floor area
50–75	250
100–125	400
250–300	900
400–450	1400

Approximate 5 sq. ft per meal

Table 8.6: Heavy duty electric equipment in medium-sized hotel kitchen

Name of the equipment	Load requirement kW(Approx.)
1. One oven	9 kW
2. One deep fryer	20 kW
3. One grill	8–10 kW
4. One deep freeze	1 kW
5. One large freeze	1 kW
6. Bain-marie	8–10 kW
7. Dish water (if required) 1500 pieces/h	15 kW
8. One tea boiler	15 kW
9. One masal grinder	1 kW
10. One micer	0.5 kW
11. One hot-case	0.25 kW

Table 8.7: Requirement of electric equipment in a good medium-sized restaurant

Name of the equipment	Load requirement kW (Approx.)
One deep fryer	12 kW
Two bain-marie	4 kW
Two oven-cum-range	8 kW
One microwave oven	2.6 kW
One refrigerator	1 kW
One automatic coffee maker	3 kW
One bulk water boiler	4 kW
One hot plate dispenses	0.5 kW
One service shelf with heating arrangement	4 kW
One toaster	1 kW

Table 8.8: General requirement of gas-cum-electrical equipment for a moderately-sized hotel

2 heavy duty solid top range with canopy (gas)
2 heavy duty industrial burner (gas)
Stockpot stove (gas)
Large single pan deep fat fryer
Hot cupboard with sliding doors
Tea boiler
Toaster
Masala grinder
Chapati puffer
Tandoor
Water boiler
Bain-marie
Idli steamer
Griller/salamonder
Hot case
Rice boiler (50 L) and pressure cooker
Work tables with shelves

Details of Food Preparation Techniques

1. **Stock soup:** Stock soup is prepared from liquid in which meat and bones have been slowly immersed for many hours in a stockpot with herbs, seasonings or vegetables added late in the cooking. For good stock soups, stimmer many hours to help extract and develop flavour. Drain, filter and refrigerate promptly to preserve

quality. Remove the top fat after refrigeration. Remove the fat that congeals on the top after refrigeration.

2. **Cream soup:** Cream soup has a thickening agent like white sauce thoroughly cooked and blended with (tomatoes or vegetables) purees.

For good cream soups:

- Use thin white sauce, made from vegetables stock
- Hold just below boiling point
- For tomato soup, add seasoned tomato cream sauce just before serving
- Add salt at the end

3. **Meat production:** The appropriate meat preparation method depends on the grade of meat and on the cut. Meat should be cleaned and cut properly. Wash with minimum of cold water. Moderate temperature is best for slow cooking.

4. **Steaks:** Broiling of steak is a method of dry heat cooking. Practice is needed to control time and temperature for boneless of various thickness of steaks. Surface should be browned and uniform.

5. **Fish:** In hotels, only limited variety of fishes are used. Sole, Arh, Pomphret, Bhetki are largely used. These must be scaled, cleaned and cut accordingly before cooking. Chilled and frozen fishes are also used.

Overcooking and overhandling should be avoided. These should be seasoned with salt, turmeric, herbs, vinegar, lemon juice as required.

Fish may be baked also with buttered crumbs and seasoning.

For deep fat frying, use bater (Nizam) and fry at 180°C.

Cooked fish should be flaky and moist, not tough and dry.

6. **Egg:** Eggs cooked in their shells are often served for breakfast or used in salads.

Eggs placed in boiling water are soft, cooked in three minutes, medium cooked in four minutes and hard cooked in 12 minutes. Cook below boiling point for tenderness. If eggs are warmed for a few minutes in lukewarm water, they are less likely to crack in hot water. After cooking, eggs should be immediately put into cold running water to halt cooking process. Hard cooked eggs are easier to shell immediately after cooking and cooling in cold running water. Slice with egg slicer for even slices.

7. **Scrambled eggs:** Scrambled eggs are easily prepared in quantity. When done, they should be tender and moist, not rubbery and tough. Undercook rather than overcook.

8. **Poached eggs:** Eggs may be poached in frying pan filled with water. High quality eggs will hold compact shape better. Water temperature should be near boiling point when egg is gently slide into hot water. Remove from water with perforated spoon. Time for soft eggs is 3 to 5 minutes.

9. **Vegetables cookery:** Purchase fresh vegetable of suitable size and maturity. Store under proper conditions. Use short cut process and machines in preparations to reduce time and water. Avoid excessive pelting and handling. Use vegetables in natural state and in whole pieces, when possible. Cover prepared vegetables with damp cloth until ready to cook. Green colour of the vegetables is retained, if cooked in alkaline medium.

10. **Cooking fresh potatoes:** Use potatoes of uniform sizes and shapes. Peel in vegetables peeler, if available. Be careful not to waste food by overloading or running the peeler too long.

11. **Preparing mashed potatoes:** Mash freshly cooked potatoes in a mixer, swing a paddle, mash while hot and allow steam to escape. Add hot milk or dried milk, and butter and seasoning. Overmashing should be avoided.

12. **French fried potatoes:** Use fry cutter for even sizes, soak briefly in salt water to reduce starch, cooking time and fat absorption.

Dry to prevent deterioration of fat. Use deep fat frier with temperature control, if possible.

13. **Onion:** Select and peel mild-flavoured onions. Cook in salted water in unperforated basket in steamer without overloading. Sliced and chopped onions should be used as and when required and should not be stored.

14. **Legumes:** Dried legumes may be cooked in pressure cooker, sometimes soaked overnight in water and eating soda added at the time of cooking.

15. **Fruit and vegetable salads:** Select fruits and vegetables for contrasting colours, shapes, textures. Prepare all ingredients, using slicers, shredders and short cut methods for speed and evenness of shapes. Refrigerate until served. Serve with appropriate dressing. Avoid long holding.

16. **Salad and salad dressings (Table 8.9):** The general conception of salad in India is a mixture of certain fresh vegetables served raw. Assorted fruits are also served as fruit salad at the end of meal.

    The salads are offered in varieties and form a major item in Western menu. Salads can be decorated and dressed with appropriate salad dressings and are served in a decorative container and in a decorated style. On the table, all the salads should look uniformed in size, design and position. Salads can be made out of leafy heart or from fruits, cold cooked vegetables. Meat and fish are also used in salads.

    Salad-dressings are mixture of certain ingredients used for making salad tasty and suitable for different pallet. Following are some of the important salad dressings used in quality hotels throughout the world.

    a. **English dressings:** Salt, pepper, mustard and two parts vinegar to one part oil, castor sugar, if guests require to taste.

    b. **French dressings:** Salt, pepper, mustard and one part vinegar to three part oil.

    c. **American dressings:** Similiar to English dressing with equal oil and vinegar and sweetened with sugar.

    d. **Lemon dressings:** Salt, pepper, fresh lemon juice and olive oil to taste with castor sugar.

    e. **Mayonnaise dressings:** Mayonnaise sauce thinned with vinegar and lemon juice to a dressings consistency.

    f. **Vinaigretta dressings:** Salt, pepper, one part vinegar to two parts olive oil, French or English mustard is often blended.

    g. **Thousand Island dressings:** Mayonnaise dressing with a little chilli sauce, chopped red pimento, chives and green peppers.

Quality—Estimation, Portioning and Pricing of Dishes

Anybody who has experience of eating out, knows that the portion and ingredients vary from place to place even for a particular dish. Amount of meat in meat curry, amount of fish in fish fry, paneer in mattar paneer all vary from place to place as also the price and taste. Then what is a standard dish? What is the authenticity of the dish? A suitable policy should be evolved by the hoteliers as regards to the portion size of a dish and as regards to the use of ingredients to maintain the character of quality and portion of a dish.

By and large, the contemporary American portions are very sumptuous and sometimes it is difficult for one to eat the quantity offered in a particular dish. In India, we may not be able to offer very liberal portions within competitive prices but some standardisation is necessary. Standardisation is generally practiced in Indian Railway Catering and other Institutional food service. But standardisation is sadly missing in restaurants in general. Following are some standard portions of food items in Railway Thali (Janata meal):

Rice	—100 gm (raw)
Vegetable	—200 gm (raw)
Dal	— 40 gm (raw)
For special chicken	—1.5 kg clean bird is used for 10 plates

For 4 plates of chicken roast	—700 gm clean bird is used
For 10 plates of mutton biriyani	—1 kg mutton 300 gm onion 1 kg rice 300 gm oil are used
For 10 plates of vegetable curry	—Mixed vegetables – 1kg Potato – 500 gms Veg. oil – 100 gm are used

In order to have good sales and business reputation through the food and beverage department, it is important to adopt some kinds of satisfactory portion size. Sometimes for an individual to go to a restaurant and order suitable food for one is very difficult. Indian portions are so designed that they suit two persons to share. This is one of the reasons why thalis meal are popular among general outdoor eaters. There is also an arrangement for standard family menu as seen in many Western countries for 4 persons, for 6 persons, etc.

Table 8.9: Examples of some salads with suggested dressing

Name	Constituents	Dressing
A la francaise	Lettuce hearts, tomatoes, hard-boiled eggs (beetroot sometimes added but only at last minute due to staining)	Vinaigrette
Allemande	Diced apples, potatoes, gherkins, smoked herrings, onions, chopped persley (if francaise)	Vinaigrette
Archduke	Julienne of beetroot, endives, truffle and potatoes mined with mayonnaise	Vinaigrette
Augustin	Lettuce French beans, tomato, hard-boiled egg, green peas	Mayonnaise
Eve	Scooped-out apple filled with dice of apple, pineapple and banana	Acidulated cream
Fanchette	Julienne of chicken, raw mushrooms, chicory truffle	Vinaigrette
Hara chana	Fresh green gram, onion, green chilli	Lemon dressing
Indian Hotel (green salad)	Beet, onion, carrot, cucumber, lettuce leaf, raddish	Lemon dressing
Nicoise	French beans, quartered tomato, sliced potatoes, decorated with anchovy fillets, olives and capers	Vinaigrette
Onion salad	Small dressed onion	Vinegar & salts
Onion capsicum carrot salad	Julienne of onion, carrot and fresh capsicum	Lemon dressing
Cole-slaw	Occasionally green chilli pieces Shredded cabbage	Mayonnaise/ vinaigrette
Waldrof salad	Shredded cabbage, apple Sultana, Walnut, capsicum (optional), onion	Cream/ Mayonnaise sugar

In buffet service, people are allowed to help themselves with the displayed food. For a party of 100, the following approximate food quantity (as purchased) should be considered sufficient.

- Egg—150 pcs. (one and half helping)
- Rice—100–120 gm per person
- Atta and flour—2 to 3 kg (for puri)
- Fish fillet for fry—16 pcs/1 kg boneless fish
- Chicken—40–45 birds of 650–700 gm each (feathered)
- Fish for curry—100–125 gm per head
- Dal—20 gm per head
- Mixed vegetables—70–75 gm per person
- Frying oil—1 kg vanaspati/1 kg flour for frying puri
- Cooking oil—1½ l

Beverage is more or less served in standard portion. Alcoholic beverages are measured by pegs or automatic dispensors and served.

One large peg – 60 ml
One small peg – 30 ml.

Tea and coffee are served between 120 and 150 ml in average size cups. One helping of juice is also equivalent to approximately 150 ml. Small coffee cups are practically not in use. Lassi, thandi and sarbat are served in large glasses with approximately 250 ml. capacity or more. The fresh green coconut water is served one-for-one basis in the coconut shell itself or in suitable glass.

Costing Procedure of Food

Portion cost or the cost of a dish in restaurants should not be determined without any rationale basis. The unscientific costing may lead to loss to the establishment because of unsold dishes. Unreasonable costing may also lead to consumer dissatisfaction.

However, for the costing of dish and for the formulation of selling price, some basic information regarding number of portions out of the purchased food, cost of ingredients, overhead loss during preparation, percentages of yield are necessary. These details can be derived by using the following methods for calculations:

1. The AP (as purchased) weight of the food minus the EP (edible portion) gives preparation loss and the percentages loss may be calculated as ratio of AP weight.

$$\frac{\text{AP weight} - \text{EP weight}}{\text{AP weight}}$$

2. The cooking time and temperature affect the quality and cooked weight of food and result in difference in yield and servings.

$$\% \text{ yield} = \frac{\text{Cooked weight}}{\text{Weight before}}$$

or

$$\% \text{ yield} = \frac{\text{Cooked and drained weight}}{\text{Raw EP weight}}$$

3. The cost of recipes may be determined by adding up the cost of each ingredient. The cost of all ingredients of the recipe is added and divided by the number of portions for the processing cost.

$$\text{Portion food cost} = \frac{\text{Total cost of recipe}}{\text{No. of portions served}}$$

If ten portions are left over and discarded, the portion's cost is accordingly higher.

Portion's cost of various recipes throughout a period may be recorded and then used to compare portion costs of similar items. These records may then be used for menu costing and for helping menus within a cost range.

If a restaurant maintains a food cost average of 52% of the selling price, the desired food cost is calculated as follows:

To calculate the cost of labour in preparing an item, time spent by cook and others to be multiplied by hourly rate of each. The time for cooking is only calculated.

In a restaurant, it is important to know the portion of food cost and also portion of labour costs in order to plan for the charges.

An item with a very little labour can be sold at a lower cost than a high labour item and still be within the budget to prepare an item that takes extra time and for which a higher price is charged. Purchasing is analysed and controlled by the purchase of foods through production and service. For example, if fruits had to be ordered and if three-fourth was used in salad and the one-fourth spoiled and to be discarded, the full supply of the fruits should be taken into the cost, thus making the portion cost of item higher. Spoiled foods add to the cost.

4. Popularity studies and checks of plate waste explain items that are popular and items that are less liked by guests and wasted. Studies in plate and scraping area can help to know preferences. Percentages of waste can be calculated as follows:

$$\% \text{ waste} = \frac{\text{Number of portions discarded}}{\text{Number of portions prepared}}$$

Amounts of foods prepared and unutilised should be recorded daily and studied by person planning amounts to prepare, in order to decrease overproduction and reproduction.

Pricing in hotel and restaurant means the system of charging the guests for food and services. In food service establishments, general profit expected is usually very high, whereas if sales are not up to the expected level with minimum wastage, then value of sales drops with obvious loss in profit. Thus, a suitable pricing policy must be adopted giving value to the customer's rupee for achievement of a desired sales volume for profit and maintain the sales value.

There are two methods of pricing usually applied. These are as follows.

1. Pricing Based on Costs

This method is based on the calculation of the food cost per dish and then a given percentage of gross profit is added to the value to arrive at the selling price per dish. The percentage is added to cover the labour cost, overhead cost, etc.

If the expected profit of 150% of food cost is considered, then the price of a dish having food cost of ₹ 1.20 will be 1.20 + 1.20 + . 60 = ₹ 3.00 or 1.20 + 5/2 (2½ times of food cost) = ₹ 3.00

The method is simple but has disadvantages also.

2. Pricing Based on Return

This method is based on the net profit in relation to the investment. This method is basically profit oriented, hence the flexibility in terms of market demands, investment strategy, etc. but gives an overall guide to the pricing. Pricing decisions are very crucial. Success and failure of an establishment often depend upon the pricing. There are many factors which affect pricing, namely:

- Charge in the establishment and services
- Charge in the menu
- Customer preference and charge in their eating system
- Devaluation and charge to the purchasing power of the customer
- Unpredictable factors such as strike, flood, drought, riots, etc.
- Imposition of sales taxes, luxury taxes, etc.

Depending upon the demand of a typical Kabab or a Chinese dish or pudding, etc. one establishment can have liberty to charge suitably for its additional profit without damaging the demand and turnover. In case of competition due to new establishment, competition due to large portion of tasty foods, etc. suitable pricing strategy should be evolved to maintain the level of profit. Sometimes it may be necessary to compromise with the lower profit level to maintain the sales volume.

Controlling Measures for the Prevention of Loss in Food Preparation

Profit may be wasted in various shapes—starting from purchase, storage, preparation and services of food. Some of the causes of loss are discussed hereunder.

Improper weighing, equipment, improper quality of foods, pilferage at delivery point, inaccurate ordering, clerical errors are responsible for loss at the point of receiving the goods.

In kitchen and service areas, losses may be due to bad menu planning, improper sale expectation, poor workmanship, improper cooking methods and waste due to faulty storage.

Lack of training of the staff, improper service implements, improper portioning and pilferage also cause loss.

In the Indian hotels, there is no suitable cold room. Only deep freezes or refrigerators are used to store fruits. Appropriate care must be taken for ordering perishable items, in particular which is based on sales pattern. Through appropriate marketing and management strategy, introduction of incentive to staff, careful supervisions on vulnerable areas, sale efficiency put control over losses. There could be short-term, medium-term and long-term measures to achieve goals by the catering establishments.

Calculations of the number of customers, service patterns, selection of menu and task allotment to the staff come under short-term measures.

Any intermediate measure between these two can be termed medium-term measures such as extension of menu, maintenance, introduction of labour-saving devices, etc.

Staffing Pattern in Hotel Kitchen

There are many factors which determine the types and number of kitchen staff requirement.

Usually, two types of staff are generally required for average Indian hotels, namely:

a. Skilled supervisory type
b. Unskilled type (picks up job detail while on work).

In most of the Indian hotels, there are no separate restaurants for Indian, continental and Chinese food. It is very common here that Indian, continental and Chinese foods are prepared in the one kitchen under supervision of a senior "multipurpose cook". Cooks in Indian hotels are usually highest paid employee and there is frequent turnover also.

But because of labour problem, trade unionism sometimes cooks try to have contract on specific terms and conditions and prefer to look after only specific cuisine, i.e. either Chinese, Indian or continental. Indian cooking basically depends on tandoor operation and making of rich gravy and curry.

In India, the pattern shown in Flowchart 8.1 is seen in general.

Number of assistant cooks and helpers vary according to the size and number of shifts. Usually, two shifts are in operation 6 am to 2 pm and 5 pm to closing.

In star hotels, kitchen staff are often designated in accordance to the traditional nomenclatures as under:

- Chef-de-cuisine   – Chief cook of the kitchen
- S'ous Chef   – Deputy to the chef
- Chef-de-partie   – Working cook
- Commis   – Cook's helper
- Apprentice   – Learner

Flowchart 8.1: Pattern of hotel's kitchen department workers in India

Senior
or
Head cook
(1 per shift or a broken only)

Junior cook/assistant cook
helper

Junior cook/assistant cook/
head cook helper

Junior cook/assistant cook
helper

Tandoor cook

Continental cook

Chinese cook

Cooking helper
(Sometimes combined)

Non-cooking helper

Cooking helper

Non-cooking helper

Cooking helper

Non-cooking helper

Food Services in Hotels

Foods are served mainly in the restaurants. Depending upon the hotels, the types and numbers of restaurants vary. In big hotels, there are a number of restaurants and some are known as speciality restaurants. Speciality items such as Italian foods, Chinese foods, Indian foods, French foods, etc. are served with typical atmosphere and service style. In general, in most of the places, we have only one restaurant serving a mixture of food items such as Indian, Continental and Chinese commonly known as multicuisine restaurants.

The hotels are also required to arrange service of foods in the rooms (room service). and also in the conference halls and in other locations such as bar, rooftops, etc. Under special circumstances, in all such cases, foods are supplied from the kitchen and pantry. In the restaurants, foods are served under certain procedures universally accepted. However, because of the style of the restaurants and because of other conditions, such rules and styles are not always possible to maintain but it is essential to have clean, decent and methodical service in small or big restaurants. The following are some of the examples of the typical restaurants services followed in different parts of the world.

1. English service
2. Russian service
3. French service
4. American service
5. Breakfast service
6. Indian sit down service
7. Banquet service
8. Buffet and cold buffet
9. Tea and coffee service
10. Wine/cocktail service

1. **English service:** In restaurants, the dish is presented to the host. The waiter portions the food on the side-board, plates the food and sets the combined plates in front of the guests, serving the host last. The portioned out food is placed in front of the guest preferably from the right (whenever not possible, it may be done from the left and cleared from the right-hand side.

2. **Russian service:** All food served is finished in front of the guests on a gueridon trolley. The gueridon trolley is equipped with a small stove or heater which is used to keep the food warm and for the preparation of small items.

   The service is carried out by commis and chef-de-rang.

   Food is partially prepared in the kitchen and finished in the restaurant.

   Semiprepared food is brought on platter to the restaurant by the commis.

Chef-de-rang takes order and finishes the food by carving, preparing and garnish and flaming the dishes.

Commis-de-rang holds the guest's plate below to receive the food.

Chef-de-rang using service spoon and service fork transfers the food from the platter to the plate.

Once the food has been arranged in a plate, the commis take the plate in his right hand and serve the food.

3. **French service:** The table is set up for hors d'oeuvre, soup, main course and sweet.

The food is fully prepared and portioned in the pantry.

The portioned food is put on the platters.

The waiter picks up the food platters and carries them with serving plates (hot or cold) to the restaurant.

He places plates before the guests and picks up the food platter from the side board and presents the main dish to the host. Serves each guest using service spoon, and fork to transfer the food. The rule of service is to set empty plates from the guest's right moving clockwise and clear dirty plates from left.

Only one waiter is needed in each station. It is less expensive than Russian service. It is much faster than English and Russian services. In this service, there is comparatively less wastage as unused food goes back to the kitchen to be served again. It gives personal attention.

4. **American service:** Portioned food is plated in the pantry by the kitchen staff. The prepared, pre-portioned food is brought by the waiter and served from the right of the guest. Serve solids as well as beverages from right and clear from right too.

5. **Breakfast service:** Breakfast service is no less important than lunch or dinner service in the restaurants. This service is of two types, i.e. food items for breakfast are prearranged in the service tray and

delivered in the rooms as per guest's order—room service breakfast. The orders may be taken in the night before, for service of breakfast in the following morning. The food items usually are limited but guests may order for items of their choice in big hotels where there are arrangements for morning shifts cooking.

There are some typical breakfast items internationally used. European breakfast consists of bread, honey, marmalade, butter, jam, coffee, tea, milk and eggs. Cold meat can also be served. Anglo-American breakfast includes hot toast, rolls, muffins, butter jam, marmalade, honey, tea, coffee, fruit juice, other items such as kippered herrings, cornflakes, porridge, milk, fried or grilled, fish, bacon, ham, sausages, egg preparations, cold meat, etc. are also served. Puri, bhaji, parantha, halwa, kachori, jalebi are popular Indian items served for breakfast. Tables are laid after dinner and before the close of the restaurants but in some places the early morning time is utilised for the purpose.

Breakfast tables are usually laid the evening before with cover and plates are brought warmed up to the table with the order. A breakfast often needed a folded napkin on the top of a glass, laid for each cover with a small knife on the right side. For the Anglo-American breakfast, often a knife and a spoon, sometimes a fish knife and fork and a jam spoon are required. The saucer is placed on the right side of the plate, the handle to the right and the spoon parallel a little higher than the cup and above this, the cream and the water jug are placed. Marmalade, jam or honey, butter, sugar and salt may be placed immediately in the centre of the table. Toasts or cakes are brought in fresh on demand, and hot breakfast dishes are best served directly on hot plates. After the breakfast, plates should be removed, an ashtray is placed in front of the guests who would like to smoke in the smoking zone.

6. Indian sit down service: This is a mixture of Anglo-American style. In comparatively less expensive places, eating plates are mostly of stainless steel and sometimes less expensive crockery. All-purpose knife, fork and a spoon, side plate, napkin, water tumblers are laid on the table with a set of desert knife and fork (Fig. 9.1). Foods are brought from the kitchen and served to the guests from donga and unserved helpings are kept on the table in front of the guests. Guests may himself take food from the donga or the waiting staff serves the food and takes empty dongas.

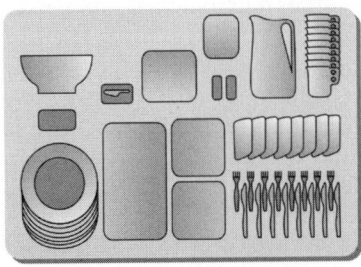

Fig. 9.1: Laying out of tables

Indian thali meals are served on arranged thalis. Additional helpings are served from multi-donga unit with a handle carried by the waiting staff. Price includes additional helpings of selected items such as rice, dal, sabji, etc. These services are very popular in South India also in restaurants run by vegetarian Marwari Basas. The service is fast and the food and eating style suit Indians with hot freshly cooked food.

7. Banquet service: This is very formal sitdown service organised in special occasions such as marriages, ceremonies in honour of VIPs, during the visit of head of the states, etc. Special attention is paid to the sitting arrangements and for suitable floral decorations. The shape of the table depends upon the size of the room, it may be T-, round, or oval. Hors d'oeuvre, soup, fish, a main dish with vegetables and salad, ice cream, biscuit and coffee are served. Each cover is laid with a service plate, a large knife and forks, a dessert spoon for the soup, fish and dessert knives and forks, a breadplate with a small knife, water, wine and a champagne glass. Formerly, it was customary to place five glasses on the table at banquets, now the glasses are changed, if more than one wine is served. Plates for the hors d'oeuvre are laid, cups for the soup and plates for the fish and the main dish are kept in the hot cupboard ready to use. A soup ladle, saucers for the soup, plates to place under the saucers and dessert plates are kept ready for use on a separate service table. Cocktail or a glass of champagne is usually served in the lounge before the start of the banquet.

At a wedding, the services always start from the centre with the bridal couple. At banquets, the most important guest is served first. The first course is served from right to left, the second from left to right, the other courses alternately. If ladies are present, they ought to be served first, but this is not customary everywhere.

8. **Buffet and cold buffet:** Here foods are displayed in chaffing dishes or in other suitable containers of various style and origin and guests pick up items of their choices. Waiter may also help in the services—foods to guest's plates behind or from the front of the buffet table. Buffets are also arranged for various occasions and for a large number of guests. Buffet for convenience, has been gaining popularity. The buffet can be for hot food as well as for cold foods. Cold buffet is particularly popular in Western countries. Convenience of the guests, space arrangements, guest movements, prevention of overcrowding at stations, decoration, etc. are to be carefully considered in this type of services.

9. **Tea and coffee service:** For the utmost general satisfaction, certain salient points for the preparation of tea and coffee may be followed.

   Tea should be made in china pot out of good quality tea only. The pot should be warmed and the water should be on continuous boil before pouring over the tea. Use approximately 2 gm for one cup of tea. It is not advisable to use boiled or hot milk for tea.

   Best coffee should be used. Proportion of coffee and water should be measured (8 level tablespoon for 1 l of water). The water must be on continuous boil as in case of tea before pouring over the coffee. Fresh grinded coffee are far better flavouring than grounded coffee. Coffee should be properly stored in airtight container in cool place. Coffee must not be reheated and coffee services should be prompt. Coffee machine should be regularly cleaned.

10. **Wine/cocktail service:** Wine services with food are usually very rare in Indian eating places. Hard drinks such as whisky, gin and beer are frequently served in restaurants and in Indian bars. During parties and cocktails, mixed drinks are also made on order. A separate table with drink glasses filled with alcoholic beverages of approximately one peg each are arranged for guests who help themselves with their choices and mix the drink accordingly with ice, water, soda, etc. which are also kept handy for the guests. Sometimes, waiter carry tray with glasses filled with alcoholic beverages and soda, water, ice, etc. to the guest who picks up glass and advise the waiter to add other ingredients of choice. A strict supervision and account should be kept particularly for the consumption of alcoholic beverages.

MENU PLANNING

Menu planning is to compose a series of dishes for meal. Composing a good menu is an art and it needs careful selection of dishes for different courses, so that each dish matches with each other.

The planning of meals in commercial catering establishments is based more on economic considerations and reputations of the establishments. The dishes produced are intended to please the eye and the palate. The planning of menus for school feeding, industrial canteen, hostels, etc. has different aspects. Well-balanced foods according to budget are to be considered.

It is essential to have knowledge about the sequence of courses in Western menus, because for Indian menus, all the dishes are served at one time in a thali. The modern trend is to give about 4 to 6 courses. A list of various traditional courses has been given below.

Sequence of Courses

1. Hors d'oeuvres (starter or appetiser).
2. Soup
3. Fish
4. Entree
5. Releves
6. Sorbet
7. Roast/grill
8. Vegetables/salad

9. Sweet

10. Dessert (fresh fruit, nuts). Coffee is almost always served.

There are mainly two different types of menus: Table d'hôte, and à la carte. Special party menu for banquets, buffets, and formal parties, etc. can be tailor made as per individual choice and budget.

Table d'hôte

A fixed menu planned for a complete meal at a fixed price. It is meal of three or four courses with a limited choice of dishes, and it is cooked in advance. It is changed daily or may be in rotation. It is set in the classical sequence starting with hors d'oeuvres or soups and so on.

À la carte

As per choice. À la carte means the production of a menu of varied sequence of dishes and courses. Each dish is individually priced. Dishes are cooked to order and the portions are often larger than a table d'hôte menu.

This type of menu is normally permanent, until either prices or change of management makes it out of date in a restaurant.

Banquet

Usually the menu is composed for a number of people and it is necessary to know the reason for the banquet. It is usually a formal affair and dishes should be compiled to suit the occasion. The dishes chosen should be such that will not require last minute changes. The menu is elaborate and of a high class quality. It is fixed menu, with no choice. The sequence may be as follows:

- First course — Fruit cocktails, hors d'oeuvres or soups.
- Second course — Fish
- Third course — Entree roasts, grills or cold meats with vegetables and potatoes or salads.
- Fourth course — Cheese and biscuits
- Fifth course — Coffee

Buffets

There are two main types of buffets in Western eateries, e.g. the light buffet and the fork buffet (lunch and dinner). The buffet table is attractively displayed. The food served is colourful and attractive and tastefully decorated. A large variety of dishes are offered, for everyone to choose.

Light buffets are given for various reasons to augment a long function, i.e. late in the evening, also could be given for tea dances and supper dances, etc. in western countries.

The fork buffet will also provide a variety of dishes and the food item can be easily eaten with a spoon or fork, while standing.

The modern trend in buffet lunches or dinners is to display the elaborate well-decorated dishes together and the guests can take as they desire. The dishes displayed are: Salads, soups, roasts, fish fried, vegetables, potato dishes and puddings of different kinds. The Indian dishes are pulaos, biryanis, kormas, roghanjosh jhalfarze, bhajees, bhurtas, raitas, papad, pickles, salads, nans, bhaturas, chhole, tandoori chicken, seekh kababs, assorted sweets, etc. There could be table arrangements for guests who like to take the food of their choice and then sit and eat comfortably.

Cocktail

The main ingredients are actually drinks. Very tiny savoury snacks are also served, such as stuffed olives, gherkins, walnuts, salted almonds, sausage, bacon rolls, cheese fritters, cheese straws, canapes, shami or goil kababs, mini, seekh kababs, fruit prawn, etc.

POINTS TO CONSIDER WHEN PLANNING MENUS

1. Type of Meal

The different types are — breakfast, luncheon, dinner, supper, tea, etc.

Breakfast

There are three types—continental, English and Indian.

Continental is a light breakfast, comprises bread, croissants or French loaf, jam, jelly or marmalade and coffee or tea.

English: It is on a larger scale and comprises fruits—fresh or stewed, cereals, bacon and eggs to order, or fish breads and beverages.

Indian: Popular breakfast is comprised of stuffed paranthas and curd or vegetables bhajee and poories, or besan cheelas and curd or dosas and chutney and pickels and beverages such as tea, coffee, lassi or milk.

Luncheon Menus

Lunch menus are usually shorter than dinner menus with less courses and simpler dishes. The emphasis is placed for steamed puddings in Western style. Luncheon is a quick affair and dinner taken more leisurely. Six sequences of dishes are given in boxes as under.

Sequence of Dishes

First course	— Appetiser: Fruit or shelfish cocktails, delicacies, such as caviar, oysters, etc. Smoked fish or hors d'oeuvres.
Second course	— Soup—thin or thick soups
Third course	— Fish—the fish could be steamed, grilled or fired
Fourth course	— Meat/chicken—stews, blanquettes, fricassees, goulash, cutlets, rechauffee dishes, braised or roasted meat. Served with vegetables and potatoes. Salads can also be served. Vegetables—a choice of vegetable dishes is given for vegetarians such as: Augratin, cutlets, vegetable bombe, kievs, etc.
Fifth course	— Sweet—hot puddings, pancakes, pies, flans, milk puddings, ice cream, fruit

	salads, bavarois, cold souffles, etc.
Sixth course	— Dessert—fresh fruits, nuts, etc. Coffee

Dinner Menu

Dinner menus comprise highly garnished, classical dishes. Here one has a scope of showing one's skill of compiling menus with a choice of the exotic dishes. Large joints may be served in the restaurant in front of the customers or flambe dishes can be served.

Dinner Menu Courses

First course	— Appetiser: Cocktail, caviare, oysters, snails, etc. smoked salmon, hors d'oeuvres.
Second course	— Soups: Consomme, cream soups.
Third course	— Fish—deep poached salmon, trout with sauce and garnishes. Grilled lobster, lobster thermoidor, fish meuniere with garnish for sole, turbot, trout, salmon. Fried whitebait. Cold fish always in aspic.
Fourth course	— Entrees/releves—large joints, chicken pole, grilled beef fillet, chicken en casserole, encocotte, served with vegetable and potatoes.
Fifth course	— Sorbat—in a long menu, dinners refresh their appetite, with a light sherbet, flavoured with champagne or liqueur.
Sixth course	— Roast—roast game and poultry served with a salad.
Seventh course	— Sweet—cold or hot—souffles, pancakes, crepesuzattes, melba ice-cream, baked alaska.
Eighth course	— Dessert—Fresh fruits and nuts Coffee

Indian Menus

There is no much clear cut differences between lunch and dinner menus. All the courses are served together on a thali. A list of Indian dishes is given to make the planning of menus easier.

Meat	— Chicken masala, chicken badam, chicken tandoori, gosht korma mutton, roghanjosh, keema matar, mutton koftas, pork vindaloo. lamb curry.
Fish dishes	— Fish Patiala, patiya, masala machi, machi jhal, Goan fish curry, hilsa with mustard, etc. fish kalia.
Vegetarian	— Malai kofta curry, aloo dum, paneer, jhalfarze, paneer pasanda, paneer matar, gobi, aloo, tinda masala, etc.
Lentil dishes	— Rajma shahi, urad dal makhana, khatte chhole, Peshawari chhole, besan kadhi, sambhar.
Sukhi sabzi	— Aloo matar, bhindi masala, karela stuffed, brinjal sag, alloo and tomato, bean mixed masala.
Raitas	— Mint, potato, tomato and onions, boondi or pineapple, chatni
Rice dishes	— Tomato and coconut pulao, biryani, kashmiri pulao, keema pulao, lime rice, curd rice, alloo-ki-tahari, pea pulao, etc.
Atta/dishes	— Nans, paranthas, roomali roti, tandoori roti, bhaturas, kulchas, luchi, etc.

Supper

A full buffet is given for supper. All the dishes are very well decorated, giving a good display.

2. Types of Establishment

Menu will vary according to the type of establishment:
1. Hotels
2. Restaurants
3. Hostels
4. Hospitals
5. Industrial canteens

The menus for restaurants and hotels will be generally à la carte buffet, banquet, or table d'hôte. The dishes will please the eye and palate and will be determined by the customer's appetite and pocket. On the other hand, the hostels, hospitals and canteens will generally have a set pattern and will offer meals to provide nutritionally balanced diets within a limited budget. As there will be no choice and food will be eaten daily, a variety given will break monotony.

3. Type of Customer

Customers can affect the type of food served because of age, sex, occupations, lifestyle, etc.

4. Season of the Year and Seasonal Availability of Ingredients

Season is important in the choice of food. Crisp and fresh foods are ideal in summer. For the cold weather, heavier, richer foods high in calorific value are welcomed. These days foods are available all the year round because of storage facilities. Foods in season should be included in menus, as they are fresh plentiful, and the colour and flavour are good. Foods selected should be easy to obtain locally.

5. Occasion

Special dishes for certain days or time of the year should be considered. For example, roast turkey at Christmas, special eggs for Oaster, halwa for Baisakhi, sweet rice for Basant Panchami, semia for Id, pongal for Onum.

6. Capabilities of Kitchen Staff

The kitchen staff's capabilities have to be taken care of. Whether they will be able to cope with the high class cookery, whether they are experienced and have the skill and the knowledge. If the staff are not capable, it will be difficult to produce good meals. Equally important is the serving staff, if they are efficient, the well dressed and garnished dishes can be served in presentable manner. Varied and sophisticated dishes can only be given, if the waiter is highly skilled.

7. Equipment of the Kitchen

While planning the menu, it is important to see that the kitchen is well equiped to cope up with preparation of various dishes (Figs 9.2–9.4).

Fig. 9.4: Chef unit assembly

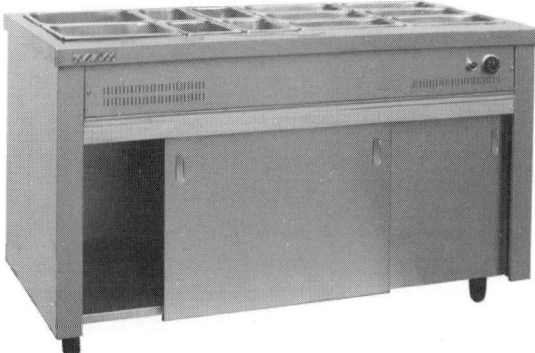

Fig. 9.2: Open top bain marie

Fig. 9.3: Bain marie with service counter and hot cupboard

MENU OF SOME COUNTRIES

Chinese Type Menu

Tomato juice
or
Egg foo yung
• • •
Chinese barbecue spare ribs
or
Mushroom chowmein with crisp noodles
or
Beef or chicken chop suey
or
Sweet and sour chicken
or
Lobster cantonese
or
Egg roll
or
Rice steamed or fried
• • •
Almond cookies
or
Pineapple chunks
• • •
Tea, coffee

English Type of Menu

Egg mayonnaise
or
Half fresh grape fruit
or
Chilled fruit juice

or
Cream of onion soup
or
Deep fried fillets of haddock only
or
Roast leg of lamb, mint sauce
or
Madras curry chicken, Patna rice
•••
Creamed sweds, garden peas
or
Boulangere and parmentiere potatoes
•••
Ox tongue, cheese, roast ham, Grosvenor pie
or
Salmon mayonnaise, roast beef
or
Fresh salads in season
•••
Black current cream cheese cake
or
Baked rice pudding
or
Gooseberry pie and custard sauce
or
Assorted ice creams
or
Cheese and biscuits
•••

French Type Menu

Asserted open-face decorated canapes
or
Spicy stuffed mushroom caps
•••
Quiche lorraine
or
Vichyssoise
or
French onion soup with croutons
•••
Coq au vin
or
Buttered fine noodles
or
French cut green beans

or
Blanquette de veau
or
Parsley potatoes
or
French cut green beans
•••
French green salad, with chef's dressing
or
French bread or French rolls with butter
•••
Crepe suzette
or
Cherries jubilee
or
Peach melba
•••
Champagne with main course
or
Cream sherry with dessert
•••

German Type Menu

Chicken soup with dumplings
or
Tongue in sweet and sour raisin sauce
•••
Spare ribs with sauerkraut
or
Knockwarst with sauerkraut
or
Roast veal with beer
or
Sauebraten with potato pancakes
or
Boiled potato, with butter or hot potato salad
or
Green vegetable with butter
•••
Beer
or
Coffee
•••

Greek Type Menu

Rice in cabbage leaves with lemon
or
Baked cabbage with tomato
or
Stuffed cabbage with meat and rice
or
Pilaf of lamb
or
Roast leg of lamb, with garlic seasoning
or
Rice
•••
Black coffee
•••

Indian Type Menu

Fruit juice
or
Eight boy curry (shrimp, beef or chicken curry with rice eight condiments from which the guest makes his choice).
or
Hard cooked eggs, chopped
or
Chutney
or
Fresh grated coconut
or
Green peppers, diced
or
Bacon, crisp, crumbled
or
Current jelly
or
Pickles, chopped
or
Salted peanuts, chopped
or
Rice
•••
Mixed vegetables salad, with French dressing
or
French bread and butter
or

Salad
or
Ice cream
or
kulfi
•••
Coffee/tea
•••

Italian Type Menu

Antipasta
or
Pizzas
or
Minestrone soup
•••
Chicken tetrazzini or eggplant Parmesan
or
Spaghetti with tomato sauce
or
Veal scallopine Marsala
or
Hunter's wild rice
or
Old-fashioned lasagne
or
Pasta atiano
or
Green salad or sliced tomato with Italian dressing
or
•••
Red rose or white wine
or
Black coffee
•••

Russian Type Menu

Borscht with sour cream (hot and cold)
or
Beef strognoff
or
Shashlik
or
Buttered noddles

121

or
Green beans
or
Vinaigrette salad
or
Dark rye or polish dark corn bread, with cottage cheese, butter
• • •
Vodka
or
Strong tea / coffee
• • •

FORMAL DINING ROOM

1. Type of Service

Service in the formal dining room is elegant. Use French service and appropriate service equipment taking full advantages of the trained skills of the Maitre d'hotel (flaming, salad making, and other preparation dishes or 'specialities') are emphasized, merchandised, and presented in an unusual and sophisticated manner.

2. Mis-en-Place

Before the restaurant is opened, all tables are covered with fresh, clean tablecloths and the 'cover' properly placed. The 'cover' consists of service plate, bread and butter plate with knife, knife and fork, water glass and napkin.

A salt and pepper shaker, an ashtray, a flower or candle decoration, and perhaps, a table number complete the table setting. Plates, silver and glassware are, polished by the waiters prior to placing them on the tables. Napkins are folded in a simple manner, to avoid contact with the waiter's hands.

A decorative display may be placed at the entrance, featuring appetizing items such as, flower, wine or speciality food items. If these are done, they must be continually checked and kept appetizing.

3. Receiving the Guests

Each guest entering the dining room is received at the door by the headwaiter or his assistants, in a cordial manner and courteously seated. Chairs are held out for the lady guests, and gentlemen, if need be. The headwaiter distributes the work load evenly between the various stations, however, he should inquire, if the table which the guest has chosen is agreeable, prior to being seated. If all guests cannot be accommodated, they should be asked whether they wish to wait.

In the bar until a table is available, or have their meal in one of the other restaurants in the hotel, ideally, somebody accompanies the guest to the other facility to ensure that they will be taken care of properly.

4. Taking the Order

While the headwaiter hands a menu to the guests, he inquires whether they wish to order a cocktail. The guests are given sufficient time to study the menu, and not hovered over and rushed in their ordering.

Orders are taken by the headwaiter or captain. In a pleasant manner, he suggests those dishes which are 'menu specialities' that evening.

Care has to be taken to avoid recommending expensive items merely for the sake of a higher average check (and consequently higher service charge). Basically, the headwaiter's duty is to direct the guests in such a way that they are satisfied with their selection.

5. Beverages

The food order taken, a polite query is made as to whether any wine is desired. The person taking the order should be knowledgeable about the wine list, and knows what type of wine is suitable for the particular menu ordered. It is unnecessary to employ an aggressive approach (such as 'What kind of wine would you like to have?'), the guest must be given a chance to order only plain glass of water, if he wishes, without feeling intimidated.

6. Completion of Cover

The 'cover' is completed according to the order, and if the guests are accustomed to it, ice water is served. Bread and butter is offered.

7. Wine

Wine is served shortly before the food, and at the correct temperature (white wine 8 to 10°C) observing the rules of good service. The opening of the bottle at the guest's table may have some merchandising effect, if proper showmanship is taken care of, particularly red wine and champagne, are not shaken. White wine, rose and sparking wine bottles are cleaned and placed in a wine cooler. Red wine bottles remain dusty as they come from the cellar and are placed label upwards in the service basket.

8. Opening the Wine Bottles

The guest who placed the order is first shown the bottle's label. The foil on the bottle is then cut at the first groove and the small piece of cut foil removed, as the wine must not touch the foil when poured. The mouth of the bottle is wiped carefully, to avoid any cork particles failing into the wine. A champagne bottle is kept at 45° angle, and opened in such a manner (without the use of an opener) that the extraction of the cork does not create any undue disturbance in the dining room for other guests (Fig. 9.5).

9. Serving Wine

The wet bottle is rapped in fresh napkin, label showing prior to the service. The waiter pours a small quantity of wine into the host's glass, so that he can taste it and give his approval. (It is suggested that the waiter enquire if the temperature is correct, or the wine is of his liking.)

10. Wagon Control

Strict controls are maintained on all items displayed, when served from a table or wagon. Extremely expensive items (e.g. caviar) are not displayed. Only the headwaiter is responsible

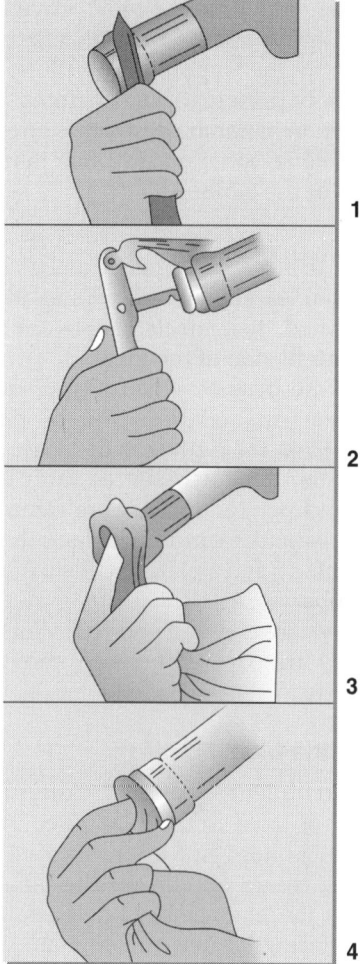

Fig. 9.5: Example showing opening of wine bottle
Step 1: Cut foil   Step 2: Wipe mouth
Step 3: Draw cork   Step 4: Wipe again

for all food items in the restaurant and is allowed to cut the meat. If expensive items, such as smoked salmon, etc. are served from a buffet or wagon, they are weighed by the chef prior to issuing them to the restaurants and again after they are served. The quantity consumed matches the number of portions accounted for as served. Also, the consumption of items from the pastry wagon is controlled.

In some restaurants, it may prove desirable to designate a cook to do all carrying and serving from the wagons and buffets. He must be extremely presentable at all times.

A selection of flambe desserts is offered. Also where feasible, some meat or fish items can be prepared at the table.

11. Cleaning the Table

The table is cleared when all persons at the table have finished their meals. Plates are removed from the right side of the guest.

Before the dessert, when all persons at the table have finished their meals, plates are removed from the right side of the guest.

Before the dessert is served, all dishes and the salt and pepper shakers are removed, and crumbs cleaned from the tablecloth (using a rolled napkin), and a plate to collect the crumbs, or a crumber.

Ashtrays are checked and replaced as necessary. They are covered before removing them from guests.

12. After the Meal

Coffee and liqueur are offered. Coffee is poured at the table from individual pots. While the coffee pot is kept hot after the first service, sugar and cream are left on the table for self service. If the management decides to have a wagon offering liquors and cognac circulating in the restaurants, only one captain is in charge of handling the wagon, so that accountability is assured.

If cash register slips are in use, the person in charge collects the slips and replaces an empty bottle from the service bar, turning in the proper amount of cash register slips. If order checks are used, they are stamped by the cashier, as an acknowledgement that the drinks have been billed.

After dinner, mints and a hot towel are good ideas to round off the service with a flair. Also an open package of foreign or local cigarettes can be presented in smoking zones.

The bill is presented only upon request. And it is placed face down on a small silver tray or plate. Change is also presented on this plate. If appropriate, the cheque may be placed in a decorative envelope or cover prior to being presented.

COFFEE SHOP

1. Types of Service

Service in the coffee shop is speedy and economical, using the simple American type of plate service. The mis-en-place is identical to that of the formal dining room, except that service plates are not used, and filled sugar bowls are on the table. In most coffee shops, mats are used instead of tablecloth. Tablecloths may be used on special occasions, holiday, etc. Less expensive china, glass, linen and silver (stainless steel) are used.

2. Seating and Order Taking

The guest is received at the door and seated by a headwaiter or hostess. This procedure is identical to that of the formal dining room, except when two ladies are seated. An enquiry should be made as to whether they wish separate checks.

The order is taken by the hostess (or headwaiter, or it can be taken directly by the waiter, if they are capable of performing this task. Again the procedure is the same as in the formal dining room, except that emphasis is placed on quick service.

3. Completion of Cover

The 'cover' has to be completed according to what has been ordered and, if the guests are accustomed to it, ice water should be served at this point and both are generally put on the same plate, by the waiter (at a service station) and placed to the guest's left side.

4. Serving the Food

The waiter receives the food items from the kitchen in a plate, and places the plate in front of the guest, using his right hand and serving from the guests right side (if possible).

Elaborate dishes requiring time-consuming preparation and serving, and flambe dishes, are not offered in the coffee shop. Pastry can be served from a tray, or from a small pastry wagon.

5. Clearing the Table

The table is cleared, when all persons at the table have finished their meal. Plates are removed from the right side of the guest. Before dessert is served, all dishes are removed. Crumbs are cleaned (using a rolled napkin, and a plate to collect).

A cup of coffee or espresso and dessert is offered after the meal. The coffee is poured from a large coffee pot, making certain that it is hot. Cream is served in a portion-controlled individual creamer. Guests are asked, prior to the coffee service, whether they prefer cream or milk, since the cost of these items can be eliminated, if the guests desire their coffee 'black'.

The bill is presented, on completion of guest dinner or has requested for the bill. The bill is placed face down on the table near the host. It is not necessary to use a plate.

6. Breakfast

Breakfast service emphasizes speed, and it is usually offered only in the coffee shop, snack bar and room service. Presently in India and abroad, breakfast buffet service is also provided.

Mats, where available, are used with a paper napkin. Small-sized cloth napkins are used only if they are less expensive than paper. Before the coffee shop opens, the covers should be placed on the tables, with ample replacement kept at the service stands. This breakfast cover consists of cup and saucer, medium-sized knife, fork, coffee spoon (placed on saucer), napkins and water glass (where water is generally expected for breakfast service). A salt shaker, pepper shaker, ashtray and perhaps a flower decoration and table number complete the table setting. The guest is received at the door, and seated by the person in charge. In Europe, newspapers are generally offered to the guest as he enters the dining room. The order may be taken directly by the waiters, if capable of performing this task, and orders are written on the bill.

After the service is completed, the bill is placed face down on the table together with a pencil (in case the guest wishes to sign for the meal). The bill may be placed on the table without the guest's asking for it, as an expedient.

The table is cleared, except for the cups, cream and sugar, when the guests have finished their meal. The guest is asked, if he desires more coffee. (Additional coffee, cream, sugar, bread and jam are free of charge). Generally, coffee shop service requires the guest to pay to the cashier directly.

COUNTER SERVICE

1. Types of Service

Like coffee shop service, counter service, emphasizes speed and simplicity of service. Check averages are usually low, eat turnover high, selections limited and a near round-the-clock service provided.

2. Mis-en-Place

Place mats, paper napkin, fork, coffee spoon and water glass at each seat. For breakfast, cup and saucer, knife, coffee spoon and water glass are placed on the table. Sugar and bulk creamer, salt and pepper shaker and ashtrays are placed on the counter, along with the bulk jam container.

3. Menu

The guests select their own seats and place the order at the counter. The menu features as simple as sandwiches, salads, egg dishes, hamburgers, steaks, soups, appetizers, desserts, ice-cream, soft drinks, beer, coffee, etc. if the counter is a self-contained unit. If all food drinks come from the kitchen, a limited coffee shop menu may be offered.

4. Service

Service consists of politely placing the dishes on the counter, and removing them as the guest finishes his meal. All food service personnel are well groomed, with a pleasant disposition as they are closely interacting with guests.

5. Bill

Bills are written directly as the order is taken. When the guest has completed his meal, the check is totalled and he pays the cashier directly.

ROOM SERVICE PROCEDURE

1. Taking the Order

The person who takes the order answers the telephone promptly in a polite manner. He thanks the guest at the end of the conversation. Room service sales volume is directly related to the sales ability of the telephone sales clerk in the room service department. The clerk must learn to pick up the name of the guest ordering along with the room number and use the name throughout the conversation.

The order is taken on his order pad in legible letters and is repeated to the guest to avoid any possible misunderstanding, and ensure the room number, spelling of the name and the number of covers to be served. The order is taken in triplicate and time stamped. The original is given to the waiter so that he can place the order with the check. The waiter retains a copy, one copy is kept by the order-taker to write out the bill.

For control purposes, the bill number is inserted on the order slip. The order is then handed over to the waiter-in-charge. If there are several waiters working in one shift, each

waiter receives an order in regular rotations. Room number and service time, be it a tray or a table is entered on the clearing chart.

2. Preparation for Service

For breakfast, a regular room service tray is covered with a clean tray cloth including the necessary service materials. Every item placed on this tray is checked to see, if it is cleaned and polished.

a. For a continental breakfast, the following items are necessary (Figs 9.6 and 9.7):
  • Small plate, butter knife, cup and saucer, sugar cubes, coffee spoon, napkin.

Fig. 9.6: Room service-tray laid for breakfast for one

1.	Small napkin	5.	Coffee cup	9.	Jam dish
2.	Dessert plate	6.	Coffee spoon	10.	Sugar bowl
3.	Small knife	7.	Bread plate	11.	Milk jug
4.	Saucer	8.	Butter dish	12.	Coffee pot

Fig. 9.7: Room service-tray laid for breakfast for two

1.	Small napkin	6.	Tea spoon	11.	Cream jug
2.	Dessert plate	7.	Bread plate	12.	Water jug
3.	Small knife	8.	Butter dish	13.	Tea pot
4.	Saucer	9.	Jam dish		
5.	Tea cup	10.	Sugar bowl		

- Ice water is not filled to the brim of the glass since water will be spilled while being carried to the guest's room. Continental breakfast comprises the following:
- Sugar—2 or 3 wrapped cubes per person
- Butter—20 gm per person
- Bread and roll—3 for the first person, (assuming rolls are small breakfast size), 2 for each additional person. If toast is specified (wrapped in a napkin).
- Jam—If possible, choice of 2 jams (or jam and honey). Each portion not exceeding 25 gm (sachet can be used).
- Beverages—As ordered.
- Coffee must be served in thermos to keep hot, captain keeps tight control on thermos servers by numbers.
- Tea served with a pot of hot water, chocolate served in pot with cover, and large creamer (4 ozs. of hot milk), fruit juice as alternative.

b. To serve a full course luncheon, dinner, or American breakfast for more than one person, the service table is used. This table is set up with the following items:

Knife and fork, bread and butter plate, small knife, napkins, service spoons and fork, water glass, soups, dessert, coffee spoons, salt and pepper shakers ladle, fish service, loose sugar, entrement service (as order dictates). Table removal sign, candle light lamp for dinner/supper, if supplies are available, they must be used for juices, ice-creams, shorbet and cold soups.

c. Depending on local hotel policy, newspaper may be included at no extra charge with continental and/or American breakfast room service orders.

3. Service

The cold food items are placed on the prepared table or tray. All hot food and warm plates in the hot food container, and the soild fuel/spirit is lighted to keep this container hot. Care is taken that the food is not turned or dried out from the heat in the warmer.

The bill is picked up from the cashier and double checked to make certain that the foods on the table or in the food container are those listed on the bill. The captain in charge checks all orders before they are released for service. Missing foods during service agitate the guest and slowdown service. All tables are covered with a plastic cloth or disposable plastic sheets prior to being wheeled into the guest's room. The waiter knocks on the guest's door, and enters at the guest's request (leaving the door open). He greets the guest by name, deposits the tray on the table making sure that the cover faces the chair. If table/service is used, the table is wheeled in an open area and the chair and silver glass and china arranged at each setting.

The guest is asked, if he wishes to be served, and if not, the fuel is extinguished before the waiter leaves the room. If a bottled beverage is served, the bottle is opened. After the guest signs the check, the waiter explains the use of the table removal card, and asks, if he may be of any further assistance before leaving the room.

The guest is allowed approximately one hour to eat, and then the tray/table is taken away by the waiter. The clearing chart indicates which rooms have to be called on for removals. When the tray/table is removed, the entry is marked off on this chart. It is the responsibility of the room service department, not housekeeping to remove all trays/tables and other room service equipment from guest rooms and guest floors.

The signed bill is handed to the cashier, and if there is any irregularity, it is reported to the captain-in-charge immediately.

4. General Information

A detailed chart of glassware, china and silver needed for each menu is prepared and placed in the room service area for the waiter's information. If there is langauge barrier, it is important that the waiter fully understands the guest's requests or call the captain-in-charge to follow up on the guest's wishes. Flowers, fruits, etc. are sent according to the local management policy.

CANDLE LIGHT SERVICE

In order to upgrade and merchandise room service, dinner/supper service, some hotels use a candle light service and the procedure for this is as follows:

When a dinner/supper order is taken, the service table includes a hurricane lamp. Each hurricane lamp is numbered and before the table is taken to the guest's room, this lamp is entered on a control chart, as well as on the check. The waiter enters the guest's room, the candle is ignited and the lamp placed on the service table. These hurricane lamps are always kept in a serviceable condition.

BUFFET SERVICE

A buffet provides an opportunity to display high standards of cuisine, but proper control is exercised to maintain a reasonable food cost. There are a number of points to consider about buffets.

1. The buffet table is suitable where it receives maximum attention from arriving guests. It must have easy access from all tables and be practical to service from the kitchens or pantry areas.
2. The tables set-up itself may take some sort of interesting form (round, oval, etc.) which can be accomplished through the use of half-round and quarter-round tables.
3. Buffet tables can be made interesting by laying the tables, or making several levels through the use of boxes or crates. The table itself can be decorated with candles, silver platters, greenery, leaves, flowers, etc.
4. The centrepiece is important, and could be an ice carving, floral decoration or some

other large eye catching presentation. Height is extremely important in buffet service and often spectacular effects are created with a little imagination.

5. The buffet is artistically set up with decorated pieces (such as turkey, salmon, or other selection).
6. The service line areas are individually defined, so that smooth service pattern and flow are established. If a large group of people congregate on the buffet line at one time, with no control of line formation, the result is chaotic. This is specially true for banquet buffets where the guests arrive together.
7. When the buffet platters, bowls and other food containers are depleted to a point where they are no longer eye appealing, they should be replaced so that the buffet retains its effectiveness.
8. Cost of decorations and displays are considered when selling a buffet.

Some useful Tips for Waiting the Service Table

A primary objective of food and beverages department is to sale the products. Good food and beverages with good presentation and service will help catering establishments to increase their sales. To perform a proper food service, some procedures are to be followed during waiting at the table. These techniques are as follows:

a. The cutleries, crockeries, glassware, etc. are perfectly cleaned before use. The dining hall should also be equally cleaned including its personnel with clean and nice dress.
b. The sideboard (dummy waiter) is completed and ready for the service session.
c. The menu of the meal should be carefully studied before offering it to the guests.
d. While taking orders, do not rest your hand on the table or on the back of the chair. Always avoid having your face coming into close contact with the guest.

e. Waiter should not make any misleading statements about the quality of any food or drink.

f. When waiter is about to take order or to serve and if the guests are busy in talking among themselves, the waiter should say in a polite and gently tone, 'Excuse me, Sir / Madam' or 'I beg your pardon Sir / Madam' which will alert the guest that the waiting staff is ready to take order or to serve. After having served the food, stand at a reasonable distance away from the table but watch for the need and call of the guest.

g. The articles of silver dropped on the floor must not be used at the table without wash.

h. Never use a chipped glass or plate and avoid serving from any such imperfect articles.

i. Articles such as teaspoons, menu cards or lumps of sugar should never be kept in waiter's dress.

j. Avoid filling glasses, cups, etc. up to the brim. Do not put fingers inside the glasses, when lying or removing them. For service of ice, use spoon or an ice tong.

k. Waiter should never put the spoon in the guest's soup, tea, coffee.

l. For wiping plates, glasses, etc. never use soiled or used napkins or tablecloth. Waiter's cloth is to be used for the purpose.

m. If the tables become crumby, all the little crumbs should be removed at a convenient time by using service cloth and on a quarter plate.

General Tradition for Service

Place clean plates and glasses from the right of the guest. Serve food from the left of the guest. Serve drink (including coffee, wines) from the right of the guest. Preplated food is served from the right. However, these rules may depend on the house custom of the establishment / country and on the restaurant layout.

Salt, pepper, and other cruets should be removed from the table before the sweet is served.

Wine should be arranged after the approval by the host. Serve guests (ladies) first, host last. White wine is served chilled and red wine at room temperature. Beer must be chilled and served in large glasses or jugs.

Some more details of alcoholic and non-alcoholic beverages service are described separately.

Guest Reception in Restaurant

The procedure for receiving a guest from the moment he or she enters the establishments till he or she leaves is mentioned. This is just a simple procedure and the style and character vary from place to place and from country to country.

When a guest enters the restaurant, he or she should be received and shown to a suitable seat—usually by the headwaiter.

Reception by Headwaiter

In large, first class establishment, there is one or more headwaiters exclusively engaged on receiving guests. This reception headwaiter takes advance bookings and enters them in the restaurant reservation book. He receives the guests at the door properly. Having received the guests, the headwaiter leads the way to a suitable table. If he gestures towards a table or to indicate a direction, he should do so with open palm to avoid any impression of pointing. He then helps the ladies to be seated and calls the head wine butler and the station headwaiter or station waiter to attend the guests.

Reservations

Allocation of tables, particularly in busy and reputed restaurants, starts before guests arrive. This is because many guests reserve their seats, usually by telephone in advance. Reservations are normally registered on register reserved for the days lunch and dinner parties. In such cases, regular guests or those who are known to the restaurants are likely to be given priority and to have their wishes met in regard to their seating. It is vital not to let new guests or less-favoured guests be aware of any priority given to the others for the interest of the business. In busy time guests may asked to wait in the waiting lounge.

Choice of Tables

The actual location of the seating depends on the number of vacant places at the time of entry, the size of the pantry and as far as possible others to be near of the orchestra or by a window and so on. It is the duty of the headwaiter to ascertain the wishes of guests. The assessment of guests and their wishes is acquired by long experience only. A group of guest should not be placed at different places as far as possible. If the restaurant is busy, the waiter should therefore know just when tables will be vacant or be ready to extend the service to other people on waiting.

Essential Tips for Setting a Dining Table

During setting a table, the food and beverage service staff should follow some procedures which will not only help them to serve food and drinks rightly and smoothly but will give a good look of his/her serving table also. The following are the tips for setting dining tables:

a. Before laying the tablecloth, you must ensure that the tables and chairs are in their correct position.
b. See that the chairs and tables are perfectly clean and perfect.
c. Some kind of flower arrangement should be provided at the table. The flower arrangement shall be on low value and heavily scented flowers should be avoided.
d. Each cover should form balanced definable unit. It must not be overcrowded. An ordinary cover will require 24" length and 18" width while in case of banquet, it should be 27" × 18".
e. Place only the required sliver needed for the particular meal. The sequence of sliver should be from outside to inside and from upwards in the orders they are to be used.

f. The knives should be placed on the right-hand side of the cover with the cutting edge towards the left. The forks are placed on the left-hand side of cover with prongs turned up, spoons are placed on the right-hand side of the cover but the spoons for sweets or cereals for breakfast or for curry or for rice preparations are placed on the top of the cover with the handle towards the right. The fork for the sweets is placed at the top of the cover with the handle towards the left. When serving farinaceous dishes, e.g. spaghetti, macaroni, etc. in the typical Italian way, spoon is placed on the left-hand side of the cover with the forks going to the right-hand side.
g. The water glass or goblet, turned upside is positioned just on the right-hand side useful to place them on left for service of Indian food.
h. Place a side plate to the left of the cover, place a side knife on the plate.
i. Butter dish should be placed on left. Butter knife must be on the dish with the handle towards the right.
j. The napkins (serviette) should be placed either in the centre of the cover or on the side plate.
k. All the cutleries crockeries should be placed half an inch away from the edge of the table.
l. Salt and pepper cruets are always placed on the tables, in the case of a long table allow one set for each two covers.
m. Avoid handling of cutleries, etc. in bare hand as far as possible.

Reception at Table

When the guest reaches the table, the waiter of that table should always greet him/her with a smile and in a courteous manner—good morning/good evening Sir to male and Madam to lady. If the guest is known, the first greeting may be addressed as 'Good morning, Mr. Sinha' but thereafter, he should be addressed as 'Sir'. A waiter aims to make sure that guests feel welcome and gain the impression that staff are glad to look after them. However, a waiter should be guided by management and his supervisor before developing informality.

When the headwaiter has shown the guests to the table, he should see that they are properly seated, he may do this himself, if necessary the assistance of the station waiter or he may leave it to the latter while he attends to new arrivals. If there is one guest only, the waiter will stand by the chair and move it slightly to make it convenient for him to sit down. If there are several guests in the party, the waiter will attend first to lady guests unless the gentlemen accompanying them do so. Similarly, at the end of the meal, when they are ready to leave, the ladies should be assisted again and the chairs should be pulled back.

The head wine butler now comes forward and after giving the appropriate greeting will enquire, whether an aperitif is wanted. When the aperitif order has been given, the station headwaiter or the station waiter approaches the host from the left, and offers/places menu in front of him.

Guest may be guided to smoking zones if they wish to do so and if there is such area marked.

Order Taking

The waiter should know what is on the menu and be able to advice accordingly. He will approach the guest from the left and enquire 'May I have your order, Sir (Madam)?' He should wait patiently facing the guest until the order is completed.

When the menus are long and varied, it is advisable to allow guests a few minutes before asking the order. During this time, the waiter may provide bread rolls, butter, etc. (in special restaurants) and fill water glasses. It is usual for a waiter to assist by unfolding table napkins, offering or helping to place them for guests. While taking an order it may be necessary for a waiter to enquire about the preparation of certain dishes such as boiled egg—'How do you

like them cooked, Sir, half boiled, full boiled or under boiled? and steak—'How do you like them cooked, Sir, under medium or well done?' If there is any doubt over the order, repeat the order back to the guest to avoid error.

While taking the order, a good waiter should keep in mind certain factors such as:

i. Dishes ready for quick service to guests who are in hurry.
ii. Items suitable for children
iii. Suggestions for vegetables, salad, etc. for roasts, grills, main courses.
iv. Suggestions for sweet dishes.
v. Suggestions for chilled/normal water/ bottled water.

Recording of an Order

In recording an order, a waiter should fold his service cloth into a neat pad on which to rest his book. The orders taken should be recorded on KOT (kitchen order ticket) or service papers with information about waiter's number, table number, number of guests, date, time, details of dishes (using abbreviation, etc). The writing should be clear as it has to be read by other people. The waiter's book of KOT is made out in duplicate. The original being given to the kitchen clerk or any responsible person in the kitchen before he will transit the order to the chef or staff concerned. The carbon copy is retained as the waiter's own record. It may serve additionally as the bill that will be presented to the guest at the end of the meal. Sometimes two carbon cpoies are made out, the original for the kitchen clerk, one for the preparations of the guest's bill and the other for the waiter.

Procedure for Wine Order and Service

By the time food order has been taken, the wine butler should attend the guest. This type of functioning is not generally found in most of the restaurants of our country. The wine butler then returns to the table and presents the wine list to the host from the left and must be ready to answer any queries and if required advise the guest on the choice of wines. While the station waiter will serve the food, the wine butler serves that particular wine to match the food. He should always co-ordinate with the station waiter with skill and intelligence.

Serving the Meal

The waiter must know the order of services of dishes that his guest has ordered. He will therefore pass on the KOT to the appropriate part of the kitchen or to the kitchen clerk or whoever is accepting the orders. In order to keep the guests waiting, the first dish in course of the menu is usually kept ready for immediate service. Meanwhile, the dishes that are to follow are immediately put into preparation. Having served one course, the waiter goes to the kitchen for the next course which he will bring to the side table in time. He should check other tables at his station before leaving for the kitchen to ensure that no other guests are trying to attract his attention. Where a waiter has several separate guests to attend at a time, he must have a clear memory and service skills to bring at a time and serve the dishes correctly and promptly.

Adjusting Covers

It may be necessary for a cover or covers to be adjusted for guest's need.

Order of Service

In a party of two, a lady and a gentleman, serve the lady first. In a party of four consisting of two ladies and two gentlemen, serve the lady on the right of the host first, then the lady on his left, the gentleman opposite the host and finally the host.

In a party of six, three ladies and three gentlemen, the host and hostess will sit facing each other. The lady on the right of the host is served first, then the lady on the left, then the hostess. Next the gentleman on the right of the hostess followed by the left of the hostess and finally the host. In a large party, if there is a top table, the top table guest is served first. During the service, if there is any undue delay in obtaining an order, the guest must be informed by the headwaiter with a suitable excuse.

Procedure for Taking Booking in Restaurant

After usual greetings and introduction, the following information are useful.

   a. Date of the party
   b. Date of the booking
   c. Name of the host
   d. Number of covers
   e. Time of the party
   f. Any special request from the host
   g. Type of party

When you have received the above information from the prospective client, it is advisable to repeat them over the telephone as confirmation and clarification, if any from the client. Telephone conversation may end after usual exchange of 'thanks', etc.

Art of Presenting the Bill to the Guests

The waiter must always check his bill before presenting to ensure that it is correct. Bills can be paid in two ways. By the guest to the waiter or by the guest on leaving direct to the cash desk. But the present mode of presentation in a sophisticated restaurant is by using a bill presentation folder. The time for presenting the bill varies with the type of restaurant. In a quick service restaurant after the waiter has ensured that the guest requires nothing else, he can usually place the bill on the table. But in a more sophisticated restaurant or speciality restaurant more service may be required after the meal. So the bill must remain open until asked for. No time should be lost in presenting the bill once it is demanded. At no time should a waiter give the impression that he is trying to get rid of his guest either because other guests need the table or he wants to go home. The bill with the money when paid should be taken to the cashier for encashment and the receipted bill with the change, if any, should be placed on the table at the left-hand side of the host. Any tip left on the plate, of no matter what size should be picked up graciously with the plate with 'thank you very much, Sir/Madam'.

NB: If the guest is on credit facility, his/her signature has to be obtained in the bill and the same must be submitted to the cashier immediately for his action. For credit card (e.g. American Express, Diner's club, credit card VISA, BOB, etc.), prescribed formalities are to be observed without any inconvenience to the guests.

Conclusion

When the guest rises from the table in order to leave, the waiter must immediately come forward and help the guest to leave his/her seat by pulling the chair. He should also check the belonging of the guest which has fallen under the table or is hidden under the napkin and finally at the end should say 'Thank you very much Sir/Madam for your visit in the restaurant', 'See you again', etc.

Restaurant Furniture, Linen and Implements

Within the restaurants, furniture varies according to the establishment. Floors may be covered with costly carpeting, polished wood or, in simpler restaurant, with linoleum or plastic floor covering. Chairs similarly vary in upholstery and covering according to the degree of luxury. Items such as curtains, decor, table lamps and other light fittings are similarly variable in quality and design and local flare. Theme of the restaurant, if any, is also important for the decoration.

Special functional qualities of the furniture should have:
a. Durability
b. Ease of storage
c. Ease of cleaning
d. Functional suitability for restaurant

Table height varies a little according to choice but does not usually exceed 2½ ft. Lower tables, sofa, etc. have a greater serving problems to a waiter because of bending.

Table tops may be of wood or sunmica covered with glass or plastic material or marble and other contemporary products. Tables should be stable and with legs well spaced to afford minimum interference to guests. In good restaurants, each party of customers has its own table and two parties are never made to share. Oval tables are suitable for seating larger parties. Round tables with rotating inner elevated portions are also used for serving Chinese foods.

In more popular restaurants, square or rectangular tables of uniform size are generally used. The advantage of sqaure table is that two or more can be put together quickly during service to accommodate large parties who have not reserved table in advance.

Cover Space at Table

Table size should allow a length of at least 2 ft per cover for simple plated service and up to 2½ ft per person for silver service (Table 9.1).

Table 9.1: Guide to table sizes and seating capacity

Shape	Seating	Approximate size feet
Circular	2 persons	3 to 3¼ dia
	4 persons	3¼ dia
	6 persons	4 dia
	8 persons	5 dia
Rectangular	4 persons	4 × 3¼
	8 persons	5¾ × 3¼
	10 persons	9½ × 3¼

Chairs

From serving point of view, a chair style is important in the restaurant. It is important to guest to have comfort and intimacy. Management is concerned with durability, ease of movement and stackability. A customary chair height (seat to floor) is about 18 inches and should neither touch nor press against the tablecloth. Wherever possible, chairs should be placed in the manner so that table legs do not obstruct seated customers.

Sideboard

For efficient service, waiter needs his own sideboard in the restaurant. This furniture is also described as dummy waiter, or station service table. It normally consists of an upper shelf on which a waiter affects all his preparations during service. A hot-plate may also be accommodated on the top surface. Under the sideboard top are drawers with compartments, open or partially open at the front. All the silvers (cutlery) available are arranged here. Below the cutlery compartment, there is usually another shelf for storing plates of various sizes and usages. Second lower shelf is spaced for spare linen, including tablecloths, slip cloths, service cloths and napkins. Sometimes the sideboard has a cupboard for temporary storage of used linen. The sideboard is indeed the focal point of service.

Cutlery stores in the compartments usually comprise table spoons, forks, dessert spoons, forks, knives, fish knives and forks and any special cutlery or serving implements. Stacked under the cutlery compartments are the various plates, coffee saucers. Coffee cups will be obtained as required from the hot cupboard. Pickles, finger bowls, toothpick, etc. are also kept in the sideboard.

Following is a broad guide to furniture for a good restaurant for 100 covers.

1. Reception-cum-billing desk
2. Buffet table
3. Tables and chairs (as per no. of covers)
4. Sideboards with hot plates
5. 1 liqueur trolley
6. Trolleys for service of appetiser and dessert

Linen

Tablecloths, napkins and other textile items of tableware are usually described in hotels and restaurants as linen, whether or not they are actually made of linen. Table linen may be of materials mixed with linen and cotton, or mixture of synthetic fibres with cotton or linen. Damask is a form of weaving in which the weave produce a self-pattern. Damask is traditionally, but not necessarily, white. The self-pattern can be simple, elaborate or even incorporate a restaurant's name or logo. Textile company produces good quality damask in India.

Linen Sizes

Tablecloths are available in variety of sizes. It is also made out of large cloth roles by cutting into desired sizes for a standard table of sizes, i.e. 60" × 40" or 60" × 80".

Napkins (Table 9.2)

Varying from small to large:

12" × 12"	(Tea)
18" × 18"	(Lunch)
20" × 20"	(Dinner)

Table 9.2: A guide to napkins and tablecloth requirement for a 100 seating restaurant		
1500	Table napkins	(20" × 20")
150	Tablecloths	(60" × 60")
75	Tablecloths	(80" × 60")
250	Small napkins	
500	Slip cloths (if used)	

Trays

Trays are chiefly used by waiters for breakfast tea/coffee service where a recatngular type is appropriate. Wine waiters use salvers (or small trays) at all meals for the service of drinks served in glasses and whisky, gin, aperitif, beer, minerals, etc. and for removing dirty glasses from tables. Square or rectangular trays are sometimes used for carrying food from kitchen to sideboard during meal service and also for clearing the dirties from the restaurant.

Silverware

As all the table fabrics are called linen in restaurants, so sliver is used to describe cutlery and metal flatware and hollowares. In fact, restaurant silver is often of stainless steel. Even when not stainless steel, cutlery and other items used are not made of solid silver, but of electroplated nicked silver (EPNS). Stainless steel is increasingly used instead of silver-plated items for reasons of cost and maintenance. Its stain resistance is due to chromium being incorporated into the iron. Knife blades are usually made of a harder type than other stainless material and are therefore tough and stain resistant.

Cutlery

The principal cutlery and their uses are:
- Soup spoons for soup, when served in soup plates.
- Fish knives and forks for fish and hors d' oeuvre.
- Large knives and forks for main course.
- Dessert or sweet spoons and forks for all sweets served on plates, small silver fruit knives and forks for fresh fruit.
- Small knives for side plates.
- There can be other varieties of fork, knife, and spoon for specific purposes.
- Sundae spoons: May provide for ice-cream.
- Coffee spoons: For coffee; tea spoons for tea, cheese knife, etc.
- Service spoons and forks are used for serving all food orders from the serving dish onto the plate. Examples of some varieties of fork, spoons, knives are shown in Figs 9.8–9.10.

Miscellaneous Equipment and their Variety for a 100 Cover Restaurant

10 Chafing dishes	60 Oval service dishes
	80 Round dishes with cover
30 Toast racks	60 Bread baskets
60 Tea strainers	20 Coffee pots
20 Tea pots	20 Water jugs

20 Egg cups	50 Butter dishes
40 Vegetable server	75 Platters
20 Sauce boat / dal server	50 Salad trays

Service dishes can be adjusted accordingly for use of donga.

Glassware

In all the eating establishments, some quantity of glassware are used except in very samll places where all the implements are of stainless steel origin. The quality of glassware, their design and variety sometime change the whole ambience of a eating place. More sophisticated use of glassware leads to more careful use and extreme attention to its up-keep. The glasswares are also generally known as china or crockery. Bone china is very fine quality of porcelain and very expensive also. Depending upon the policy and budget of the management, the crockeries are to be selected for any hotel. Crystal and cut glass items are also used in very class restaurants.

Dishes and plates are of different types used for different purposes so are the wine glasses. Following is a rough guideline for estimating crockery need of a restaurant.

Dinner plate (full plate)	2 to 3 times the number of restaurant seats
Small plate (half plate)	3 to 4 times the number of restaurant seats
Quarter plate	4 times the number of restaurant seats
Soup plate	3 times the number of restaurant seats
Tea cup	3 to 4 times the number of restaurant seats
Saucer for the above	3 to 4 times the number of restaurant seats

Because of limited wine service in Indian hotels and restaurants, we practically do not come across the varieties of wine glasses.

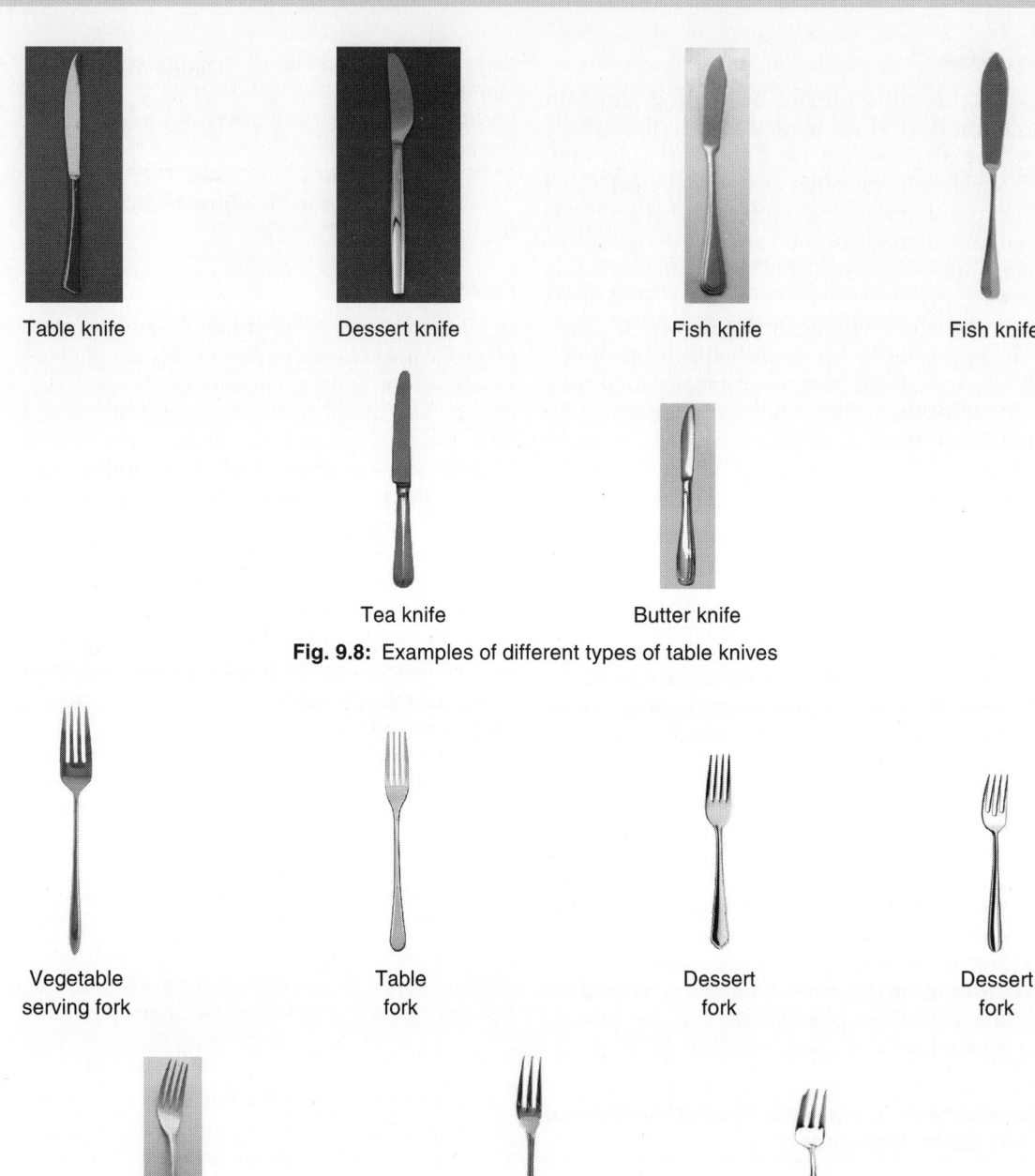

Table knife   Dessert knife   Fish knife   Fish knife

Tea knife   Butter knife

Fig. 9.8: Examples of different types of table knives

Vegetable
serving fork   Table
fork   Dessert
fork   Dessert
fork

Fish fork   Tea fork   Pastry fork

Fig. 9.9: Examples of different types of fork

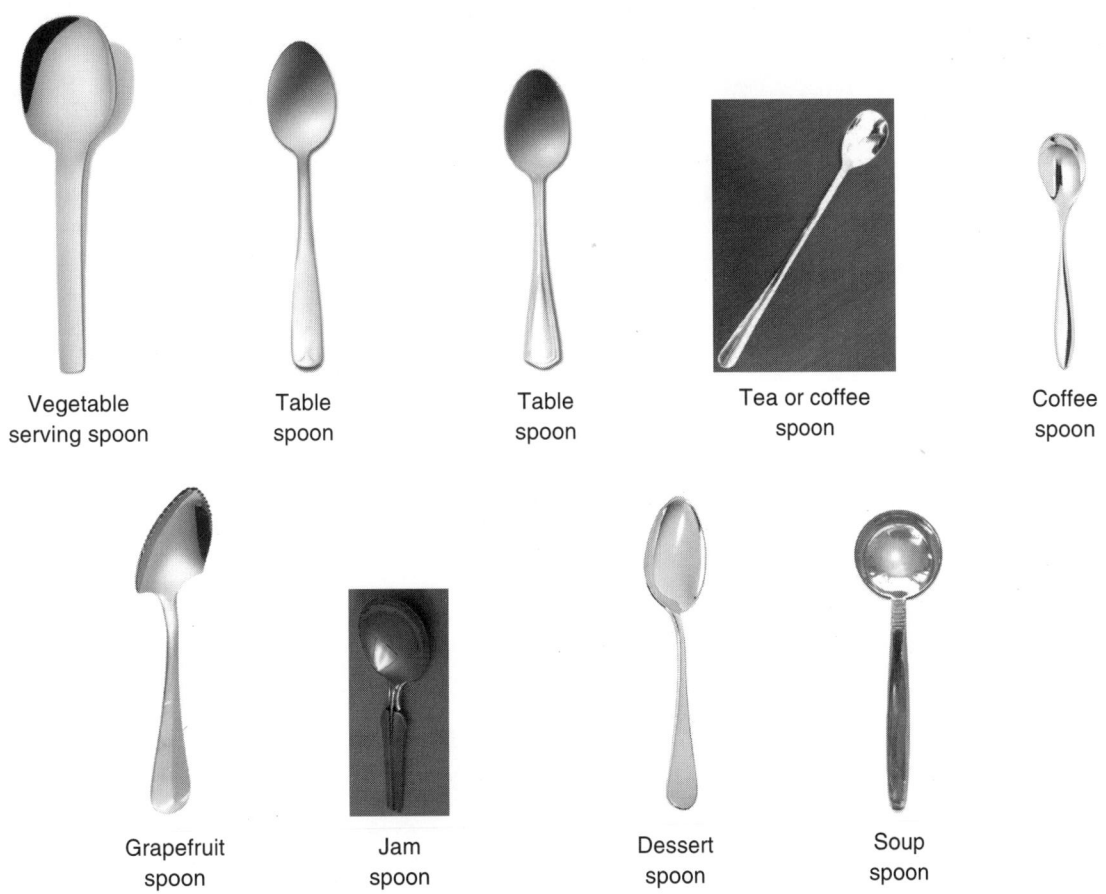

Vegetable serving spoon	Table spoon	Table spoon	Tea or coffee spoon	Coffee spoon
Grapefruit spoon	Jam spoon	Dessert spoon	Soup spoon	

Fig. 9.10: Examples of different types of spoon

Otherwise specified glasses are used for specific wine and cocktails. Beer is served in large beer glasses or in beer mugs.

Some typical glasses used in restaurants are shown in Fig. 9.11.

Care of Crockeries, Cutleries and Glasses

The best of restaurant services and restaurant's reputation not only depends on the food but also on the sparkling clean and choicest crockery, glass and cutlery. Appropriate methods need to be introduced for proper removal of dirty item, cleaning and storage for repeat use. A separate washing area is often provided. One must be trained to take meticulous care in the whole process, otherwise heavy breakage will happen. Very fragile and delicate china or cutglass may only be introduced considering the provision of trained staff, washing, storage facilities, etc. as well as the nature of customers. Following are some important guidelines for cleaning and caring various implements of restaurants.

1. Glass

In India, we now have many good glass manufacturing companies. Glasses are usually purchased in gross or in dozens. Because of

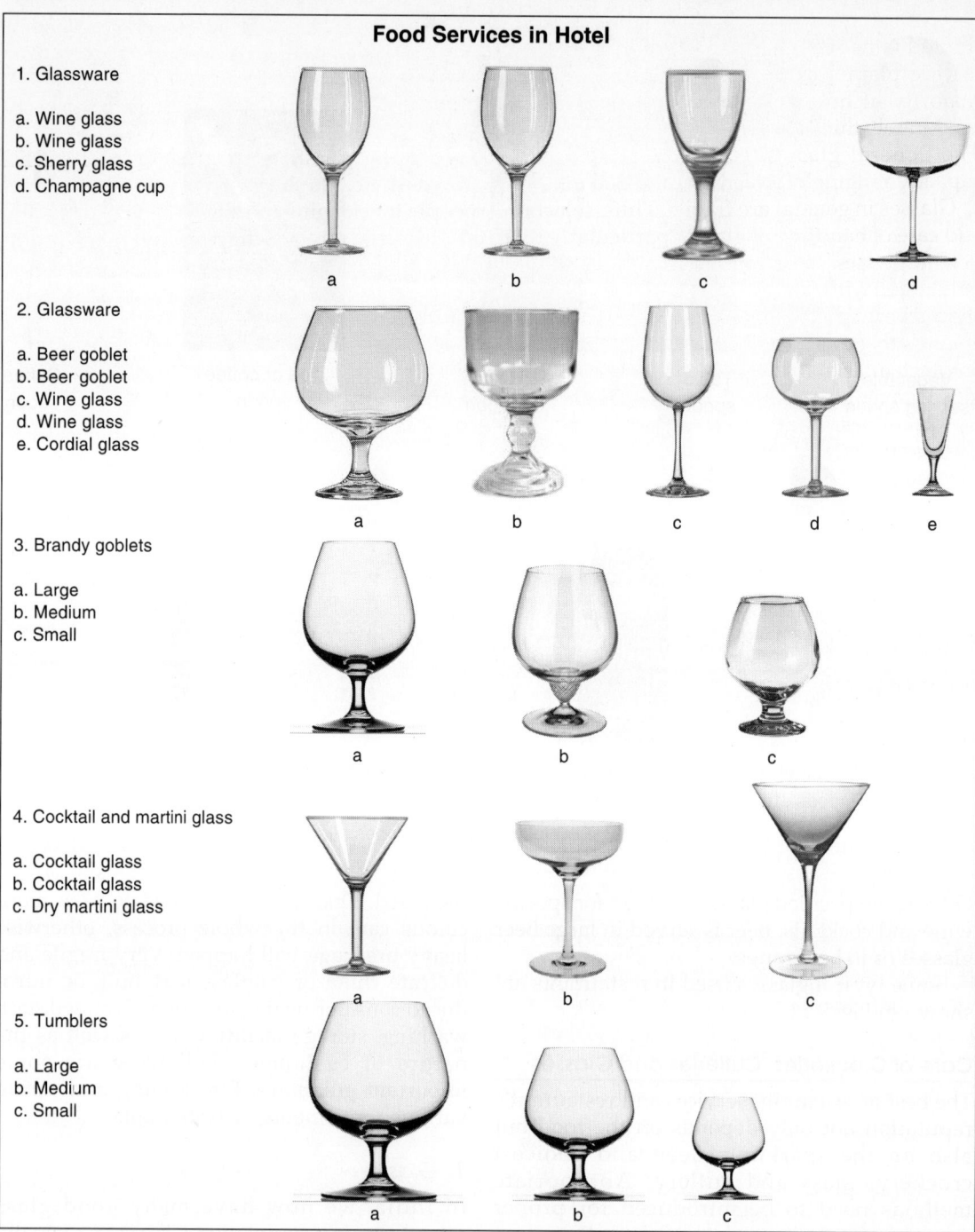

Food Services in Hotel

1. Glassware

a. Wine glass
b. Wine glass
c. Sherry glass
d. Champagne cup

2. Glassware

a. Beer goblet
b. Beer goblet
c. Wine glass
d. Wine glass
e. Cordial glass

3. Brandy goblets

a. Large
b. Medium
c. Small

4. Cocktail and martini glass

a. Cocktail glass
b. Cocktail glass
c. Dry martini glass

5. Tumblers

a. Large
b. Medium
c. Small

Fig. 9.11: Some typical drink glasses used in hotel

limited wine service in the country, only long-lasting plain all purpose glasses are used in majority of hotels. Decent, light weight and moderately thick glasses are preferred for wine. The general glass sizes that are used have capacity ranging between 200 and 300 ml.

Glasses in general are fragile. Thus, selection and care of handling of glasses particularly that of wine glasses is very important. Glasses should be handled with care and proper style. All glasses should be washed in hot water and cleaned with glass cloth. Some cleaning agents like "Teepol" are particularly good for glass cleaning. Clean glasses may be lifted and can be examined for the cleanliness against light. For hotel rooms glasses are first clean and wrapped in cellophane or similar papers. Very special care must be taken to see that there is no chipped rim or crack in any glass for the use of customers.

2. Crockeries

Large and small plates comprise the bulk of the crockeries used in majority of average Indian hotels. These are generally hand-washed in soap solution, rinsed and dried. Soft warm water (60°C–70°C) is reported to be very ideal for crockery wash. Strong surface abrasion because of careless scrubbing, etc. spoils the design and decorations. If the dishes are washed in dish washing machine, particular care must be taken for the proper use of the machine as per instructions. The cleaned plates are usually kept hot on plate warmer till the time of service. Before offering to the guest, checking must be made regularly for chipped or cracks in plates, should there be any of those then they must be discarded.

3. Cutlery

Hotel cutleries are mainly of metallic origin. The most common metal is stainless steel. The hotel silver are simply items silver plated over a base metal (copper, zinc, nickel alloy). The life of silver plating depends upon the thickness of silver coat, washing methods and atmospheric conditions. Sulphurous connections either from food or other sources damage the silver through chemical interaction. Egg and onion very sharply react with silver plated cutleries. Appropriate polish such as silvo or polish powder, etc. should only be used by trained people for cleaning the silver. Stain on stainless steel is very rare and implements made out of this metal is relatively easy to clean and keep. Electrical cutlery washing machine is now available in the country. Apart from service of food and cleaning duties, the restaurant's staff are also responsible for care of glasses, china and cutleries used in restaurant.

The cleaning and arranging of the restaurant at the time of opening and organising things at the closing time are also part of restaurant staff duties. The golden rule for the restaurant's staff is to arrange, clean and keep the things in proper order and as per policy of the proprietor.

Basic Etiquette for Restaurant Staff

The hotel and restaurant business is an admixture of showmanship, diplomacy and salesmanship as well. All front line personnel are required to have an ability to communicate effectively coupled with certain manners and etiquette associated with gentleness. The etiquettes that a waiter should exhibit in a restaurant are as under:

1. Attend the guest as soon as they enter the restaurant.
2. Wish guests as per the time of the day and welcome them to the restaurant.
3. Assist guests to remove warm, heavy coats in winter and help to put them on when they leave.
4. Be polite to guests.
5. Help to seat ladies first.
6. Provide extra cushion or special chairs for children, if required.
7. Keep away from eating during service.
8. Avoid putting service cloth in trouser's pockets.
9. When speaking to a guest, do not interrupt him, if he is speaking to another guest.

10. Do not soil menu cards.
11. Do not overhear guests' conversation or show any interest in their talks.
12. Be attentive to guest's calls.
13. Communicate softly.
14. Always maintain right posture and smartness.
15. Avoid touching hair or nose, etc. in front of the guests.
16. Do not hurry guests.
17. Light a match away from the guests and hold the flame only in front of guest to enable a guest to light his cigarette or use lighter.
18. Avoid arguing with service staff and guests in restaurant.
19. Carry pencil in the pocket and not behind ears or in hairs.
20. Never add up bills wrongly.
21. Avoid chewing gum or pan, etc.
22. Do not show interest in tips but receive them politely.
23. Remove tips after the guests leave the restaurant.
24. Do not ignore guests by talking among fellow waiters.
25. Enter and leave the restaurant through the service door only.
26. Never put on spotted or greasy uniform, unpolished or unsuitable shoes.

Model Staff Organisation for a Good Restaurant

Staff in the restaurant are designed with nomenclatures in use in different countries in the USA, the UK or France. Junior staff in some places are known as waiters but some staff are known as stewards in the USA and commis-de-rang in France.

In large restaurants, there should be a manager and even a separate receptionist. In most places, there is a restaurants clerk to process the bills and receive the payments. In general staff organisation in restaurants is of the following pattern (Flowchart 9.1)

Flowchart 9.1: Staff organisation in restaurant

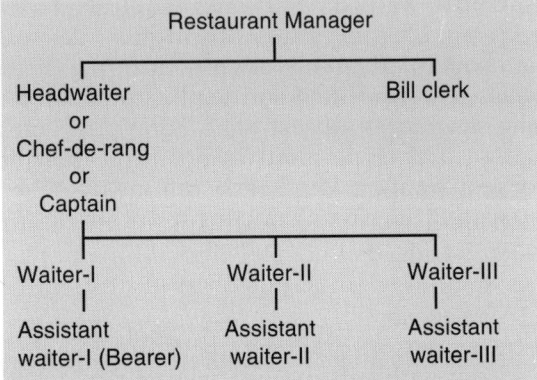

Depending upon the policy and volume of business, the number and type of restaurant staff varies. In general for 100 cover restaurant, approximately 40 staff are required per 8 to 10 hourly shift to attend the guest properly. If there is any beverage services, then wine waiter is needed. In Railways and other Government places, restaurant staff are also designated as masalchi, bearer and orderly, etc. Whatever may be the descriptions, the restaurant owner must see that right persons have been selected for the task. It must be kept in mind that because of untrained and unmotivated waiters, there can be irreparable loss to the business.

Bar Operation in Hotel

Bar is traditionally defined as a restricted or exclusive area in a tavern. The age old concept is still being carried for centuries. The purpose of making a restricted area was to provide separate identity and facilities for the exclusive customers who preferred their drink to be shared with fellow drinkers closely and enjoy the cosy ambience. This concept is being carried out till date almost in all countries. In many countries, the sale of alcoholic drinks remained confined in the bars only. Further there are many places where eateries and restaurants are allowed to serve alcoholic drinks remained confined in the bars only. In Europe and in many other countries, gradually excise rules and regulation are introduced. Such rules and regulations are also introduced in our country by the British rulers. Prior to that we had indigenous Sarab Khana or Sari where drinks were available to the visitors. During the British days, " Desi" Sarab Khana or Bhati Khana or country liquor bars were introduced. Functioning of these is now regulated by excise rules. In these places, only locally brewed spirits are sold. As per excise regulation, no women are allowed in these places. Gradually, quality drinking places were established in major cities with different decor. Liquors, spirits and wines are stocked there for sale in retail. No women were also previously allowed

to have drinks in these places. But gradually permission were granted to women consumers as well, if they are accompanied by male companions. During British days, restricted drinking places were established in our cities—specially at Kolkata (Calcutta)—the former British Capital of India. With the change of time, the concept of original bar changed and it did not signify restricted drinking 'area'. Bar is now understood as a place where drinks can be available on retail measures and foods and snacks may also be available along with drinks. It is a specific Indian habit to have some namkins, snacks, etc. with drink and post-food drinking sessions.

Temporary Bar

In order to cater the demands for drinks in garden party, farmhouse party, outdoor catering party, etc. special day licence or function licence is available for restricted hours on specified dates. Licence holders are allowed to sale alcoholic products on such dates at specified venues.

In large establishments, bar also provides facilities for mixed drinks (cocktails) as well as non-alcoholic fizzy drinks. However, such operation does not come under excise rules and regulation.

It is the house policy of the operator as to how he sales his products in a licenced bar. In Europe and America, there is no restriction for women to work in bars as bar tender or bar staff. But Indian excise provisions do not allow women to work in bars.

Bar Area

Traditional bar designs include counters of various sizes and designs; minimum height 36". Bar stools for guests provide comfortable leg rests, etc. No hand rests are provided. At the back of the counter, arrangements are provided for dispensing drinks, with ice, soda, tonic water and cold water. Cold beer dispensing machine, granulated ice, ice cube machine, soda fountain, etc. may also be provided, when designing a modern bar. On the back wall, bar products are stocked suitably, aesthetically and functionally. Varieties of glasses of different sizes are needed for bar. These are well-stocked properly. Bar design is a professional work and helps from interiors conversant with such works should be called for. There is also arrangement for dealing cash. After the specified period of bar operation, cleaning, cash counting, spillage and removal of empty bottles should be organised for proper functioning of bar.

Proper stock taking as per excise rules is must. This is also necessary for stock and new purchases.

BAR EQUIPMENT (Fig. 10.1)

In order to arrange a bar for full operation, the following tools and equipment are necessary.
1. Corkscrew opener
2. Ice crusher
3. Cigar cutter
4. Ice shaver
5. Ice picks
6. Ice scoops
7. Ice bucket and tongs
8. Cocktail shaker
9. Mixing glass
10. Bar spoon
11. Decanter with stopper
12. Hawthorn strainer
13. Sprinkler pots
14. Peg measures 30 ml and 60 ml or as per State Excise Laws
15. Fruit knife
16. Juice extractor/squeezer
17. Cutting board
18. Cocktail/swizzle sticks
19. Cutters
20. Fine grater
21. Strainer/tunnel
22. Wine coolers
23. Drinking straws
24. Coasters
25. Bottle/can opener
26. Ashtrays
27. Doilies/paper napkin
28. Silver/glass bowls
29. Tray/salver cloths
30. Glass cloths
31. Serviettes
32. "Dry day" display board/plate
33. a. Dusting cloth
    b. Waste bins
34. Various types of glasses (Figs 10.2 and 10.3) with different capacity:
    • Beer glass/tumbler/mug
    • Collin glasses
    • Goblet glasses
    • Old-fashioned
    • Brandy balloon/inhaler
    • Cocktail glass
    • Champagne saucer/tulip
    • Red wine/claret
    • White wine glass
    • Sour glass
    • Herry
    • Port glass
    • Liqueur glass
    • Rolly-polly
35. Bar counter with top and shelves
36. Bottle cooler
37. Store room
38. Ice cube machine
39. Bottle display rack

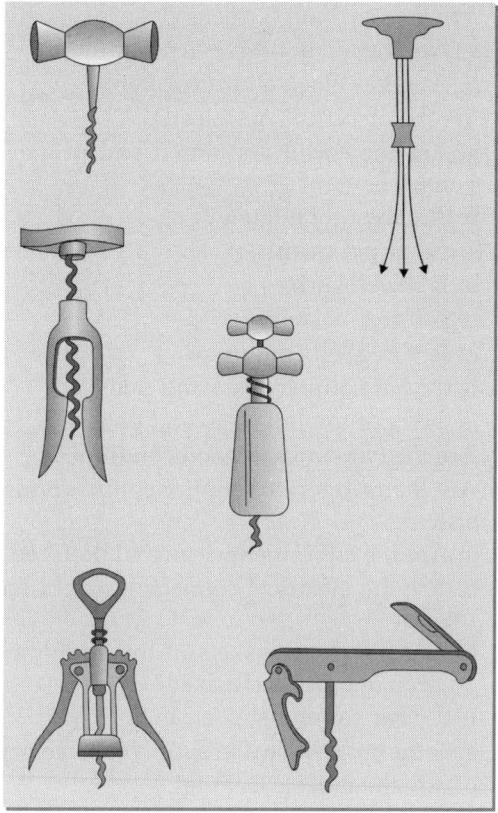

Fig.10.1: Bar equipment

Fig. 10.2: Types of wine glasses

40. Recharged battery
41. Sink and work space
42. Bar stock and seating arrangements
43. Billing machine / credit card handling machine, etc. if there is control billing system

Wine Glass Capacity

1. Water goblet 10 oz
2. Red wine glass 7 oz
3. Champagne tulip 9 oz
4. Parfait glass 5 oz
5. White wine glass 5½ oz
6. Wine goblet 14 oz
7. Brandy mug 14 oz
8. Beer goblet 14 oz

Fig.10.3: Types of wine glasses

9. Sherry 4 oz
10. Beer mug 14 oz
11. Champagne saucer 6 oz
12. Cocktail glass 4 oz
13. Rolly-polly 9 oz
14. Liqueur cordial 3 oz
15. Old fashion 9 oz
16. Pool glass 12 oz
17. Tom Collins 3 oz
18. High ball glass 8½ oz
19. Pony tunbler/juice glass 5 oz. (1 fl. oz = 30 ml)

BAR CHECK LIST

Check Points

1. Is the bar name board distinct and well appointed?
2. Are the directional signs prominent and in proper place?
3. Is the entrance clean?
4. Is the door clean and well polished?
   A. Is the door glass clean and polished?
   B. Has the glass door a painted sign?
   C. Is the door in good working condition?
5. Is the bar air-conditioned?
   a. Is the AC working and effective?
   b. Are the AC grills clean?
6. Are all the light fixtures clean?
7. Are all the light in working condition?
8. Are light shades?
9. Do the curtains drape well?
   a. Are the curtains clean and in good condition?
   b. Are the bead conditions ok?
   c. Are the beads clean and complete?
   d. Are the beads in working condition?
   e. Do they drape well?
   f. Are they clean?
10. Are the windows clean?
    a. Are they in good working conditions?
    b. Are the window glasses clean and polished?

11. Are the partition/screens clean?
    a. Are they in good repair/condition?
    b. Are they clean and presentable?
12. Are the objects d' Art Clean?
    a. Are they well appointed and properly fixed?
    b. Are they catalogued?
13. Is the carpet clean?
    a. Is it well laid?
    b. Is it free of stains?
    c. Is it in good condition?
14. Is the bar counter clean and polished?
15. Is the bar foot rail clean and polished?
16. Are the bar stools in good condition?
17. Are the refrigerator equipment in working order?
    a. Are the equipment clean and polished?
    b. Are the electrical connections right and safe?
    c. Are the door gaskets of the equipment clean and properly fixed?
18. Is the bar counter sink clean?
    a. Is the hot/cold water supply satisfactory?
    b. Are the faucets leaking?
    c. Is the drain board fixed at the correct angle?
    d. Is the drain pipe leaking?
19. Is the bar display counter/rack clean and polished?
    a. Are the mirrors clean and polished?
    b. Are the bottles clean?
    c. Are all the labels on the bottle intact?
    d. Does the display look complete and impressive?
20. Is the bar adequately stocked?
21. Are the bar equipment and ingredients as per list available and if yes are they in good condition and sufficient quantity?
22. Are the bar cards/wine lists clean?
23. Are the tables clean and well polished?
    a. Are they firm on legs?
    b. Are the table tops smooth?

c. Are the table linen clean and unfaded?

d. Are they of right size and well laid?

24. Are the chairs firm on their legs?

a. Are they clean and polished?

b. Is the upholstery of the sofas in good condition?

25. Are the sofas in good condition?

26. Is the upholstery of the sofas in good condition?

27. Is the bar furniture laid out as per plan?

28. Is the bar staff well groomed and in clean and proper uniform?

29. Is the floor behind bar counter dry?

a. Is it made of non-slippery materials/ tiles?

b. Is it in good condition?

30. Are the control books for various purposes in good condition?

31. Is the excise register available and up-to-date?

32. Is the bar-stock store door clean and well polished?

33. Is the bar-stock store clean and neatly arranged?

a. Is the store clean?

b. Are the shelves clean and properly labelled?

c. Is the refrigerator to store white wine is ok?

d. Is the store well lit and ventilated?

e. Is the store cool?

f. Are the bar-store records and registers up-to-date and in good condition?

As detailed out earlier, the bar operation is very critical, though apparently appears to be simple.

Its operation has to be guided by many procedures and legal as well as excise provisions. All papers, registers and explanations for natural deviation has to be provided readily and to the satisfaction of the competent authority.

Bar is not only a service point for beverages but it has a special and silent responsibility to satisfy the consumers from their stress and other physical and mental tensions. Thus, the bar's ambience and environment are of great value for those who gather around the place not only for simple drinks but also to socialize and relieve of their tension.

Hence, depending on the policy, size of the establishment, and local demands, a suitable bar is established for business, entertainment and reputation.

The above check lists provide lines for proper management and day-to-day check. Any laxity in any area should be dealt by the authority in time to maintain the reputation. Standardized business policy, honesty of service, personal attention to regular as well as for the first timers must carefully be handled to build business reputation.

In order to assess the guest satisfaction and proper management, a guest comment card with good quality paper having scope to note address, etc. should be recorded by the hostess, and maitre-d-hotel. The card should then be forwarded to the F & B manager.

PREPARING BAR AT THE OPENING TO CLOSING

Morning Shift: Bar Opening Tasks

1. Cleaning all bar area including bar counter, furniture, glass, etc.
2. Stock drawn from main stores.
3. Any repair required in the bar, report to maintenance department.
4. Linen arranged.
5. AC system checked.
6. Display rack cleaned and bottle displayed.
7. All bar requirements cleaned and kept in place.
8. Fresh fruits, cherries, cocktail, olives, lemon slices, lemon juice, etc. kept ready.
9. Stock of ice cubes checked.
10. Bar stock checked as per stock register.
11. B.O.T and bill book made ready for use.
12. Dry-day/closed board removed.

SAMPLE GUEST COMMENT CARD

Dear guest

It is our endeavour to provide you with quality service. You are requested to kindly fill up this card to help us serve you better.

Name ....

....

Address ....

....

Phone Number .... Cell phone Number ....

Birthday ....

Wedding Anniversary: ....

Please insert your Visiting Card/Business Card

Please tick	**Excellent**	**Good**	**Poor**
Decor	☐	☐	☐
Air-conditioning	☐	☐	☐
Ambience	☐	☐	☐
Entertainment	☐	☐	☐
Service	☐	☐	☐
Prompt	☐	☐	☐
Courteous	☐	☐	☐
Settlement of bill	☐	☐	☐
Food	☐	☐	☐
Taste	☐	☐	☐
Portion	☐	☐	☐

We thank you for visiting us. It would be a pleasure to welcome you again.

EVENING SHIFT

Bar Closing Tasks

1. "Closed" sign/board closing time.
2. Totally clear all tables and counter. No dirties and left over to remain under any circumstances.
3. Wash and polish all equipment and store them.
4. Store all perishable items properly.
5. Take physical stock inventory and enter in bar register.
6. Lock all liquor bottles.
7. Bottles cooler stocked with various bottles should be chilled.
8. Close Bill book and complete picking sheet.
9. Deposit cash collected.
10. Lock the main door of bar.
11. Deposit bar main key to security control or other authorised person.

PREPARING BAR FOR OPERATIONS

Adequate care and pre-planning is necessary everyday for bar operation to begin in schedule time. The work and service should be uninterrupted and guest should not be made to wait for execution of his/her orders at the counter. Overcrowding should not be allowed to happen. Defective or wrong delivery must be immediately rectified and replaced.

Following are some standardised steps for preparing bar operation in an establishment.

- Obtaining supplies
- Laying supplies
- Arranging bottles according to the plan
- Squeezing fruits
- Refilling and arranging juice and syrup bottles
- Preparing cocktail decorations
- Arranging cutting boards and knives
- Arranging cocktail making equipment
- Arranging trays and salvers
- Preparing and arranging spice and bitters
- Preparing and arranging mixers
- Filling ice containers
- Arranging drinking straws swizzle sticks, bottle openers and corkscrews
- Arranging service and glass cloths
- Arranging cocktail lists
- Refilling the cigar and cigarette stand and arranging cigar cutting equipment and match boxes
- Starting the drought beer machine
- Arranging for waste disposal
- Arranging and laying of linen
- Operate drought beer wherever applicable
- Recognise and report malfunctioning of equipment and machine

These are major steps of bar operation to be attended to. Therefore, other occasions where make shift bars required to be set up, for example, at the banquet or at exclusive parties on the gardens or by the poolside or on rooftop parties, adequate preparations are necessary in respect of glassware and products to be dispensed. Therefore, the host pre-negotiate the service arrangement of products to be supplied. Thus, there is no question of charging the customer/guest at the time of beverage service for these parties. Attention should be made to see pilferage/waste, etc. Attention should also be paid for proper washing of glasses and removal of broken glasses at once so that no injury takes place to the customers. Customer should not be kept waiting unreasonably during the large party gathering. Adequate manpower is required and to be planned accordingly.

In order to clear the rush and avoid over-crowding, wine waiters with prepared drinks and separate mixes and ice are rotated among guests for the convenience of the guest as well as for the operation.

In many restaurants, alcoholic drinks are served and there is no specific bar area located within the dining hall/restaurant areas. These drinks are served from kitchen. Guests are presented with drinklist/bar menu along with food menu and waiters take orders. In many Indian restaurants there are no special bar waiter for easier and economic operation.

Spirit/Wine Bottle Capacities

Wines are usually served as full bottle because bottles once opened must be consumed unlike spirits, etc. The practice is the same with beer. However, presently small bottles of beer and can beers are now available in the market which are sold as such. In foreign countries, wines are available retail in glasses and one can order one or more glasses as required.

The standard spirit bottle (full) contains 750 ml, ½ bottle and quarter bottles are also available.

1 l, 5 l, magnum containers for spirits are also available. There are miniature spirit bottles which are also on sale for tourists and airline beverage services.

Wine bottles are of 750 ml capacity. However, magnum size and ½ size bottles are also in the market.

The sizes, shapes and colour of wine and spirit bottle vary in accordance to the trade practice. Wine bottles are usually dark green, whereas spirit bottles are made of white glasses, amber colour bottles and blue colour bottles are also often used in bottling plants. For wine making, labelling is mandatory regulation and essential factor before marketing.

BAR PROVISION

Alcoholic Bar Provision

It is synonymous that bar provides alcoholic beverages. But one should understand that such old-fashioned association with bar for alcoholic drinks is no longer there and there are milk bar as well as coffee bar in and around our cities. However, the major product association with bar is still alcoholic beverages. In order to serve alcoholic beverages in style and with appropriate mixture with other liquids, e.g. water, soda, aerated water, lemonade fruit juices, etc. the bar must be appropriately equipped and store provisions to satisfy the need of the customers.

In India, dispensing of spirits, beer, etc. still dominate over dispensing wine varieties because of price constraints and drinking habits.

However, following are the major producers of alcoholic products with special reference to Indian market.

M/s Shaw Wallace & Co

M/s United Breweries

M/s Mc Dowell & Co

M/s Haywards & Co

M/s Mohan Mekins & Co

M/s Khodey Distilleries

M/s Kalyani Breweries

The above companies have their marketing and distribution all over the country. Some companies are also selling their products outside the country.

With proper import licences under excise rules, imported spirit, wines are now also available from "off shop" and in licensed bars.

STAFF ORGANIZATION IN THE BAR

Though the bar has a special set up such as bar with stools and counter and bar tender behind the bar to serve and take payments, in most of the bars (drinking places) having medium to large space where sofas, tables, etc. are laid out for guests to enjoy their drinks in more comfortable style.

However, in order to run bar services methodically, following are some typical requirements of staff and their organisation pattern.

Example 1

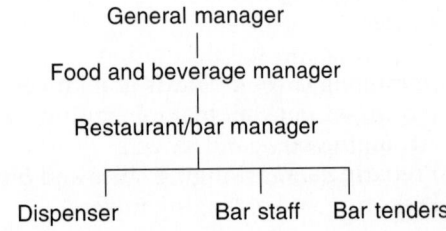

Example 2

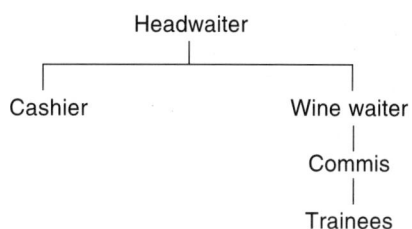

Headwaiter

Cashier — Wine waiter — Commis — Trainees

Example 3

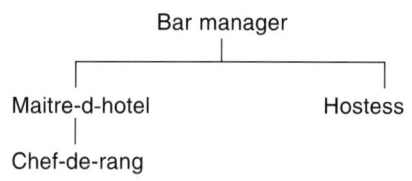

Bar manager

Maitre-d-hotel — Hostess

Chef-de-rang

Example 4

F & B manager
|
Maitre-d-hotel/chef-de-rang
|
Commis-de-rang
|
Apprentices (Trainees)

In foreign countries, bar tenders, wine waiters are mostly female. They add grace and mood to the guests who assemble in the bar. This practice is not yet introduced or seen in Indian bars or restaurants. The major manpower or human resources come from various catering institutes who are more or less trained and aware of their duties and responsibilities. They are also knowledgeable to some extent about materials and material handling in bars. Further training and teaching the trade practices are easier because of their institutional background.

But in many small and disorganised sectors, ordinary low paid people are hired for running the show and doing the business. It becomes difficult for the management to train them for best satisfaction of the employer and guests both.

Following are typical job descriptions of the key staff in the bar/bar-cum-restaurant.

JOB DESCRIPTION	
Job title	: Food and beverage manager
Responsible to	: General manager/ resident manager

Scope and Purpose

To achieve marketing, sales, profitability and quality service goals for the Food and Beverage Department by developing and executing marketing strategies, preparing and executing the budget, providing quality service to the guests and employing leadership and managerial skills effectively.

Duties and Responsibilities

- Attains food and beverage sales goals and targets by executing marketing strategies and controlling costs:
  - Prepare market plan by developing strategies to increase market share, analyse sales, review competitive surveys and develop new plan.
  - Execute market plan by implementing agreed strategies, evaluate results and adjust strategies as required.
  - Ensure that menu engineering supports marketing goals and recommending price, based on competition and market trends.
  - Maintain marketing and merchandising standards of operation by following the laid down service standards.
- Achieve profitability goals for entire department while providing the guest with quality service:
  - Develop the food and beverage budget by reviewing the outlet head's recommendations and trends, preparing a budget package and presenting the

complete to the general manager for approval.

- Implement the approved budget. Monitor revenues and costs on daily basis and take corrective action where necessary.
- Control cost by adhering to standards of operations for forecasting, budgeting, overtime control, and other cost control measures.
- Ensure that each department is run in accordance with the food and beverages standards of operations.
- Maintain control of food, beverage and supply costs and inventory by adhering to standards for purchasing and inventory control.
- Assist chef in setting up specifications and standards of food materials (raw, canned, and any other) and beverage items for the purchasing manager being a PFA nominee. Testing, guarding and approving of new products in the market.
- Do surprise checking of raw materials to confirm to standards and specifications as stipulated.

• Utilize leadership skills and motivation techniques in order to maximize employee productivity and satisfaction.
- Help in selection of qualified employee and provide orientation and training.
- Conduct employee meetings and counselling sessions in order to maximize employee morale and productivity.
- Determine the communication standards of performance to employee. Evaluate employee performance on a regular basis.
- Develop employees to maximize potential, and prepare them for future promotional opportunities through career development schemes.

• Ensure that all new developmental training goals are executed on an ongoing basis:
- Ensure that all new employees receive departmental orientation and go through on the job training programmes.

- Ensure that management utilize the trainer skills while conducting training programming.

• Achieve goals by ensuring that marketing and sales strategies are executed in order to maximize sales and that guest service standards are adhered to:
- Maximize banquet sales by ensuring that banquet sales personnel utilize sales promotion guidelines such as direct selling through verbal merchandising techniques.

• Keep immediate superior promptly and fully infromed of all problems or unusual matters of significance coming to his/her attention so that prompt corrective action can be taken, when appropriate.

• Perform all duties in a timely and efficient manner in accordance with established company policies.

• Maintain a favourable working relationships with all other company employees to foster and promote a cooperative and harmonious working climate, which will be conducive to maximize employee morals, productivity and efficiency/effectiveness.

• At all times, project a favourable image of Group's aim and objective. Foster and enhance public recognition and acceptance of all of its areas of endeavour.

• Ensure all licences related to his department are processed timely, perform other duties as requested.

• Perform other duties as required.

AUTHORITIES

• To ensure availability of all officers under his control.

• To recommend rewards for the outstanding performances and disciplinary action against defaulting employees within the department as per standing orders.

• To recommend purchases and condemnation of articles and indent material.

• To cancel/amend guests bills after full justification.

- To entertain CIPs with Food and Beverage to be ratified by GM
- To extend courtesies to CIPs and VIPs within the hotel such as cakes/bouquets/hampers, etc.
- To send give away like cakes/fruit baskets, hampers to CIPs/VIPs on special occasions or otherwise, to be ratified by GM.
- To recommend refurbishing/replacements of interiors, equipment, etc.
- To recommend advertising/promotional plans to GM.

Job Description

Job title	:	Maitre d'hotel
Responsible to	:	Outlet manager
Purpose and scope	:	To ensure quality service as per standards. To ensure smooth operations of his area.

Duties and Responsibilities

Overall responsibility of his area and to ensure high standards for product quality.

1. To ensure upkeep, maintenance and cleanliness of the entire restaurant.
2. To ensure that all registers and forms to be filled in and are maintained in the specified manner.
3. Handling all guest complaints with regard to quality of service and staff discipline.
4. To ensure that all records of the outlet are maintained.
5. To ensure staff discipline and grooming.
6. Maintain liasion and cordial relations with other departments.
7. To accord personalized attention and service to all VIPs/CIPs.
8. To maintain good and cordial relations with guests.
9. Briefing to be taken daily with the sevice staff.

10. To assist the manager in his work and to look after his jobs in his absence.
11. Any other jobs assigned from time to time.
12. To possess thorough knowledge of the menu/bar card, style and standard of service and all operational procedures and policies.
13. To assist in the planning and execution of special event.

EMPOWERMENT

1. To recommend disciplinary action to the manager.
2. Deployment of staff after normal hours as per requirement.
3. To recommend cancellation, amendment and/or replacement of order and bills to the manager.
4. To present cakes, fruit baskets, welcome drinks to guests of choice for promotional purpose.

Job Description

Job title	:	Hostess
Responsible to	:	Maitre D' hotel/ Outlet manager
Purpose and scope	:	To maintain guest relations

Duties and Responsibilities

1. To receive and welcome guests and escort them to the table.
2. To present menu/bar card to guest after they are seated.
3. Paying attention to all guests, specially to children and VIPs.
4. Seeing off all guests and to present bouquets, flower baskets and souvenirs to guest, if so required.
5. To possess thorough knowledge of the menus, restaurant and the hotel.
6. To obtain opinion on guest comment card.

7. Assisting in handling problem situations.
8. To maintain the following forms and registers:
   a. Table book
   b. Log book
   c. Guest history cards
   d. Record of events
   e. Guest comment cards
9. To send birthday/wedding anniversary cards to regular guests.
10. To perform any other tasks as assigned.

Job Description

Job title	:	Chef de rang
Responsible to	:	Maitre d' hotel
Purpose and scope	:	To provide quality service, preparation of restaurant

Duties and Responsibilities

1. To perform, organize and check mis-en-place and mis-en-scene.
2. Attending to the guest, once the hostess/ maitre d' hotel has seated them.
3. Presenting menu, taking order and executing them as per the standards specified.
4. Presenting the bills as per bill presentation standards and completing transactions.
5. Receiving/escorting the guest in and escorting the guest out.
6. All housekeeping and maintenance needs to be informed to MDH.
7. Maintaining inventory and stocktaking.
8. Maintaining good and cordial relations with the guest.
9. Reporting any untoward incident to maitre d' hotel/manager
10. Coordination with commis de rang and doing actual food service/clearance to ensure prompt, timely and efficient service to each guest.
11. To assist maitre d' hotel in special dishes
12. Any other job as assigned.

Job Description

Job title	:	Commis de rang
Responsible to	:	Chef de rang
Purpose and scope	:	Perform mis-en-place. To provide quality service to the guests

Duties and Responsibilities

1. Responsible for the purpose set up of all tables in his station.
2. To ensure linen, silver, china, glassware and all other table items and his area is clean and in proper condition before use.
3. Receives order from the guest or through chef de rang for food and beverages and places them in the kitchen/bar.
4. He should promote sales through suggestive selling.
5. Must be able to describe all dishes on menu to the guest, if needed.
6. He should know daily special/items not available, table reservations, etc. before the start of service.
7. To pick up orders for station in kitchen bar according to sequence and serve them to guests.
8. To refer complaints on food beverages items or service to his superior.
9. Prompt clearance of dirties from the tables/ station to dishwashing and getting them cleaned.
10. To exchange dirty linen with fresh linen and to store in the appropriate place.
11. To draw service wares, consumable from stores as and when requisitioned.
12. To accept payment for orders served, remit cash or signed restaurant check to cashier and if cash transaction returns full change to guest.
13. To show due courtesy and respect to the guest.
14. To perform any other task as assigned.

BRIEFING OF THE EMPLOYEES

As a routine, the briefing of the workers is essential for getting best out of them. Depending upon the policy, the briefing may be everyday before start of work or at the end. Feedback should be ascertained. The following are important check points for briefing:

1. a. Wet cloth
   b. Ball pen with small pad
   c. Bottle opener
   d. Handkerchief
   e. Name plate identity card
   f. Match box/lighter
2. Discussion instructions
   a. Recap on previous days' operation/and feedback
   b. Important functions
   c. Group/party handling
   d. VIP guest impact of any
   e. Update management policy/instructions
   f. Mini/bar card/menu
   g. Not available items/day special
3. Questioning
4. His briefing time will enhance job knowledge.
5. Ask for some problem faced by staff on their job.
6. Guide staff to ensure that they follow laid out standard and directions.
7. Motivate the staff from time to time.
8. Listen and ask for suggestion to increase efficiency/sales.
9. Inspect and check premises/tables stink, etc. personally.
10. Briefly emphasis on sales promotion through suggestion selling, sales gimmicks.

GROOMING OF BAR STAFF

Strict supervision is essential for grooming and for personal and oral hygiene in particular. No bad or foul smell mouth or bad body odour be allowed from the service staff. This is very critical in bar.

Lady employee

Shoes	:	Flat, well polished and closed heeled
Hair	:	Properly tied and well groomed
Nails	:	Well manicured and polished
Perfume	:	No strong perfume be used
Excessive jewellery	:	Should be avoided
Make up	:	Only light
Uniform	:	Should wear decently and in smart manner

Male employee

Hair	:	Close cut
Uniform	:	Clean to iron complete in all respects to socks/name badge proper fit and polished
Nails	:	Manicured
Shave	:	Close shave and beard properly trimmed
Hygiene	:	Nobody likes bad breath
Physical optima	:	Should not be sloppy or overweight. Must look smart and alert

BAR SERVICE STANDARDS

1. Bar will open punctually at scheduled time, as per local excise rules.
2. All guests will be greeted at the door within 10 seconds by hostess/maitré, chef de rang/Assistant Manager.
3. All guests will be escorted to the table by the person receiving them.
4. All guests will be addressed by their names, wherever means of identification exists.
   Note: The bar staff should make an effort to remember the names of the regular guests.
5. No guest will ever be seated at a table which is not clean.
6. The guests will be seated by bar man/commis escorting them chair will be pulled back

for the eldest lady first and the gesture will continue till the last guest is seated.

7. Bar card will be presented within two minutes of the guest being seated. Presentation of the card will be done as follows:
   a. Present bar card with a polite word "May I have your order Sir, Madam?" from the right-hand side of the guest.
   b. Present individual bar card to each guest.
   c. Order will be taken and suggestion offered by recommending in respect of cocktails and premium brands of spirits. Order will be taken on a BOT.
8. The drinks will be served within 5 minutes of taking the order in appropriate glasses and at the right temperature. Ask for ice, if required.
9. The snacks menu will be offered after the drinks order has been taken. If asked to come back, menu will be presented only after the drinks have been served.
10. On receiving a verbal or non-verbal indication from the guest, the snacks order will be taken as per standard specified.
11. When about to serve the order to the guest reading a magazine or has his hands on the table, courteously say "Excuse me Sir".
12. All drinks will be served from the right-hand side and cleared from the right-hand side.
13. All snacks will be served in the appropriate manner.
14. Presentation of snacks on the plate would confirm to the standards laid down by the chef.
15. All complimentary snacks will be placed on the table.
16. Bar man/commis de rang would be watchful of the guest's needs. Next order will be taken, when the drinks in the glass is about to finish.
17. The service of all drinks will be presented, when asked for.
18. The bill will be presented, when asked for.
19. The bill will be charged correctly and checked before presentation by the bar man. It will be presented in a folder along

with a ball pen within 3 minutes of the guest asking for the bill.

20. The money paid for, will be discreetly checked and received by the cashier and returned to the guest within 5 minutes.

Order Taking and Service in the Bar

- Presenting bar menu/wine list
- Explaining the wine/spirits/cocktails
- Assisting the staff to make drinks
- Writing wine order

The staff in charge should have the ability to:

- Tender wine list
- Suggest wine suitable for meals at table, when it is so needed and required.

The staff should have knowledge of:

- Wine terminology
- Wine available in the bar
- Vintage years
- Name of various wines and major origin
- Prices
- Relevant legislation
- Various wines in relation to food
- Quality and characteristics of various types of wine.
- Establishment's marketing policy

Attitudes

- Salesmanship
- Tact
- Accuracy

Technique of Service of Beer

1. Take the order.
2. Obtain the beer bottle.
3. Present it to the guest and open the bottle with the opener.
4. Ask the guest whether he wants it with or without crown (forth).
5. When the bottle is finished, asked the guest whether he would like to have another bottle of beer.

Serving Technique of Red Wine (Fig. 10.4)

1. Red wine is served at cool room temperature, i.e. 18–20° C.
2. Present the bottle to guest as usual.
3. Cut the foil as in white wine.
4. Clean up the cork with napkin.
5. Pull out the cork with the cork screw.
6. Present the cork to the guest, for him to ascertain the year of the product.
7. Clear the tip of the bottle with a clean napkin.
8. Pour a little wine to the host for tasting and approval.
9. Serve to all other guests as in case of white wine and then to the host. Red wines which

have sediment are brought in a wine cradle to avoid any disturbance. This wine is decanted in a carafe (or decanter) and used from the decanter.

Serving Technique of Champagne

1. Present the bottle of champagne in wine cooler at 5–7° C.
2. Present it to the guest as in white wine.
3. Keep it on the table, remove the foil.
4. Loosen the wire around the cork and remove it.
5. Keep your left hand thumb on the cork while loosening the cork.
6. Arrange all the champagne glasses in straight line on the table, touching each other.
7. Release the cork slowly.
8. When the cork is pulled, some wine will ooze out, so keep the bottle on top of glasses so that such overflow should go into the glasses.
9. After this, present the cork to the guest, for him to ascertain the year of the product.
10. Pour a glass of champagne to the host for tasting and move for other as in the case of white wine.

TECHNIQUE OF HANDLING FAULTS IN WINE

Corky Wine

Corky wine complaint comes from the guest because of smell of cork in the wine.

The wine waiter or sommelier should apologize to the customer, remove the wine, check it himself and if it is out of condition, he should replace the bottle with another of the same type. If the wine is in the correct condition, it is prudent to offer a replacement wine of another type rather than having an argument about it. If the sommelier has detected this corkiness before serving the wine, he should replace it with

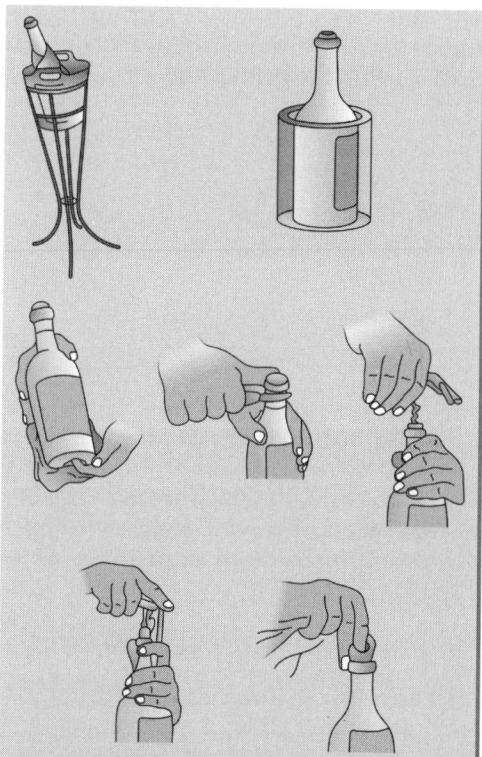

Fig. 10.4: Cooling of wine bottle, presenting and opening of wine bottle

another bottle of the same type without offering the defective one to the customer.

In busy bar in Western counties, wines are sold per glass basis instead of the full bottle. Thus, there is no difficulties or problem with any bottle which is opened but returned by the customer based on his assessment even if the condition of the wine is ok.

Broken Cork

If a cork breaks and part falls into the bottle of wine, it should be removed with a cork extractor and decant the contents of the bottle. This work should be done away from the table.

Effervescent Wine

If the wine is seen to be fizzy or slightly effervescent, then it should be discarded. This condition will make the wine smell yeasty.

Attention should be given so that replacement bottle should not have the same defect.

Wine waiters should be careful to see that right type of glasses are used and they are meticulously clean. A careful check should be maintained by the waiter. Measures are poured from the peg measure or from other device.

Wine waiters should be careful to see that right type of glasses by the handle, if there is one or by the stem or the bottom half of the glass. The fingers around of the hand must never be placed in and around the top of a glass whether it is clean or used of one containing drinks. The waiter should stand and remove from right of the guests and glass should be placed on the right-hand side.

General Rules for Serving Wines (Fig. 10.4)

- Light wines should be served before rich or full-bodied wine.
- Dry wines are served before sweet wines.
- The white dry wines should be served before the red wine.
- Do not advise dry wine for foods that have sweet taste.

SERVING TECHNIQUES OF COCKTAILS

Cocktails are the combination of alcoholic drinks and other ingredients which are mixed according to the set standards (recipes). They should taste without any one ingredients predominating.

Cocktails are offered as short drinks which are suitable to be drunk as apertif stimulating the gastric juices for the meal to come. Others are suitable as after dinner drinks which are popularly known as mixed drinks.

Cocktails come under two basic categories:

1. The one, prepared by shaking the ingredients together with ice in a cocktail shaker (Fig. 10.5), then straining the drinks into a glass.
2. The other one prepared by stirring the ingredients together through ice in a mixing glass, then serving the drinks into a glass.

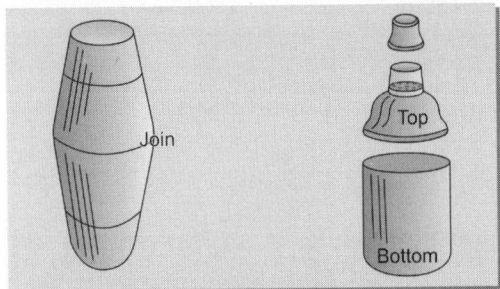

Fig. 10.5: Type of cocktail shaker

There are cocktails which are made up of just two ingredients. The vast majority comprises three, sometimes more than three as well (Fig. 10.6).

The major three parts consists of:

1. A base	: Usually a spirit
2. A sweetening	: Either syrup sugar or liqueur
3. A souring	: Bitter fruit juice of other similar ingredients

Fig. 10.6: Layered drinks

Examples are as Under

White lady contains lemon juice, gin and contreau. Bronx contains vermouth, gin and orange juice. Old nick has Drambuie and rye whisky and lemon juice.

Both alcoholic and non-alcoholic cocktails may be prepared by shaking or stirring. Other mixed drinks are prepared by combining various ingredients together.

In Mumbai, Goa, Kolkata, Kerala, etc. coconut water, kokam mixed with gin and vodka are very popular. Lassi can be made by alcoholic drink, when mixed with vodka, gin or cointreau.

In fact there are some internationally well established combinations. Some of which are listed below. But because of individual choice and availability of serving ingredients, many spot cocktails can be prepared for service.

Examples of Some Cocktails

Angel face	: ½ dry gin ¼ apricot brandy ¼ apple brandy Shake and remove in cocktail glass
Angel kiss	: Mixture of cocao, brandy and cream
Alexander	: ½ Cognac ¼ cream de cocao Shake and remove in cocktail glass

Bloody Merry : 1 part vodka, lemon 4 part and tomato juice

A dash of Worchester sauce and lemon juice. Some people like a dash of Tabasco sauce in the mixture.

This is served in small brandy balloon or in a high ball glass with salted rim.

Bamboo

Equal portions of sherry and vermouth serve with a twist of lemon in a martini glass.

Black Russian

Mixture of coffee, liqueur and vodka.

Brandy Punch

Mixture of egg, sugar and rum.

Champagne Cocktail

The sugar cube is placed in a champagne glass soaked with Angostura bitter, champagne is added and topped with Cognac, finish with half a slice of orange or cherry pierced in a cocktail stick.

Cuba Libre

It is a mixture of white rum, cola and juice of lemon (half).

It is made by adding rum and lime juice in a light glass half-filled with ice and topping up with cola.

Rum Cooler

It is a mixture of sugar syrup, lime juice, rum and soda water.

John or Tom Collins

1 part London dry gin, juice of medium-sized lemon, tea spoon Gomme syrup, and soda water. The glass is half-filled with ice, then gin is added with syrup over it. Soda is added and stirred, decorated with a slice of lemon and straw.

Dry Manhattan

It is a mixture of ½ rye whisky and ¾ dry vermouth. Dry martini or sometimes known as American dry/martini. It is a mixture of gin and dry vermouth.

Fizz and Frappers

Fizz is similar to collins except that all the ingredients except the soda water are shaken. Frappers are made by pouring liqueur in short stemmed glass filled with crushed ice and serving with two half straws.

Gin Sling

It is a mixture of sugar, gin and lime dissloved in a little water and then ice added, thereafter gin.

Hores's Neck

It is a mixture of brandy, a ginger ale and the lemon skin peeled in a long spiral placing one end in the bottom of a high ball glass and the other over the top edge, place ice into the glass, add the brandy and top up with ginger ale.

High Balls

This is a long drink and is a mixture of spirit and some effervescent such as soda water lemonade, ice-cream, soda, etc. They are all served in high ball glasses.

Harvey Wall Banger

1 part vodka, and small bottle of orange juice and little galliano.

Kir Royal

It is a mixture of half a measure of Cream de cassis topped up with champagne and served in champagne glass.

Manhattan

There are there types of Manhattan—sweet, medium and dry.

1. Sweet Manhattan

1½ measures dry whisky, ¾ measure sweet vermouth, dash of angostura bitter. Stir and strain before service.

2. Medium Manhattan

1½ measure of rye whisky, 3/8 measure of sweet vermouth, 3/8 of dry vermouth. Stir and strain before service with garnish of cherry or lemon silce.

3. Dry Manhattan

½ measure of rye whisky, ¾ measures of dry vermouth service as of other Manhattan.

Martini Cocktails

Martini cocktails are three types—sweet, medium and dry.

1. Sweet Martini

½ measure of gin, ¾ measure of sweet vermouth. Service style is the same as Manhattan and garnish with cherry.

2. Dry Martini

½ measures of gin, ¾ measure old dry vermouth, stir and strain in a cocktail glass before services with a twist of lemon. A dryer version is known as "American Dry Martini". This is mixed with five parts of gin and one part of vermouth.

Old Fashioned

It is a mixture of 1 large measure of whisky, angostura bitter, castor sugar and little water.

A small cube of sugar is placed into old-fashioned glass saturated with Angostra bitter. Some water is added to dissolve the sugar. Then the glass is half-filled with ice, over which whisky is added. The drink is garnished with cherry and orange slice and a cocktail stick is provided for stirring.

Pink Lady

It is a cocktail of 1 large measure of gin, ½ measure of Grenadine, 1 egg white. All the ingredients are shaken and strained into a small cocktail glass.

Pink Gin

It is a gin-based cocktail. The original pink gin was made with play mouth gin and this is still recognised as the right base. The gin is served with little bitter pouring iced water on the top.

Pina Colada

It is a cocktail of white rum, pineapple juice and coconut cream.

Pausse Café

These drinks are made by layering syrups, liqueurs and spirit on the top of each other in a narrow glass, to give a multiple coloured layers appearance. The order in which the liqueurs are added depends on the specific gravity of each layered syrups, the heaviest settle at the bottom, over it liqueurs and on the top the spirit being lightest. Pouring should be done carefully without disturbing the layers.

For World Cup Football 2006 in Germany, "D-cocktail" was made having colours of German flag.

Tri-colour national flag for surprise welcome drinks can be served in this style.

Screw Driver

It is a mixture of vodka and orange juice.

Side Car

It is a mixture of Scotch whisky, Cointreau and lemon juice.

Tequila Sunrise

It is a cocktail of tequila, orange juice and little Grenadine.

White Lady

It is a mixture of gin, Cointreua and fresh lemon juice.

Whisky Sour

It is a mixture of 1½ scotch whisky, 1½ lemon juice, measure Gomme and ½ white of egg.

Non-alcoholic cocktails are also served from bar on request. Orange juices with lemonade are very popular. The best known non-alcoholic cocktail is "Pusy Cat"—a mixture of orange, lime and lemon juice with a dash of Grenadine and egg yolk.

For ladies who do not prefer alcohol in cocktail in India, "Widow Marry" has taken over the place of "Bloody Marry" without the vodka.

Many guests venture drinks in company of ladies or families to order mixed drinks of their choices. This can be attended to. New cocktails or "cocktails of choices" can be made on the spot in the bars.

However, it is the duty of the bar man to guide and help the guests for their satisfaction, whims, and ego.

Some guests behave on whims during drinking beverages other than cocktails. There is a saying in India that "Beer before whisky, no fear, Whisky after beer can be risky". A bar man should discourage tactfully the possible risky situations in his bar.

The bar staff should be well conversant about mixing the cocktails as per recipe and proper addition garnish and serving style. Nothing, however, prevents him from adding his own artistic flare while garnishing mixed drinks. He/she must ensure that the bar has at least the following ingredients in adequate quantities.

a. Lemon, lime, mint, cherry, oranges, olives, stuffed olives (both black and green), juices and syrups of different varieties should be in stock.
b. Castor and cube sugar
c. Cream
d. Perl or pickled onion

e. Eggs

f. Green chillies (for vodka in India)

g. Salt and pepper

h. Tabasco and worchester sauce

i. Cucumber, tomato, tomato juice

j. Pineapples and pineapple juice

k. Plain nuts and salted nuts

l. Cheese cubes

m. Chips, wafers, papad, namkin, bhujia

n. Ham, pork, salami, etc. whenever there is a demand. Otherwise, arrangement of refreshly fried pakoras, baby corn fries, etc. should be available.

o. Soaked lentils, or green bangal gram (in season) is very popular in Indian bars.

In India, bars have limited capacity at the counter like many other countries. Hence, in most of the places, remaining floor areas where bar is located are used in restaurants. Sometimes, sofas are also placed for relaxation while drinking. Hence, more number of waiters are needed and some service time has to be allowed for carrying out orders.

In India, many bars and restaurants had developed new cocktails and their garnish are well accepted even among foreigners who visit the country. All these are added to the satisfaction of guests and creativity in the bar menu.

Examples of wine bottles are shown in Fig. 10.7.

New concoctions with Classics Daiquiri and Margarita have also been developed recently. Rendezvous (with cherry brandy, campari and cheries), Prince Edward Martini (with Drambuie, lemon and honey), mango, mint Daiquiri,

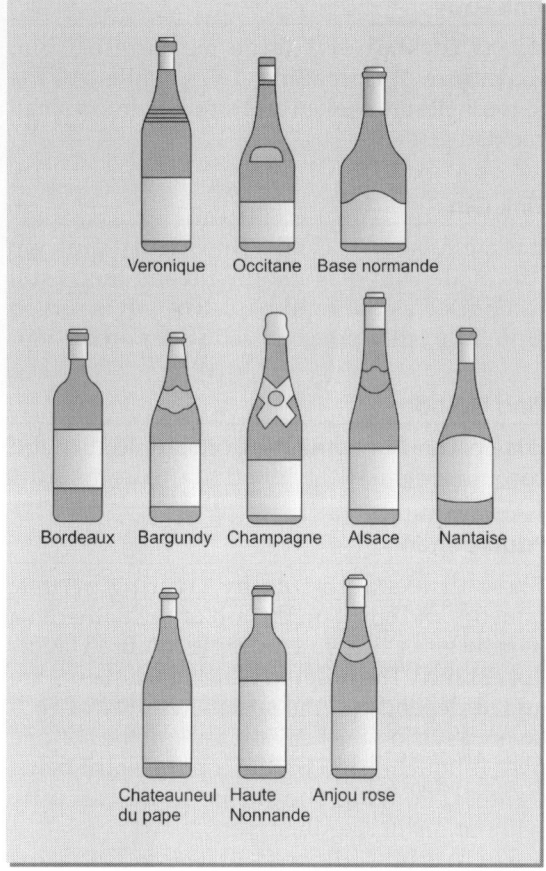

Fig. 10.7: Examples of wine bottles

Frozen Daiquiri are some of the latest twists in the classics. Flambe' cocktails are also interesting and magical in bars for parties.

Computer in the Hotel Industry

A computer system is made up of several components, including hardware, software, and the user, which work together to perform various tasks. Each of these is independent, but is only productive when used with the other components. For example, hardware, the parts of the computer that you can physically see and touch, will do nothing unless given instructions by the user through the software.

Hardware includes both the actual computer itself, and the various peripherals (short for 'peripheral devices') which allow data to input, output and stored. There are many different types of computer, ranging from large mainframes, which are expensive and can support many simultaneous users, to personal computers, which are relatively cheap and designed for use by a single person.

Conceptually, all computers are based on the same principle. Each is composed of a central processing unit (which does the actual work), a system bus (which is an electronic pathway along which data travels) and memory (which is used to store data). On a physical level, these components are incorporated into tiny chips made of silicon which are mounted on cards inside the system's unit—the case which most people refer to as the computer.

Software, on the other hand, is basically a series of instructions which tell the hardware what to do and how to do it. Software operates at several different levels. The bottom layer is known as an operating system. In simple terms, this controls the use of computer peripherals (Table 11.1).

Table 11.1: Computer peripherals		
Input	*Output*	*Storage*
Keyboard	Visual display units	Magnetic disk
Mouse	Printers	Magnetic tape
Bar-code reader	Voice synthesizers	CD-ROM
Magnetic-strip reader		DAT
Touch screen		Mini-disk
Pen entry		
Voice entry		
Direct entry		

The hardware supervises the running of the other programmes. Two different types of operating system are common. A command line interface is textbased and is used by typing specific commands with a particular format and syntax. A graphic user interface, on the other hand, uses a more intuitive, picture-based system to perform the same task, and this requires less technical knowledge from its users.

Application software lies on the top of the operating system. These are the programmes with which the user works directly and uses as tools to perform various tasks. Some applications softwares have general purpose in nature. For example, packages such as spreadsheets, wordprocessing packages and databases are relatively flexible and can be applied to a variety of tasks. While, as can be seen from Table 12.2, each has a particular purpose, the boundaries between different types of packages are rapidly being broken down as new variations are launched. Other applications softwares are both industry-specific and function-specific. Applications of this type are highly specialized, and can only be used for a very specific set of tasks. Sometimes, specialized pieces of hardware are combined with software

to automate a particular series of tasks. Some examples of such system from the hospitality industry are shown under hybrid computer systems in hotel industry (Fig. 11.1).

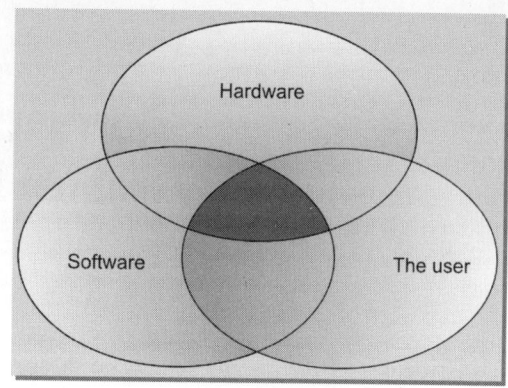

Fig. 11.1: Computer system

Each of the systems outlined in Tables 11.3 and 11.4 can be, and often is, used independently. However, efficiency and productivity are greatly increased, if the systems are integrated, as data can flow freely between the interlinked systems and thus improve guest service, security and control. Unfortunately,

Table 11.2: General purpose applications

Application type	Main functions
Word-processings package	Allows text to be typed, stored, have its appearance manipulated and be printed.
Spreadsheet	Allows numerical models to be set up modified interactively.
Database package	Allows data to be stored and processed using powerful sorting and selective retrieval facilities.
Graphics package	Allows graphics, messages and data to be sent electronically from one computer to another.
Communication package	Allows messages and data to be sent electronically from one computer to another.
Utilities package	Adds extra feature to a computer system—for example, to enhance case of use or security.

Table 11.3: Hospitality-specific applications

Applications	Main functions
Reservation system	Processes enquiries for room availability; tracks the number of rooms booked for each future data; accepts and stores reservations for both individuals and groups; tracks advanced deposits paid and travel agents commissions due; provides a variety of operational and management reports.
Property management system	Stores a list of the guests registered in the hotel; identifies which rooms are occupied; helps maintain guest foils by tracking

(Contd.)

Table 11.3: Hospitality-specific applications *(Contd.)*

Applications	Main functions
	charges and payments; provides a great variety of operation and management—level reports to both the front office and most other departments in the hotel.
Recipe-costing system	Generates an accurate and up-to-date cost for both individual dishes and complete menus, automatically recalculates the cost of all recipes, when an ingredient changes; generates a store requisition list detailing both the ingredients and quantities needed to produce a specific number of portions of any menu.
Stock-control system	Manages and controls by identifying the variance between the amount of each ingredient used and the amount which should have been used based on the number of portions sold; generates a variety of management and operation-level reports including usage rates and automatic recorder lists.
Conference and banqueting	Assists in the management of the banqueting department by accepting and storing reservations for conference and banqueting events, tracking audio-visual and other equipment needs, co-ordinates the provision of services from the food and beverages department, and simplifying the process of billing clients for services provided.

Table 11.4: Hybrid computer systems in the hospitality industry

System		Main functions
Telephone system	:	Automatically posts charges for telephone calls to the guest's bill, and provides a variety of other services such as voice mail and wake up calls.
Electronic point-of-sales system	:	Assists in food and beverages service by electronically transmitting orders to remote printers in production areas such as kitchens or dispense bars; increase control by automatically posting charges on the guest's bill and by providing a variety of management information and analysis.
Robobar system	:	Provides beverages facilities in bedrooms and automatically posts charges for the items consumed to the guest's bill.
Electronic door-lock system	:	Improves security by generating a unique electronic key for each new guest.
Energy-management system	:	Helps reduce energy costs by automatically shutting off services to unoccupied areas, and by controlling temperature more precisely than it is possible using manual or mechanical methods.

many computer systems in use in hospitality industry are not integrated. Poor planning and the lack of an accepted technology standard for hospitality computer systems have resulted in majority of systems operating in isolation, as a result, losing many of the benefits which the consistent use of a computer system can bring.

Why use a Computer System?

Before discussing the benefits which the use of a computer system can bring to an operation, let us examine some of the characteristics which make them useful:

* Speed	:	Computers work at electronic speeds and can process thousands of transactions per second. As a result, large and complex tasks can be completed very quickly.
* Accuracy	:	Computers always do exactly what they are told to do. As a result, they do not make mistakes and all calculations are performed correctly.
* Discipline	:	Computers can perform the same tasks over and over again, and never get tired, bored or distracted.
* Capacity	:	Computers can process large amounts of data easily. As a result, they can perform more in-depth analysis and consider more variables than would be possible manually.

As a result of the above four characteristics, the use of a computer system brings many benefits when compared with manual procedures. Firstly, there is a reduction in the amount of clerical work which must be carried out. Many boring, repetitive tasks can be automated, which make employee jobs more varied and fulfilling, thus helping to increase job satisfaction. The accuracy of the computer helps to reduce mistakes, which leads to increased guest satisfaction and better control over operations. Computers also increase productivity, because the same amount of work can be completed with less effort. This can be translated into cost savings by reducing staff numbers, or can help to further increase guest satisfaction as staff have to concentrate less on routine clerical work and thus have more time for personnel to interact with the guest. Computer system also allows larger amount of data to be processed, in a wider variety of ways, than would be possible manually, which results in more timely, accurate and relevant management information.

COMPUTER HARDWARE

One does not have to be a computer system expert to buy or use a computer. However, just a knowledge how a car works can improve your driving, so having a basic understanding of how a computer works can help you to use it more effectively. In addition, a knowledge of computer terminology can be useful, when dealing with sales people or reading advertisements. You have a better idea of what to expect from different types of computer system and can therefore be chosen an appropriate one with confidence.

As an introduction, following outlines the development of computer terminology from the mainframe computers of the 1950s and 1960s to the personnel computers of today. The internal structure of a computer and its peripheral devices are examined and many common technical items are explained. Particular attention is paid to two components, the central processing unit (CPU) and the computer's memory, because of its importance in the overall performance of the computer.

BRIEF HISTORY OF COMPUTERS

The concept of a computer is generally regarded to have been developed by Charles Babbage, who devised his engines in the 1930s. They bore an uncanny resemblance to the modern computer, with the ability to perform mathematical operations, to input and store data, and to output results. However, Babbage's devices were never produced because the technology of the period was not capable of manufacturing the parts required. Babbage was clearly ahead of his time, as all modern computers more or less follow his basic design.

The first electronic computer was built during 1950 in the University of Pennsylvania. The use of valves in computers of this era meant that they generated vast amounts of heat, and as a result, could only be used for a few minutes at a time, before they overheated and shorted out. However, in these short bursts of activity, they were capable of processing thousands of calculations per second and could, therefore, carry out a tremendous amount of work.

Batch processing was used to maximize the amount of work which could be carried out in the periods when the computer was operational. Work from different people was placed in sequence and coded onto punched cards by a special data-processing department. These cards were then feed into the computer and processed in the 'batch' thus, keeping the amount of time that the computer was in actual operation to a minimum.

The major problems associated with batch processing were the time lag between submitting work for processing and receiving the results, and the difficulty in detecting and correcting errors. All work had to be submitted to the data-processing department punched onto cards, 'batched' and processed. The results then had to be translated back into text and taken back to their owners. As a result, the work cycle could take anything from a few hours to several days. The gap between submission and receiving results was greatly extended, if an error occurred. The owner of this work did not become aware of the error until the results of the batch were obtained, perhaps a day or two later. The error than had to be corrected and the work resubmitted to be processed again.

The development of transistors and then integrated circuits in the early 1960s allowed computers to be built which were smaller, consumed less power and generated less heat. An integrated circuit is basically thousands of electronic components etched onto a tiny silicon chip (sliver of silicon). These chips can be mass produced, a fact which allowed IBM to launch the first commercial computer (the IBM 360 mainframe) in 1964. Computers then began to fall in price. Mini-computers which were far more powerful than the original mainframes but much cheaper, appeared on the market. Although still expensive to purchase and operate, computing power was now within the reach of large organizations.

As computers became more sophisticated, a new type of processing emerged. Instead of sending their work to the data-processing department to be punched onto cards and batch processed, people began to work directly on the computer themselves, using a keyboard and a screen. On-line processing, as this became known, is interactive in the computer process commands as they are entered and gives results straightaway. Errors are immediately apparent and can, therefore, be corrected, and work continued, without any delay.

Having a single person using a powerful computer interactively is not very efficient. Even when the time spent thinking is ignored, the power of the computer is not being used most of this time.

Computers are capable of processing many thousands of transactions per second, but the fastest human typist can only reach a speed of may be a hundred words per minute. As a result, the computer lies idle while it is waiting for the typist. Literally thousands of processes could be completed between the strokes.

To make better use of the computing power, a process called "time-sharing" was developed. The power of the computer is divided among several users, each using a terminal, which is basically a keyboard and screen. Each user connected is allocated a period of computer time called a "time slice", during which the computer processes his or her work. This is then saved temporarily and the computer moves onto each of the other users time slices. When every user has received his or her slice, the computer returns to the beginning, leads the first user's work and starts the cycle again. This process occurs at tremendous speed, so far for all intensive purpose; it appears that each user has exclusive use of the computer.

However, 'time-sharing' is problematic. Complex (and therefore expensive) software is required to control the allocation and management of the time slices. Furthermore, as there is only a finite amount of computing power available, a time-sharing system tends to become slower as the number of users increases. Eventually, if the number of users become too large, the computer 'trashes'—each user's time slice becomes so small that there is no time available to do anything apart from load and then immediately save the work before moving on to the next user's time slice. Although this problem can be controlled by limiting the number of simultaneous users, this unreliability in terms of speed (along with a massive reduction in hardware costs) fuelled the growth of the personal computer.

The development by Intel of the first microprocessor (computer on a single chip) at the beginning of the 1970s began a path which ultimately lead to massive cuts in the computing power. The first personal computers (PCs) appeared in the 1970s. Personal computers are designed specially to be used by a single person. Each has its own central processing unit and operates independently. As a result, the number of people using computers has no effect on the speed of operation of each user's machine. However, independence also has disadvantages. Information is not shared among users, as is the case with a mainframe system. Data entered on one machine is only available to the user of that machine. Each PC must also have its own peripherals such as printers and disk drives, while multiple users connected to a mainframe can share these expensive devices.

To overcome these drawbacks, methods of allowing personal computers (PC) to communicate with each other were developed. While each machine remains standalone and thus retains a reliable speed of operation, the use of a network allow computers to share both information and peripherals.

The IBM PC, which was the first personal computer to become a standard throughout the entire industry, was launched in 1981. After this, the personal computer revolution occurred, and computers have continued to fall drastically in price and rise rapidly in power. It has been estimated that computers double in speed, processing power and storage capacity every two years, while also halving in price. As a result, the dividing line between different categories of computer has become blurred. Apart from a rapidly closing speed difference, the main method to distinguish is by the number of simultaneous users or more technically 'terminals'—the computer in question can support. A personal computer is normally used concurrently by just a single user, and a mini computer by five to eighty users.

HARDWARE IN THE HOSPITALITY INDUSTRY

Computerization in the hospitality industry has followed a similar development pattern to that in many other sectors. Initially, because of the expense of purchasing and operating a mainframe computer, only the large hotel chains were able to afford and use computers. The 'superhuman' processing capabilities and level of accuracy given by the computer were used to automatic large scale and repetitive tasks such as reservations and guest folio maintenance.

Alvarze, Ferguson and Dunn documented experience of the New York Hilton, when it attempted to use a mainframe to manage front-office operations in 1963. Because of the number of users, the system slowed down at busy times, such as check-out in the morning. When broke down, the hotel was effectively deaf, dumb and blind. Instead of increasing efficiency and productivity, the system actually reduced guest service and had to be abandoned less than a year later, at great financial loss to the company. Naturally, this failure made diffusion of computer technology across the hotel industry by ten or fifteen years. During this period, the use of computers was limited to the less time-critical areas of hotel operation, such as in back office processsing, where a delay has a little or no effect on guest service.

The development of personal computers and networks did much to reduce the fears of hoteliers. In addition to being much cheaper (and thus financially more justifiable for smaller hotel), the fact that each machine has its processor eliminated the limitations on speed and reliability of using a mainframe. Both PCs and networks of PCs are now commonly used in the hospitality industry. Many new softwares are developed during recent years which are cost-effective and simple for operations.

HOTEL COMPUTER

The use of dedicated computer software in hotels has become widespread. This, however, operates much more efficiently, when linked together to form an integrated hotel system. Each system is explained briefly below:

Reservation Systems

Reservation systems are used to display room availability, sell individual and group reservations, track guest deposits and travel agent's commission, and generate reports such as arrival lists, reservation forecasts and pre-registration cards. Reservation systems operate on different levels as detailed below.

Property-based Systems

These display availability and accept reservations for just a single hotel.

Central Reservations Systems (CRS)

These display availability and accept reservations for a group of hotels. There are two general types of CRS: Those operated by a hotel chain or a marketing consortium (such as Holiday Inn or Best Western), which are sometime called affiliated systems or those which have been outsourced and are operated by an independent service company, such as Utell.

Statistics show that in excess of 50% of all reservations in the US hotels come through a CRS. In Europe, the figure has traditionally been much lower, but trends are changing. For example, the Forte group estimates that, in the future, two-thirds of their reservations worldwide will be made electronically.

Traditionally, CRS operated independently of the reservation systems in individual hostels. Reservations made on the CRS have to be transferred manually onto the property-based systems periodically, so that two systems would often be out of step with each other.

However, automatic real-time posting of reservations directly into the individual property's reservations system is now available, known as seamless or type. An integration leads to more accurate room inventory figures, and allows reservations office to sell up to maximum, including the last available room.

For a hotel group, using of a CRS can bring important marketing benefits, as it acts as a valuable channel of distribution. Customers and the direct clients or travel agents have access to availability and rate information for the entire group from one source. Some companies, such as Travellodge in the UK, use this facility to cross sell their hotels: If a requested hotel is booked out, the CRS will automatically suggest the nearest. Travelodge hotel with rooms available try to keep the sale within the group. Valuable management information is also provided by the CRS. For example, a detailed breakdown of the number of room-nights sold, the percentage made, can be found for each travel agent with which you do business. As a result, the hotel knows each bulk buyer's previous pattern of business, which can be very valuable when negotiation of room rates or commission levels.

GLOBAL DISTRIBUTION SYSTEMS (GDS)

CRS may, in turn, be linked to other larger reservation systems known as global distribution systems (GDS). These are generally based on the various airline reservation systems, such as Sabre, Apollo, Worldspan, Amadeus and Galileo, which have diversified from solely distributing airfares and availability to accepting reservations for hotels, car hire and other tourism-related products. Although many of these systems currently serve distinct geographical areas, global alliances are currently being formed which will lead to some truly 'global' systems in the not too distant future.

Listing a hotel on an airline system means that it can immediately be booked by travel agents worldwide. Since travel agents are suffering from shrinking commission because of the fall in the price of airfares, they are keen to find replacement income. Hotel rooms, as they are a complementary product, are ideal. The ability to see whether rooms are available and find the room rates electronically, is particularly attractive, because telephoning each individual hotel to find this information is expensive in terms of both time and telephone charges. Using a GDS, a travel agent with a client flying to Glasgow can check availability in hotels to find in the area on the required dates, see what room rate each is offering and make the booking electronically in seconds and at minimum cost. Marketing the same booking by telephones could prove expensive. Long distance phone calls and a fax to confirm the details, which together could make the transaction unprofitable for the travel agent. As a result, many agencies will now only make bookings for hotel rooms, if they can be made electronically.

Some GDS suppliers are experimenting with CD-ROM technology to help sell hotel rooms. The traditional way to sell a hotel to a client has been to use hotel brochures, but these are expensive to produce, are heavy and bulky, and go out-of-date quickly. CD-ROM-based systems (such as Sabre Vision and Apollo Spectrum) allow clients to see full-colour images of the hotel on a computer screen. The equivalent of thousands of individual brochures can be stored on a single CD, and this can be updated regularly and comparatively cheaply. The effect on sales in travel agencies which has been enormous. For example, Sabre estimates that travel agencies which use Sabre Vision book three to four times more hotels reservations than others.

GDS are also increasingly distributing their services to non-travel agents. Using Videotext technology (such as AERTEL in Ireland, PRESTEL in Britain and MINI-TEL in France) availability and rate information can be accessed directly by potential customers in their own homes. Potential clients can search for suitable accommodation and make reservations by telephoning the GDS supplier and paying using a credit card.

Advanced Deposits

In the past, guests have to confirm their reservations by sending a deposit (usually the cost of the first night's stay) in advance to the hotel. This policy ensured that clients did not make reservations and then fail to show up, thus losing revenue for the hotel. Although deposits have largely been replaced by a guarantee method by the use of credit card, most reservation systems still provide the facility to accept a deposit of the client does not have a credit card. When such a reservation is made, the system will request a deposit by a particular date. If the deposit is not received by this cut-off date, the reservation is cancelled and any room booked is added to availability again. The amount of any deposit received is stored with reservation, and is automatically posted as a payment on the guest's folio at registration.

Travel Agent Commission

Travel agents who send to a hotel are paid a commission of approximately 10% of the room revenue for their services. However in general, most hotels are very slow to pay this commission, which makes travel agents unenthusiastic about selling rooms. Centralized commission payment systems help to speed up and simplify the payment process. Each travel agency receives a single cheque representing all the commissions due from member hotel are reduced. A monthly report accurately details business received from each travel agency. A single cheque, made out to the clearing organisation, can then be used to pay all the commissions due.

Reservation Systems Operation

Irrespective of the level of reservation systems, the method of actually making a reservation is relatively standard. The process starts with an availability enquiry. The date of arrival needed is entered, along with type (s) of room and the number of nights required. The system will respond by displaying room availability for the requested period and the rate to be offered to the client. If the requested accommodation is unavailable, the system allows overbooking up to pre-determined limits.

If rooms are available, the client's name, address and telephone number are entered, along with details such as method of payment, the source of business and any special requirement. Utilities to help speed up the reservation process may be provided. For example, some systems allow the zip or postal code to be entered first from the most of the address can be filled in automatically by the computer, and only minor details such as the street number need to be edited, similarly, if the guest has stayed in the hotel before, his or her details may be automatically drawn from the guest history system.

When all the details have been entered, a confirmation number is generated by the reservation system, which the guest can quote, if the reservation needs to be changed at a later date. Individually addressed letters, confirming the details of each reservation, are then printed as part of the night audit.

Because availability is always up-to-date, the hotel can see the number of rooms booked or vacant on any particular date in the future. This is useful where yield management is being used, as up-to-the minute reports showing both short-term reservations can be accessed instantly. Many systems can also forecast how many rooms are likely to be sold, if past booking trends continue. Each night, as part of the night-audit procedure, an arrival list and pre-registration cards for the following day are printed, based on the reservation made in the system. All the dates held about each system so that data does not have to be entered unnecessarily.

Most systems also accept group reservation, which operates in a slightly different manner. First of all, a master reservation is set up with the group details and a 'block' of rooms is allocated to the group. Special group rates may be established, and special accounting instruction (such as billing a master folio for all accommodation and breakfast charges and the individual room folios for all other charges) may be set up for the group as a whole in a single step, thus, helping to eliminate unnecessary work for the front office staff. Individual group members can then make their own reservations and allocated rooms from the reserved block.

PROPERTY MANAGEMENT SYSTEMS (PMS)

The front office has been described as the centre of all hotel activities. It not only acts as the main contact point between the hotel and the guest, but also provides information to and receives information from practically every other departments in the hotel.

A property management system (PMS) helps manage these guest interactions and at the same time acts as an information 'hub' for the other computer systems.

These functions of the PMS may be broken down into the following different categories, which are discussed in more detail on the next page:

- Registration : Allocating vacant rooms to incoming guests and marketing those rooms as being occupied.

- House-keeping : Tracking which rooms are occupied, waiting to be cleaned, waiting to be inspected, or ready to be passed back to the front desk for allocation to incoming guests.

- Guest accounting : Tracking all guests charges and payments and producing the final guest bill.

- Night audit : Automatically performing end-of-day routines such as posting room charges to each guest folio.

Registration

Upon arrival, a guest must check-in or register in the hotel.

Where the reservation system and the PMs are integrated, most of his personal details will already have been printed as part of the previous night's audit, which the guest can simply sign to confirm the details. Guests without reservations can fill in a registration form and this information can then be entered quickly into the computer system.

Most systems allow reservations to be retrieved using either the guest's name or the reservation is displayed by the system. This is then marked as being occupied to prevent it being allocated again to another incoming guest. Similarly, group registration is greatly simplified using a computerized system. Rooms can be pre-allocated on the basis of a rooming list sent in advance by the group organizers. On arrival in a single step—literally at the touch of a button.

On an integrated system, the process of room allocations makes all the auxiliary systems aware that a new guest has registered. As a result, each system provides its service to the newly occupied room. For example, the telephone system will allow call to be made from the room's telephone, the energy management system will blast the room with warm or cool air to get it to an acceptable temperature, and the electronic door-locking system will issue a new magnetic key specifically for the new guest. A billing folio is also opened automatically for the guest so that charges in the hotel's bars and restaurants can be posted to the room number by the EPOS system. Naturally, any deposit paid before arrival automatically appears as a prepayment on this folio.

HOUSEKEEPING

The housekeeping or accommodation management department is responsible for cleaning and maintaining both the guest rooms and the public areas of the hotel, and its work is closely co-ordinated with that of the front office. Good communication between those two departments is essential because the front office needs accurate and up-to-date information on the status (vacant, occupied or dirty) of every room in order to operate effectively. Some systems facilitate this using the telephone system. When the room attendant has finished servicing a room, he or she types a code into the telephone which alerts the computer that the room is ready for inspection. The room can then be checked by the floor supervisor, who clean and ready for allocation to incoming guests, and does not have to keep guests waiting unnecessarily.

The PMS also assist the accommodation manager by automatically providing lists of guests who are departing or staying over. Some systems will even distribute the cleaning load between room attendants and produce assignment sheets automatically.

GUEST ACCOUNTING

As has already been mentioned, a folio is opened at registration to allow charges to be posted to the guest's account. This folio must always be accurate, up to date and capable of being produced for the guest on demand. Many systems allow each room to have more than one folio which guest needs. One folio for business expenses and another for personal extras, such as drinks or films.

Charges may be divided into two categories:
1. Some (such as the room rate) are posted automatically.

   This is important as today because of the use of yield management, most hotels have many different room rates. This makes it easy to post an incorrect rate accidentally, which either loses revenue for the hotel or infuriates the guest. A PMS, however, will always correctly identify the rate originally quoted to the guest at the time of reservation, and will post it to the guests folio. Other automatic charges, such as taxes and service charges, are also always calculated correctly, which help strengthen the professional image of the hotel.
2. Other charges are posted as the guest uses various hotel services such as bars, restaurants and leisure facilities. Sometimes these are posted manually from a paper docket system, but recently the trend has been to use of integrated EPOS system to post charges directly and instantly onto the guest's account. This helps to reduce clerical errors and also prevents guests checking out without paying for services.

When posting systems (for payments) manually, several security features may be encountered. The clerk posting the transaction normally has to enter an identification number, which can be used to identity from person who made in the event of a dispute at a later date the room number and the amount to be posted to, etc. accounts are then entered. A security code (such as the first four letters of the guest's surname for his or her signature) may then have to be entered to complete the posting. This helps prevent items being charged to the incorrect room number or by someone who is not staying in the hotel.

Any payment received from guest is summarized on the cashier's shift report, which helps to improve cash control. All transactions are also recorded on an audit trail, which is automatically printed onto paper several times a day. This lists the details of every transaction and can be invaluable to reconstruct guest bills, if the computer system breaks down.

To check out, the guest must either pay the total due on his or her account, or (usually by pre-arrangement) have the balance transferred on account to the debtors system. Upon checkout, the PMS alerts housekeeping that the room is ready to be cleaned, and also informs each of the auxiliary system that the room is no longer occupied. As a result, the telephone system will no longer allow calls to be made from the bedroom's telephone, the EPOS will not accept charges for that room number, and the electronic-locking system will not allow the guest back into the bedroom.

NIGHT AUDIT

Each night, various tasks, such as automatically posting the room charge to each guest's account, must be performed. In addition, all the accounts must be cross-checked to ensure that everything balances. These tasks were traditionally carried out manually by a team of night auditors. However, these tasks are routine and very repetitive, which ultimately makes them boring. For example, imagine posting the room charges manually in a 100 bedroom hotel. Each guest folio would have to be examined in turn, the quoted room rate found, the charge posted and then the new balances due calculates. Exactly the same procedure would have to be repeated for each of the other 99 rooms.

However, this 'routine' makes these tasks very suitable for computerization. The night audit modules automated these procedures and used the power of the computer to ensure accuracy and reliability. And, because the computerized system works at electronic speeds, the procedures are completed in minutes rather than in hours.

Some common procedures carried out automatically as part of the night audit include:

* Posting room and tax	:	As discussed above, the correct room rate must be posted to each guest's folio each night. Using a manual system, this alone could take several hours and can be troublesome. The amount of time saved, and the increase in accuracy achieved, by automating this one procedure can often be sufficient reason to install a PMS in the first place.
* Changing the system date	:	The night audit is usually the last transaction in the hotel's day. Once everything is balanced, the system date is changed and all daily summary totals are reset to zero.
* Performing system back-ups	:	Where a computer is used in the front office, a vast amount of valuable data (such as reservation information and details of guest charges) is collected and stored electronically. If the system failed and all these data were lost, the hotel would be in a very difficult situation. For that reason, a system back-up (making a copy of all the hostel's data files) must be performed on a regular basis. In the event of a system failure, data can be restored for the back-up and only the transactions entered since the last back-up are lost. Such back-ups are normally carried out nightly, as part of the night audit procedure.
* Printing historical reports	:	Various management reports summarizing the previous days business and the current date business (such as a nationality analysis, a departmentalized sales analysis report, or a report summarizing revenue by source of business) are generated by the system.
* Printing operational materials	:	These include status reports such as for the next day expected arrivals and departure lists, and other operational items such as pre-registration cards and confirmation letters. Folios for guests who are expected to depart in the morning may also be printed to help speed up the check-out process.

CASE EXAMPLE: USING COMPUTERIZED SYSTEMS IN SMALL HOTELS

Mr Suleman, Manager of the Claridges Hotel, describes the effect of installing a computer system in a fifty-bedroom transit hotel.

With most guests only staying one night and an averages of 90% occupancy, we have an extremely heavy load of paperwork.

Before the computer was introduced, all the confirmation and invoices were typed and room bookings were kept in the traditional way. Now the computer is used for everything from the initial telephone enquiry to the final billing.

The staff like it, because it gives them more time to spend on more interesting work, and it gives the hotel a more professional image, but above all relieves us all of the tedious paperwork.

At the end of everyday, the computer totals the transactions performed in the previous 24 hours, breaking down payments into payment types (Access, American Express, Visa, cash or cheques). At the moment, the daily information is printed out and then sent to the Claridges accounts department in Delhi, although it is hoped that soon the daily totals will be sent to the accounts department automatically over telephone lines.

As well as performing the end-of-day routines by 10 or 11 in the morning, rather than the middle of the next afternoon as before. Suleman is able to access and analyse the performance of the hotel with great ease. The revenue is broken down into accommodation, no. of shows, room hire, VAT, restaurant, bar, telephone, newspapers and other extras, so that management is able to see how areas of the business are performing, feel that all the analyses are a lot more reliable now. Earlier, there was lot of errors.

Before the system was installed, Suleman and his staff had to keep the same records, generate the same acknowledgement letters, draw up the bills and analyse the business to the same degree as does the computer. The difference is that everything is now done automatically. Previously we had one member of staff permanently tied up doing the work which the computer does now. No one has lost his/her job, but our staff are now able to spend a lot more of their time at the front desk looking after the guests, which is obviously more pleasant.

Ancillary Systems

This section gives an overview of various systems which, although not part of the PMS itself, interface with it and increase efficiency and control. The number and complexity of these systems are growing rapidly and while the list below mentions the ones most commonly found in the hotel industry, it is by no means exhaustive.

- Telephone systems
- Electronic door-locking systems
- Energy-management systems
- In-room guest services

Many catering-related systems which operate in the hotel environment such as EPOS systems and Robobars, also interface with the front office.

Telephone Systems

Telephone systems are one of the most common uses of technology in hotels. Their basic function is to direct dial facilities to be provided in guest bedrooms. The number dialled, the duration, and the charge for each call are recorded by the system. This data can be printed onto paper and then posted on to the guest's account bill.

The main advantage for the hotel is increased control. Becasue the number dialled is recorded, it is more difficult for the guest to dispute having made the call and the charge is posted automatically as soon as the call is completed. The guest cannot check out without paying for all his or her telephone calls. Most systems will also not allow calls to be made from unoccupied rooms, which prevent fraudulent use of the telephones system by staff.

Other facilities provided by systems include automatic wake-up calls and voice mail. The latter acts like a kind of mini answering machine for each room, and allows spoken messages to be left for guests who are not in their rooms. All messages are automatically stamped with the time and date they were recorded and can be replayed with the time and date they were recorded.

Electronic Door-locking Systems

Given the public nature of hotels, security is obviously important. The locks on hotel doors are usually good quality, which has the side effect that their keys are expensive to cut. Unfortunately, guests have a habit of accidentally taking the room key with them when they depart. When this happens, the door lock has to be replaced because someone could return with the 'stolen' key at a later date and get back into the room. A further disadvantage with conventional keys is that some members of staff (such as housekepeers or duty managers) have special keys, known as sub-master, which are capable of opening most of the locks in the hotel. If one of these is lost, every lock affected has to be changed.

An electronic door-locking system uses small plastic cards instead of metal keys. The combination which opens the door can be recorded on these cards in one of two ways; either by punching holes in the card, or by storing it on a magnetic strip. It does not matter, if the guest forget to return the key at check-out because the combination in the door lock is changed and a new, unique key issued for each new guest.

Electronic door-locking systems generally work in one of the two ways. Some systems use a standalone 'in-the-door' microprocessor, while others use an online system which is connected by wiring to a computer at the front desk. The standalone systems operate by storing a predetermined sequence of combinations in each lock and on the computer which issues the keys. The door lock 'knows' that a new guest has checked in when it reads the key with the next combination in the sequence. However, problems arise when the door locks and the front-office computer becomes unsynchronized. For example, if a door key is issued but the door lock will not.

As a result, when the next guest checks in and is issued a new key, it will not open the door, because the lock is one step behind in the sequence and is expecting a different combination. With an online system, the computer communicates directly with the lock and cancels the previous access code as soon as the guest arrives and a new key is issued, the lock is immediately informed of the new combination. However, online systems tend to be much more expensive, particularly because of the cost of installing wiring between each door lock and the front office computer.

With an electronic door-locking system, staff keys are also more secure. If a master key is lost or stolen, the combinations in the door locks can be scrambled quickly and easily to prevent anyone gaining access to the guest rooms. Keys can be time-limited (thus preventing their use, when the employee is off duty) or limited to particular areas (e.g., a floor housekeeper's key might open all doors on one floor, but not any other floor). Most systems can also track who has entered each room, and this computerized record can now be submitted as legal evidence.

ENERGY MANAGEMENT SYSTEMS (EMS)

Energy management systems help to minimize the power costs of the hotel, while at the same time not affecting the level of comfort of guests or employees. Such systems can be used in a variety of ways. For example, the system may automatically reduce heating or air-conditioning in unoccupied areas of the hotel. If a guest is allocated a room in that area, the system blasts the area with warm or cold air to return it quickly to an acceptable temperature. Energy management systems also allow more accurate control to be maintained over temperatures, which can lead to further energy savings.

IN ROOM GUEST SERVICES

In these systems a variety of facilities are available such as Robobars in-house pay-per-

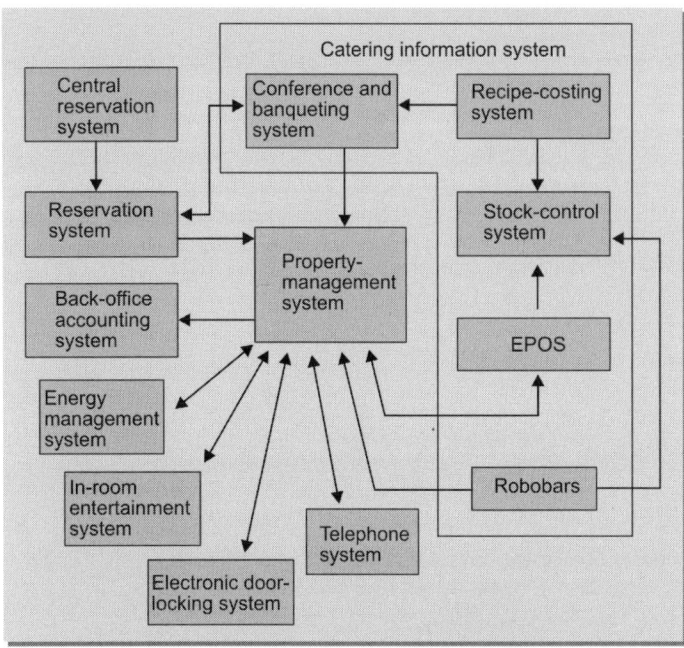

Fig. 11.2: Hotel-oriented computer systems

view-films, in room check-out and guest messaging. Both Robobars and films provide extra services to guests, while at the same time increasing revenue for the hotel. For example, the television screen can be used to display a welcoming message, in the language of the guest, immediately after check-in. Messages left for guests, and other information such as special promotions available on screen. Some security systems automatically switch on televisions to broadcast evacuation information orally and visually in the event of an emergency.

Many PMS now allow the guests to examine their bill on the television screen, and allow check-out from the guest bedroom. Guests simply reveiew their bills on the screen and, if everything is in order, then press a one-digit approval button on either the telephone handset or the television remote control. A printer at the front desk produces a copy of the bill, which the guest can either collect on the way out, or have posted to the address given at the time of registration. Once the guest checks out and leaves the room, the electronic door-locking system will no longer accept his or her key, thus preventing re-entry into the room.

Figure 11.2 depicts all the hotel-oriented computer systems.

Appendix I

Specimen Guest Activities in Hotel

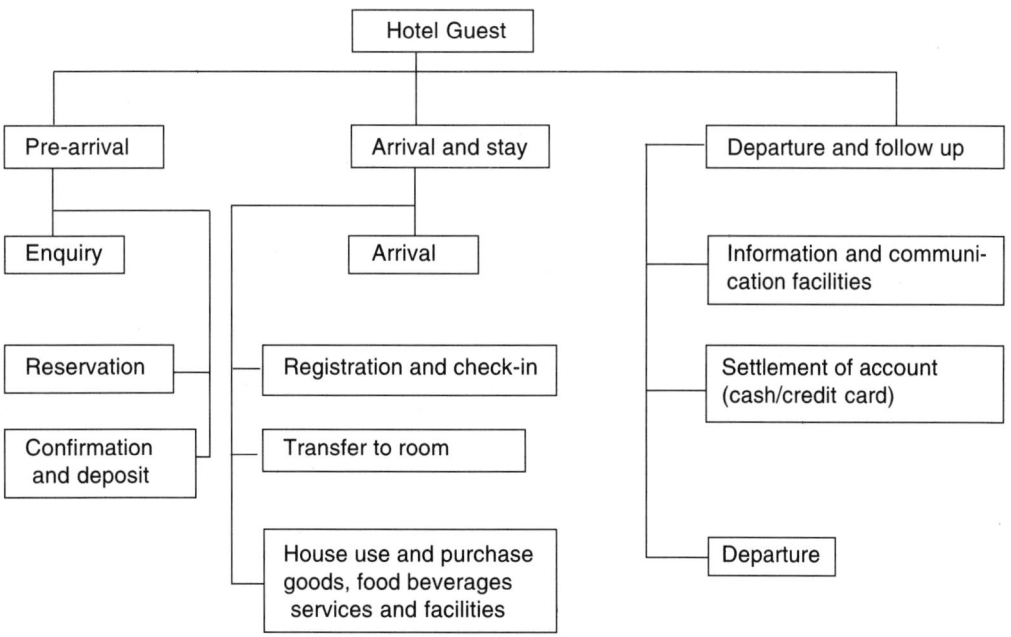

Appendix II

The Front Office and Guest Arrival in a Hotel

Arrival of guest: A typical flowchart

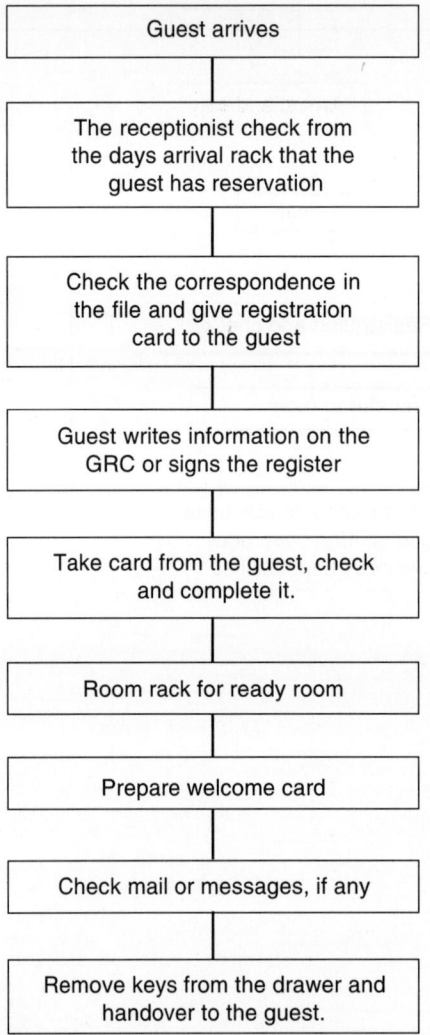

| Guest arrives |

| The receptionist check from the days arrival rack that the guest has reservation |

| Check the correspondence in the file and give registration card to the guest |

| Guest writes information on the GRC or signs the register |

| Take card from the guest, check and complete it. |

| Room rack for ready room |

| Prepare welcome card |

| Check mail or messages, if any |

| Remove keys from the drawer and handover to the guest. |

Appendix III

The Front Office Activities and Guest Activities in a Hotel

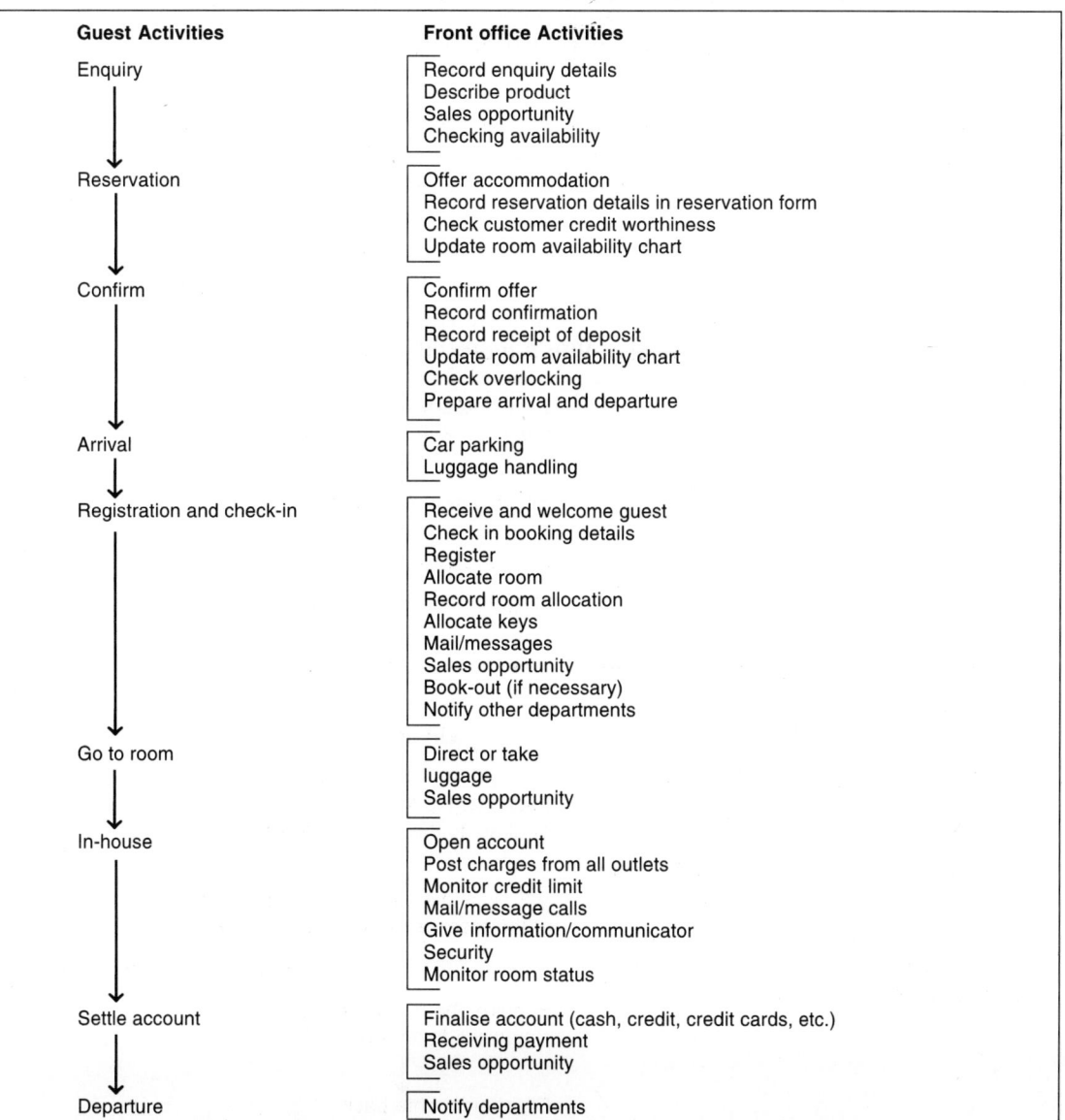

Guest Activities	Front office Activities
Enquiry	Record enquiry details Describe product Sales opportunity Checking availability
Reservation	Offer accommodation Record reservation details in reservation form Check customer credit worthiness Update room availability chart
Confirm	Confirm offer Record confirmation Record receipt of deposit Update room availability chart Check overlocking Prepare arrival and departure
Arrival	Car parking Luggage handling
Registration and check-in	Receive and welcome guest Check in booking details Register Allocate room Record room allocation Allocate keys Mail/messages Sales opportunity Book-out (if necessary) Notify other departments
Go to room	Direct or take luggage Sales opportunity
In-house	Open account Post charges from all outlets Monitor credit limit Mail/message calls Give information/communicator Security Monitor room status
Settle account	Finalise account (cash, credit, credit cards, etc.) Receiving payment Sales opportunity
Departure	Notify departments

Appendix IV

Registration Card: A typical flowchart

Registration card
details duly filled by guest

Ist copy with reservation slip goes to be filed systematically	2nd copy is 'C' form for foreigners only sent to F.R.R.O	3rd copy attached with folio is sent to L. Manager for his signature.

Guest folio with 3rd copy
of registration card is sent
to F.O. Cashier

Arrival of VIP: A typical flowchart

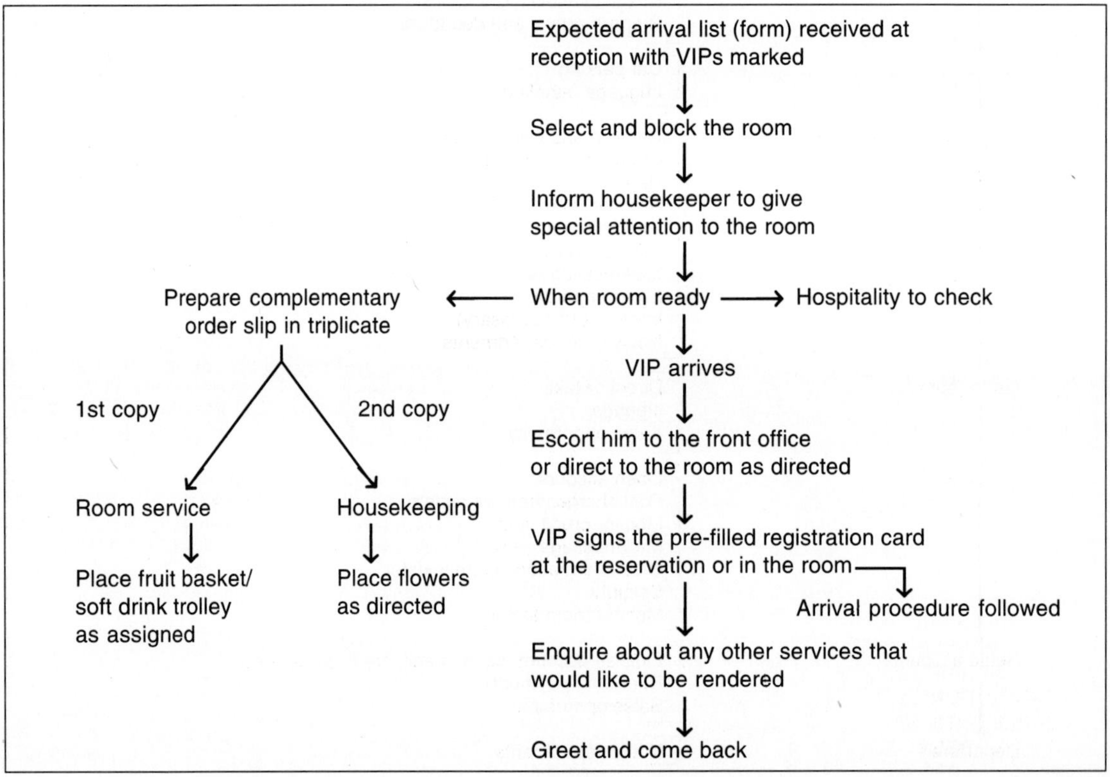

Expected arrival list (form) received at
reception with VIPs marked

↓

Select and block the room

↓

Inform housekeeper to give
special attention to the room

↓

Prepare complementary ← When room ready → Hospitality to check
order slip in triplicate

1st copy   2nd copy

↓   ↓

Room service   Housekeeping

↓   ↓

Place fruit basket/   Place flowers
soft drink trolley   as directed
as assigned

VIP arrives

↓

Escort him to the front office
or direct to the room as directed

↓

VIP signs the pre-filled registration card
at the reservation or in the room

→ Arrival procedure followed

↓

Enquire about any other services that
would like to be rendered

↓

Greet and come back

Appendix V

Specimen of a Guest Bill

HAVE YOU DEPOSITED YOUR ROOM KEY

AND THE LOCKER KEY

HOTEL   ABC

| ARRIVAL |
| DEPARTURE |
| NO IN PART |
| RATE |

ACCOUNT NO.   ROOM NO.

S. NO.	DATE	DESCRIPTION	AMOUNT

	COMPANY	STREET

| **BILLS ARE DUE ON PRESENTATION REGARDLESS OF INSTRUCTIONS, GUEST IS ALSO LIABLE UNTIL BALANCE HAS BEEN PAID** | CITY   STATE   PIN |
| | GUEST SIGNATURE |

Appendix VI

Specimen of a Guest Bill Details

HOTEL ABC

Phone:
Cable:

Continuation Sheet No. .... of G.R. No.

Name/s .... Room No. .... G.R. No. ....

Date and Time of Arrival .... a.m/p.m   Date and Time of departure .... a.m/p.m.

No. of Guests .... Rate ....

Date	₹	P	₹	P	₹	P	₹	P	₹	P	₹	P	₹	P
Rooms														
Restaurants/Bars														
Telephone														
L'distance														
Telephone Local														
Telex														
Laundry														
Miscellaneous														
Paid outs														
Transfers														
DAILY TOTAL														
Brought Forward														
GRAND TOTAL														
Cash/Credit														
Allowances														
Balance C/Fd.														

CHECKED AND FOUND CORRECT
Please forward the bill to
M/s ....
....
....
Signature

OUR FOREIGN GUESTS
Bills to be settled in
convertible foreign
exchange:
(i) Exchange vouchers No. ....
(ii) Exempted vide
category No. ....

Amount Due ....
Cash Receiver No. ....
Allowance Voucher No. ....
Transfers ....

E and O.E   Bill Clerk/cashier

Bills are payable on presentation. Cheque not accepted

Appendix VII

International Hotel Symbols (Graphics)

   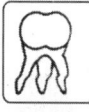  

 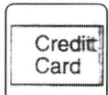   

(Contd.)

International Hotel Symbols (Graphics) *(Contd.)*

(Contd.)

International Hotel Symbols (Graphics) *(Contd.)*

Motel Traveller Lodge
Beach Resort
Forest Lodge
Tourist Reception

Telephone
Baggage Locker
Elevator
Toilets, Men

Toilets, Women
Toilets
Information
Hotel Information

Taxi
Bus
Ground Transportation
Rail Transportation

Car Rental
Restaurant
Coffee Shop
Bar

Hotel
Shops
Duty Free Shop
Lost and Found

Ticket Purchase
Baggage Check in
Customs
Immigration

No Smoking
Smoking
No Parking
Parking

No Entry
Entertainment
Sound and Light Show
Mail

(Contd.)

International Hotel Symbols (Graphics) *(Contd.)*

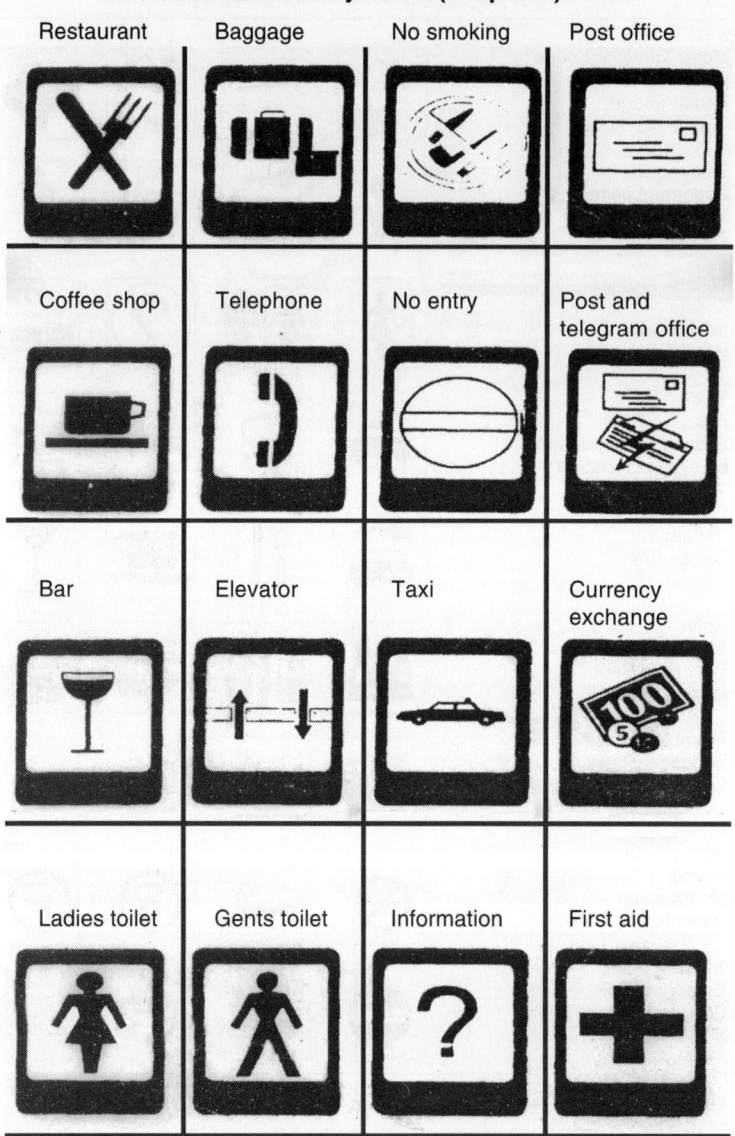

Restaurant	Baggage	No smoking	Post office
Coffee shop	Telephone	No entry	Post and telegram office
Bar	Elevator	Taxi	Currency exchange
Ladies toilet	Gents toilet	Information	First aid

Appendix VIII

CHILDREN'S MENU

Spidy's Broth

Creamy sweet corn chicken soup ₹ 80.00

Asterix Magic Potion

Little Tomato soup ₹ 70.00

MOWGHLI'S FAVOURITE

Tom & jerry Double Burger CHICKEN ₹ 200.00

Two mint burgers stuffed with chicken or cottage VEG ₹ 180.00
patty with creamy coleslaw tomatoes and tangy gherkins

Fried Dynasour Wings ₹ 250.00

Crumb fried chicken winglets served with honey mustard glaze

Nemo's Delights With fries ₹ 250.00

All time favourite fried fish with tartare sauce and French fries

Winnie's Cheasy snack ₹ 175.00

Cheese stricks with tomato dip

Scooby Dooby Doo... Non Veg ₹ 250.00

10 inch pizza with your favourite toppings VEG ₹ 200.00

Onions, capsicum, mushrooms, tomatoes, asparagus, olives
Shereded chicken, shrimps salami, ham

SWEET DELIGHTS

Mickey Mouse Magic ₹ 100.00

Strawberry ice cream topped with fruits and jelly rings

Pokemon Delight ₹ 100.00

Mango jelly served with fresh whipped cream and gummies

SIPPERS

Dexter's Nuclear shake ₹ 100.00

Crunchy chocolate shake

Simbe's Roar

Classic banana and vanila shake ₹ 100.00

Appendix IX

Name and Address of Important Hotel Consultants and Hotel Equipment Suppliers

a. Hotel Consultants

1. Hotel and Restaurant Equipment
   Consultants
   103 A, Anjali Building
   187 Floor, Seven Bungalows
   Andheri (W)
   Mumbai-400161

2. Consultancy Bureau
   1-33, Naraina Vihar
   New Delhi-110028

3. ITDC's Consultancy Services

4. M/s Vadhera and Co
   Hotel Architect and Consultant
   New Delhi

b. Hotel equipment

1. M/s Mazda Hospital and Industrial
   Equipment Pvt. Ltd.
   6, Datta Mandir Road
   Mumbai-400 078

2. LL Equipment and Machines Pvt. Ltd.
   35/36-C, LK Arcade
   Marol Naka
   Sir M.V. Road
   Andheri (E), Mumbai-400 059

3. Ardashir Jamshedgi and Sons
   Tata Housing Society Bldg.
   1/B, 36, 8th Floor
   Elphinstone Road
   Mumbai-400 012

4. Neptune Equipment Pvt. Ltd.
   24 SA Brelvi Road
   Near Homimen Circle
   Mumbai-400 001

5. M/s N.Vee Engg. Co. Pvt. Ltd.
   E-B/2, Vasant Vihar
   New Delhi-110057

6. Meta Die Engg. Pvt. Ltd.
   2/3 Vijay Industrial Estate
   1/B, Patel Road Goregaon
   Mumbai-400 063

7. Diwakar and Bros.
   6, Amrapali Industrial Estate Premises, Co.
   Opp. Society Ltd.
   Flam Mandir Road
   Goregaon
   Mumbai-400 104

8. J.B.B. Engg
   Shop No. 2, Shed No. 3, Behind Diamond
   Restaurant
   Kondivita Road
   Andheri
   Mumbai-400 059

9. Airawat Engg.
   Unit No. 82, Municipal Industrial Estate
   Parashuram Pupala Marg
   Bapti Road
   Mumbai-400 008

10. Design Centre
    5B/166 Mital Industrial Estate
    Andheri-Kurla Road
    Mumbai-400 059

11. Pheonix Appliances Pvt. Ltd.
    405, Ashirwad Building
    Iron Market, Ahmedabad Street Carnac
    Bunder, Mumbai-400 009

(Contd.)

12. United Works Pvt. Ltd.
    7–8, Mahalakshmi Bridge
    Mumbai-11

13. Nagpal Brothers
    2789, Zorawar Singh Marg
    Morigate, Delhi-6

14. Multifrig Marketing Co. (P) Ltd.
    1/12, Kirti Nagar
    New Timber Market
    New Delhi-110 015

15. Continental Equipment (I) Pvt. Ltd.
    1, E/1, Jhandewalan Extn.
    Link Road
    New Delhi-110 055

16. Sri Rajalakshmi Industrial Agency
    Rajalakshmi Corner House
    30/1 Silver Jubilee Park Road
    Bengaluru-560 002

17. Prestige Equipment Co.
    W-2, Basai Darapur
    Najafgarh Road
    New Delhi-110 015

18. Iqbal Equipment Corpn.
    Z-98, Gali No. 4 M
    Anand Parbat Industrial Estate
    New Rohtak Road, New Delhi-110 005

19. Paramount Industries
    Moti Ram Road Shahdra
    Delhi-110 032

20. Sriram Refrigeration Industries Ltd.
    19, Kasturba Gandhi Marg
    New Delhi-110 001

21. Thakar Equipment Co.
    66, Okhla Industrial Estate
    New Delhi-110 020

22. Canteen Equipment Trading Co.
    22, Shyampukur Street
    Kolkata-700 004

23. Mittal Rolling Mills
    Budh Bazar
    Moradabad-244 001

24. Udyog Bharati
    A-90/3, Wazirpur Industrial Area
    Delhi-110 052

25. Kelvinator of India Ltd.
    28, N.I.T.
    Faridabad-121 001

26. Refrigeration Equipment (P) Ltd.
    70, Diamond Harbour Road
    Kolkata-23

CUTLERY/CROCKERY

1. Brite Sales Corpn.
   3068, DB Gupta Road 2
   Paharganj
   New Delhi-55

2. Excell Glasses Ltd.
   Udya Nagar
   Pattirappally
   Alleppey, Kerala

3. Todi Metal Industries
   35, Saki Vihar Road
   Saki Naka, Mumbai-400042

4. Crystal Marketing Service
   240, Adrash Industrial Estate
   Sahar Road, Chakola
   Andheri (E)
   Mumbai-400099

5. Venus Industries
   WZ-I Basai
   Nazafgarh Road
   New Delhi-110015

6. Eagle Potteries (P) Ltd.
   P.O. Hindone Nagar
   Dasna
   Ghaziabad-201001

7. Rattachand Harjasri (Moulding) Pvt. Ltd
   54, Industrial Area
   Faridabad

8. Holy-Land Harphool Singh
   5804, Basti Harphool Singh
   Sadar Thana Road
   Delhi-110017

(Contd.)

9. J.S Tablewares
    J.S House
    Sahu Street
    Moradabad-244001

10. Ajay Mertal Finishing Industry
    H-36-D Saket
    New Delhi-110017

FURNITURE

1. Ashoka Furniture House
    21/1, Punchkuin Road
    New Delhi

2. Orday Foam Enterprises
    5/5777 Dev Nagar
    Karol Bagh
    New Delhi 110005

3. Ajanta Rubber (New) Shop No. 90
    Punchkuin Road
    New Delhi

4. Foam Tex India
    Libaspur Road
    Delhi-42

5. Naresh Rubber co.
    4, Ist Floor, MCD Bldg
    Pahar Ganj, New Delhi-55

6. Nawab Interior's
    1/115-116, Subhash Sadan W.H.S
    Kirti Nagar
    New Delhi-110015

7. Ahuja's
    65, Furniture Block
    Kirti Nagar, New Delhi-15

8. Panban (Furniture) Pvt. Ltd
    WZ-572, Naraina village
    (Opp. C/148/2, Narain Vihar)
    New Delhi-110028

9. Featherlite Products (P) Ltd
    Timmer Yard Layout
    Mysore Road
    Bengaluru-562026

10. Sleepa Mattress Co.
    5, Stringer Street
    Chennai-600018

11. Blow Past Ltd.
    Leo House
    88 C Old Prabhadevi Road
    Mumbai-400025

12. Gem India Ltd.
    P-2 Connaught Circus
    Opp. Rivoli Cinema
    New Delhi-110001

OFFICE EQUIPMENT

1. Kilburn Reprographics Ltd.
    7, Red Cross Place
    Kolkata-700001

2. Macheill and Magor Ltd.
    7, Red Cross Place
    Kolkata-700001

3. M/s Electronic & Computers India Ltd.
    1008, Akashdeep
    Barakamba Road, New Delhi-1

4. Hindustan computers Ltd.
    96, Nehru Place
    New Delhi

5. Modi Xerox

6. M/s G.R Electronic Industries
    110, Ripon St.
    Kolkata-6

7. M/s Kheraj Electronic Industries
    56 A, 11 B, Old Angriwadi, Mazagaon
    Mumbai-10

8. Indian Telephone Inds. Ltd
    16, Museum Road
    Bengaluru-560001

9. M/s Pentaz Engg. Pvt. Ltd
    Bharat Velevet Compound
    Safed Pool M. Vassanji Road
    Mumbai

(Contd.)

10. Omki Finance and Inds. Ltd
    523-25, Chanderok Complex
    S.D. Road, Secunderabad-500003

11. M/s Mahashtra Electronics Corpn.
    Radie Communication Div.
    J/5-6 MIDC Area, Hinge Road
    Nagpur-410016

AC GENERATOR

1. M/s Best & Crompton Engg Ltd
   29, Rajaji Salai
   Chennai-I

2. M/s Bharat Heavy Electrical Ltd.
   18, K Gandhi Marg
   New Delhi-1

3. M/s Crompton Greaves Ltd.
   1, Dr. VB. Gandhi Marg
   Mumbai-23

AC REFRIGERATION

1. M/s Air Conditioning Corpn. Ltd
   17, Taratola Road
   Kolkata-53
2. M/s Blue Star Ltd
   23-24 Line Beach
   Chennai-1

CALCULATION MACHINE

1. M/s Blue Star Ltd
   Kasturi Building
   J. Tata Toad
   Mumbai

2. M/s Kelvinator India Ltd
   Faridabad
   Haryana

3. M/s Rimington Rand of India Ltd.
   3, Council House
   Kolkata-1

4. M/s Western Electronic Pvt. Ltd
   43, Okhla Ind. Estate
   New Delhi-20

DIESEL GENERATOR SETS

1. M/s Belliss & Macroco Pvt. Ltd.
   6, Little Russel St,
   Kolkata-75

2. M/s Betlibboi & Co. Pvt. Ltd.
   Udhana
   Surat

EMERGENCY LIGHT

1. M/s Coronet Electronic Co.
   1127, Gurudev Nagar
   Ludhiana-1

2. M/s Piece Electronic India Ltd.
   7, JC Madhab Road
   Kolkata

Appendix X

List of some National and International Associations related to Hotel Catering and Tourism

1. American Hotel and Motel Association
    888 Seventh Avenue
    New York, NY-10019

2. American Hotel & Motel
    Kellogg Centre
    East Lansing, MI 48823

3. American Hotel Association Directory Corpn
    888, Seventh Avenue
    New York, NY-10020

4. American Management Association
    (AMACOM)
    135, West 50th Street
    New York, NY-10020

5. Association International de i' Hotellerie
    89 Rue de Faubourg
    Saint Honre, 75008, Paris, France

6. California Hotel Association 20
    Capitla Mall, Sacramento, CA 95814

7. Hotel Association of New York City Inc. 141
    West 51st Street, New York, NY-10019

8. Hotel Restaurant Employee and Bartenders
    120, East Fourth Street, Cincinnati, OH 45202

9. International Foodservices Manufacture
    Association
    1, East Wacjer Drive, Chicago, IIm 60601

10. International Restaurant Association
    Suite 2600, One IBM Plaza,
    Chicago II, 60611

11. Hotel & Restaurant Association of Eastern India
    Everest Building J.N Road
    Kolkata-700071

12. Hotel Restaurant Association of Northern India
    4.6/75-76, Manisha, Nehru Place,
    New Delhi-110019

13. Federation of Hotel & Restaurant Associations
    of India
    Flat No. 312, New Delhi House,
    27, Barakhamaba Road,
    New Delhi-110001

14. South India Hotel & Restaurant
    Association Spencer's Building, 769,
    Mount Road, Chennai-600002

15. Hotel Restaurant Association of Western India
    Roose Velt House-2nd Floor, Behind Taj Mahal
    Hotel, Mere Weather Road
    Mumbai-400039

16. Indian Tourism and Hospitality Society
    U-112 A, Vikas Marg
    Shakarpur, Delhi-110092

17. Hotel & Restaurant Association of Orissa
    College Square, Cuttack-753003, India

18. Travel Trade Club of Bihar,
    Maurya Centre, South Gandhi Maidan,
    Patna-800001, India

19. National Restaurant Association of India
    L. Block, Connaught Circus,
    New Delhi-110001, India

20. Restaurant Association of Kashmir, Srinagar,
    India

21. Jharkhand Restaurant Association Jamshedpur
    (Jharkhand)

22. ICMR, 92, Hem Naskar Road, Kolkata-10

23. Culinary Association of India, New Delhi

Appendix XI

List of some Important National and International Chain of Hotels

Taj Group of Hotels
Indian Resort Hotels Ltd
Mandlik Road, Mumbai-400039

Clark Group of Hotels
U.P Hotels Ltd
1101, Surya Kiran
19, Kasturba Gandhi Marg
New Delhi-110001

Desprakash Group of Hotels
C/o Hotel Ambassador
Sujan Singh Park, New Delhi-3

Oberoi Group of Hotels
East India Hotel Co.
Mango Lane, Kolkata
Welcome Group of Hotels I.T.C. Building
Jawaharlal Nehru Road, Kolkata

Hyatt Regency Group of Hotels
Bikaji Cama Place
Ring Road, R.K Puram, Delhi

Holiday Inn Group of Hotels
USA

Trust House Forte Group of Hotels
England

Sheraton Group of Hotels
USA
Le-meridian Group of Hotels
Western Group of Hotels

Accor Group of Hotels, France

Ramad Group of Hotels (USA)

Travel Lodge Group USA
USA

Inercontinental Group of Hotels, USA

Hilton Group of Hotels, USA

ITDC's Asoka Group, India

Le Meridan Group, N. Delhi

Marriott Group, N. Delhi

Tulip Group of Hotels (UK)

Sahara India, Lucknow

Hilton Group of Hotels, USA

Radison Group of Hotels, USA

ITDC Asoka Group, India

Ritz Group of Hotels

Welcome Group of Hotels, India

Indone Taj, New Delhi

Peerless Group of Hotels, Kolkata

Leela Group of Hotel, Mumbai

Nirala's group of Hotel, New Delhi

Radison Group of Hotels, N. Delhi

Quality Inn Group of Hotels, India

Marriott Group of Hotels, USA

TOP 25 U.S. Chains			
Rank	*Brand name*	*No. of properties*	*No. of room*
1.	Holiday Inn	1,373	262,002
2.	Best Western	1,796	162,887
3.	Days Inn	935	122,309
4.	Sheraton	339	96,456
5.	Hilton	271	96,304
6.	Ramada	517	86,427
7.	Marriott	194	85,199
8.	Motel 6	520	59,447
9.	Howard johnson	448	55,684
10.	Comfort Inn	564	52,186
11.	Hyatt	94	51,359
12.	Quality Inn	375	49,772
13.	Super 8	617	38,995
14.	Econo Lodges	490	37,748
15.	Radisson	137	328,313
16.	Travelodge	416	29,654
17.	Hampton Inn	211	26,430
18.	La quinta	203	25,883
19.	Embassy Suites	94	23,035
20.	Red Roof	209	22,930
21.	Westin	33	20,589
22.	Rodeway Inn	177	20,011
23.	Courtyara	136	19,854
24.	Residence Inn	134	15,624
25.	Knights Inn	138	15,155

Appendix XII

List of Hotel Conference Facilities in some Selected Cities in India

Delhi hotel conference facilities		*Capacity*
Ashok	Convention hall (divisible into 3)	2500
	Party rooms (4)	50–200
	Banquet hall	350
	Conference rooms	15–25
Holiday Inn	Ball room	800
	Party room (5)	300
Hyatt Regency	Ball room (divisible into 3)	600
	Senate/Maytair rooms	100/150
	Board room/crystal	35/35
Imperial	Ball room	600
	Gold room	350
Kanishka	Banquet hall	450
Meridien	Napoleon hall	1000
	Raisina hall	150
Oberoi Maidens	Banquet rooms	500
	Conference room	350
Siddharth	Manadala hall	400
	Board room	75
Sofital Surya	Elysee	450
	Smaller halls	200–350
Taj Mahal	Diwan i Am	550
	Diwan i Khas	150
	Aftab & Mahatab	180
Taj Palace	Durbar hall	1600
	Shah Jahan	1100
	Mumtaj Mahal	250
	Roshan Ara/vazir Lounge	80/50
The Oberoi	Zodiac hall	220
	Suites 1,2,3 (All combined)	750
Welcome Group	Kamal Mahal	1000
Maurya	Kamal Mahal I/II/III	175/225/400
Sheraton	Dynasty/Sakya/Chaitya	80/40/40
Mumbai hotel conference facilities		
Centaur (Santa Cruz)	Nalanda	325
	Smaller rooms (2)	200 each

(Contd.)

(Contd.)

Mumbai hotel conference facilities		Capacity
Centaur (Juhu Beach)	Banquet hall	600
	Conference rooms	250 each
Radison Centre	Centre	2000
	Open air	500
Hoilday Inn	Main hall	350
	Rooms (2)	200/150
Leela Penta	Conference rooms	1000
	Small rooms (2)	200 each
Oberoi Towers	Regal room	1200
	Rooms (7)	1500–20
President	Banquet hall	700
	Ball room	150
	Conference halls	200–510
Taj Mahal/Taj Inter	Ball room	700
	Crystal room	450
	Room (8)	140–35
Welcome Group	Imperical room	350
Sea Rock	Anchorage	120
	Rooms (3)	40–25
Agra hotel conference facilities		
Ashok	Conference room	75
Clarks Shiraz	Conference room	550
	Akbar room	300
Taj View	Banquet hall	175
	Party room	175
Welcome Group	Diwan i Khas	200
Mughal Sheraton	Majlis	40
Bangalore hotel conference facilities		
Ashok	Convention hall	500
	Banquet hall	250
	Conference hall	250
Holiday Inn	Banquet hall	500
Taj Residency	Convention hall	1000
	Meeting rooms (4)	
Welcome Group	The Regency	350
Winds or Manor	Westminster room	100
West End	Conference hall	600
	Banquet rooms (4)	20 to 50
Chennai hotel conference facilities		
Taj Coromandel	Ball rooms I	1000
	Ball rooms II	200
	Conference I/II	150/80

(Contd.)

(Contd.)

Chennai hotel conference facilities		Capacity
Taj Connemara	Ball room	500
	Wallajah room	120
	Nataraj room	25
	Arcot/Oakshott rooms	30/30
	Binny room	180
Welcome Group	Mandapam	450
Chola Sheraton	M I/M II/M III	150/80/80
	Rarendra hall	250
	Aaditya suite	40
Welcome Group	Mowbrays hall	500
Adayar Park	Chamiers hall	500
	Arcot hall	50
Savera Hotel	Conference hall	50
	Conference hall	250
Bhubaneswar hotel conference facilities		
Kalinga Ashok	Banquet hall	250
Konark	Main hall	125
Oberoi	Mandap	125
Swoati	Main hall	200
Goa hotel conference facilities		
Fidalgo	Banquet hall	150
Fort Aguada	Conference hall	150
	New Conference hall	60
Oberoi Bogmalo Beach Resort	Conference hall	100
Welcome Group Cidade de Goa	Sala de Banquet	175
Kolkata hotel conference facilities		
Hindustan	Banquet hall	300
International	Peacock hall	800
Oberoi Grand	Grand ball room	800
	Viceroy room	150
	Rooms (4)	250/50
Park Hotel	Banquet hall	1000
	Rooms (4)	250/50
Taj Bengal	Banquet hall	550
	Meeting rooms (2)	50/70
Sonar Hotel ITC	Banquet hall	1000
	Suderban (open air)	2000
Hyatt	Banquet hall	1000/750
New Kenelworth International Tower	Banquet hall	250/450
Golden Hall	Banquet hall	300

Other than above, new conference facilities and special banquet facilities are being added every year in almost all major cities of India. Shiar-Kashmir convention centre, Srinagar, Hyderabad, Jaipur, Ahmedabad, Kochi, Guwahati, Nagpur, Pune are having excellent banquet facilities.

Small Indian towns are also making efforts to make ceremonial hall and large catering facilities.

Appendix XIII

<table>
<tr><td colspan="2" align="center">**Metric/Imperial Conversion Factors**</td></tr>
<tr><td>*Imperial to metric units*</td><td>*Metric to imperial units*</td></tr>
</table>

LENGTH

1 in	= 25.4 mm		1 cm	= 0.394
1 ft	= 30.5 mm		1 m	= 3.28 ft
1 yd	= 0.914 m		1 m	= 1.09 yd
1 mile	= 1.61 km		1 km	= 0.621 mile

MASS

I oz	= 28.3 g		1 g	= 0.0353 oz
I Ib	= 4.54 g		1 kg	= 2.20 Ib
1 ton	= 1.02 tonne		1 tonne	= 0.984 ton

AREA

1 in^2	= 6.45 cm^2		1 cm^2	= 0.155 in^2
1 ft^2	= 929 5 cm^2		1 m^2	= 10.8 ft^2
1 yd^2	= 0.836 m^2		1 m^2	= 1.20 yd^2
1 ac	= 0.405 ha		1 ha	= 2.47 ac
1 sq. mile	= 259 ha		1 km^2	= 247 ac

VOLUME

1 in^3	= 16.4 cm^3		1 cm^3	= 0.0610 in^3
1 ft^3	= 0.0243 m^3		1 m^3	= 35.3 ft^3
1 yd^3	= 0.765 m^3		1 m^3	= 1.31 yd^3
1 bushel	= 0.0364 m^3		1 m^3	= 27.5 bushets

VOLUME (FLUIDS)

1 ft oz	= 28.4 ml		1 ml	= 0.0352 ft oz
1 pint	= 568 ml		1 liter	= 1076 pint
1 galoon	= 4.55 liter		1 m^3	= 220 gallons

(Contd.)

(Contd.)

Imperial to metric units		Metric to imperial units	
FORCE			
1 lbf (pound-force)	= 4045	1 N (Newton)	= 0.2251 bf
PRESSURE			
1 psi (lb/sq in)	= 6.89 kpa	1 kpa (kilopascal)	= 0.145 psi
VELOCITY			
1mph	= 1.61 km/h	1 km/h	= 0.621 mph
TEMPERATURE			
°C	= 5/9 (°F–32)	°F	= 9 °C/5+32
ENERGY			
1 BRU (British iternal unit)	= 1.06 kJ	kJ (kilo joule)	= 0.948 BTU
POWER			
1 hp (horse power)	= 0.746 kW	1 kW	= 1.34 hp
FUEL CONSUMPTION			
mpg	= 282/litre/100 km	Litres/100 km	= 282/mpg
L.P.G-cylinder	= 14.5 kg each		approx.
Do (commercial)	= 18.5–19 kg		

Appendix XIV

Approximate Floor Area Requirements for Hotel Kitchen	
Number of meals per day	*Approximate floor area sq. ft.*
50–75	250
100–125	400
250–300	900
400–452	1400

Approximate 5 sq. ft. per meal

Heavy Duty Electric Equipment in Medium-sized Hotel Kitchen	
Name of the equipment	*Load requirement kW (approx.)*
1. One oven	6 kW
2. One deep fryer	8 kW
3. One grill (sale mander)	8–10 kW
4. One deep freeze	1 kW
5. One large freeze	1 kW
6. Bain-marie	6–8 kW
7. Dishwasher (if required) 1500 pieces/h	10 kW
8. One tea boiler	10 kW
9. One masala grinder	1 kW
10. One mincer	0.5 kW
11. One hot-case	0.25 kW
12. One plate warmer	2 kW
13. One microwave oven	

Appendix XV

List of Largest Hotels in the World

1000 or more rooms

Rank	*Name* ▶◀	*City* ▶◀	*Number of rooms* ▶◀	*Floors* ▶◀
1.	Izmailovo	Moscow	7,500	4 towers 30 stories each
2.	The Venetian	Las Vegas	7,117	52, 37 and 14 floors (3 towers)
3.	First World Hotel	Gening Highlands	6,118	(Tower 1), 28 floors (Tower 2)
4.	MGM Grand Las Vegas	Las Vegas	4,734	Includes signature Skylofts, and the mansion
5.	Wynn Las Vegas/Encore Las Vegas	Las Vegas	4,734	48/50 floor (2 towers)
6.	Luxor Las Vegas	Las Vegas	4,408	22/22/36 floors (3 buildings)
7.	Mandalay Bay/THE Hotel	Las Vegas	4,332	43 floors
8.	Ambassador City Jomtien	Pattaya	4,219	
9.	Excalibur Hotel and Casino	Las Vegas	4,008	28 floors (2 towers)
10.	Aria Resort & Casino	Las Vegas	4,004	60 floors
12.	Bellagio Las Vegas	Las Vegas	3,993	36 floors
13.	Circus Circus	Las Vegas	3,774	
14.	Shinagawa Prince Hotel	Tokyo	3,680	
15.	Flamingo Las Vegas	Las Vegas	3,565	28 floors
16.	Hilton Hawaiian Village	Honolulu	3,386	7 towers
17.	Caesars Palace	Las Vegas	3,340	
18.	Disney's Port Orleans Riverside and French Quarter [1]	Lake Burna Vista	3,044	
19.	The Mirage	Las Vegas	3,044	

Appendix XVI

About SPA

SPA in hotel or resorts means a health club which offering various kinds of health therapies such as traditional massages, facial and body cleansing like face or body mask, sauna. Some SPA clubs also offering advise on how to live healthy, like what kind of food and drink, diets, various kinds of exercise or aerobics, etc.

THE TRUE MEANING OF SPA

Growing number of Americans are trying a new, but ancient approach to holistic living called "thalassotherapy". But what does this seldom spoken word mean? In order to understand the meaning, perhaps we should make a further inquiry about the definition of the word "SPA".

SPA is actually an acronym originating from the time of the Roman empire, when battle weary legionnaires tried to find a way to recover from their military wounds and ailments. They sought out hot springs (wells) and then built baths so that they could heal their aching bodies; calling these places 'aquae' and naming the bathing treatments undertaken there "Sanus Per Aquam" (SPA)—*meaning health by or through water*. During this period, the town Spa in Belgium was founded for this purpose, rising to fame in the 14th century and still existing today.

Having originated from this time, the culture of Spa developed in different ways throughout Europe, from the **ongoing use of mineral water, to using sea water and marine substances** (thalassotherapy) and a wide range of body and other therapies. What developed in SPA, as it is far from the ocean or Mediterranean sea, is more likened to **Balneotherapy**, which involves **the treatment of disease by bathing**. It may involve hot or cold water, massage via moving water, relaxation or stimulation. The concept of health or healing forms the basis of the modern SPA culture worldwide and hydrotherapy is seen as its defining feature.

The whole concept of *healing by water or water-based substances* is, therefore, known as "thalassotherapy" or "balneotherapy", with thalassotherapy bringing the "original SPA experience", probably on the coasts of oceans and seas.

Here are some of the thalassotherapy services and products provided by Atlantispa:

Services: An initial SPA detoxification Program lasting from 4–6 weeks using all sea and plant-based products. We feature ionized drinking water in our lounge. We recommend ongoing SPA service of at least once per week, preferably two.

Products for sale or used in services: Jupiter Science ionizer drinking water dispenser, chlorella, chlorella growth factor, chlorophyll, Himalayan and Dead Sea bath salts, Acupeds foot detox pads, sea clay, french green clay, Alkalife alkaline drops, Dr. Willard's Catalyst-Altered Water Concentrate, and loofahs are some examples.

In the United States, Atlantispa is a leader in bringing back the original meaning of "SPA" and to once again include "thalassotherapy" and "balneotherapy" in common, spoken English.

Appendix XVII

Formal Western Dining: Seating Plans

Woman	Woman	Man (VIP)

Host   Hostess

Woman (VIP)	Man	Man

Host	Woman	Man (VIP)

Woman (VIP)   Hostess

Man	Woman	Man

Man	Woman	Man (VIP)

Host   Hostess

Woman	Man	Woman

(The guests of honour always sit to the right of the host or the hostess)

The Formal Table Setting: Western
(As the guest approaches the table)

Appendix XVIII

The table below tell you how much energy you consume through various devices. You save a lot of energy for the nation and cut your electricity bills by switching off the devices when not required.

Devices (Capacity and size)		Wattage	Monthly electricity consumption (kWh)		One unit of power will be consumed when you run the device for ...
			One hour/days	Six hours/day	
Bulb		25	0.75	4.5	40 hrs
		40	1.2	7.2	25 hrs
		60	1.8	10.8	16 hrs 40 min
		100	3	18	10 hrs
CFL	5 watt	7	0.21	1.26	143 hrs
	9 watt	11	0.33	1.98	90 hrs 55 min
	11 watt	13	0.39	2.34	77 hrs
	25 watt	27	0.81	4.86	37 hrs
Fluorescent tube lights 48*	with Copper choke	55	1.65	9.9	18 hrs 11 min
	with Electronic choke	35	1.05	6.3	28 hrs 34 min
Night lamp		15	0.45	2.7	66 hrs 40 min
Ceiling fan	36"/48"	50	1.5	9	20 hrs
	56"	60	1.8	10.8	16 hrs 40 min
	60"	70	2.1	12.6	14 hrs 17 min
Table fan 12"/16"		40	1.2	7.2	25 hrs
Electric iron	Domestic	450/700	13.5 to 21	81 to 126	2 hrs 13 min to 1 hr 25 min
	Dhobi	1000	30	180	1 hr
Immersion rod		1000	30	180	1 hr
Geyser	Storage 15–50 l	2000	60	360	30 min
	Instant	3000	90	540	20 min

(Contd.)

Some Ready Calculations for Energy Consumption *(Contd.)*

Devices (Capacity and size)		Wattage	Monthly electricity consumption (kWh)		One unit of power will be consumed when you run the device for ...
			One hour/day	Six hours/day	
AC	1 ton	1400	42	252	43 min
	1.5 ton	1800	54	324	33 min
Air cooler		170	5.1	60.6	5 hrs-53 min
Refrigerator	Small	225			2 units/day
	Big	300			4 units/day
Toaster		800	24	144	1 hr 15 min
Hot plate		1000/1500	30 to 45	180 to 270	1 hr to 40 min
Electric kettle		1000/2000	30 to 60	180 to 360	1 hr to 30 min
Mixer-juicer (big)		450	13.5	81	2 hrs 13 min
Washing machine	Automatic	325/1000	9.75 to 30	58.5 to 180	3 hrs 5 min to 5 hrs
	Semi-automatic	200	6	36 6 hrs	
Vacuum cleaner		700–750	21 to 22.5	126 to 135	1 hr 26 min to 1 hr 20 min
Radio		15	0.45	2.7	66 hrs 40 min
Tape recorder		20	0.6	3.6	50 hrs
TV		60 to 120	1.6 to 3.6	10.8 to 21.8	16 hrs 40 min to 8 hrs 20 min
Video		40	1.2	7.2	25 hrs
Mosquito repellant		5	0.15	0.9	200 hrs
Water purifier		25	0.75	4.5	40 hrs
Computer		100 to 150	3 to 4.5	18 to 27	10 hrs to 6 hrs 40 min

1. Remember the figures given will serve only as guidelines since wattage ratings differ from model to model.
2. Electricity consumption is measured in kilowatt-hours (kWh) and is calculated by multiplying the watt rating of the machine by the number of hours the machine runs and dividing this by 1,000.
3. When 1,000 watts are burnt for 1 hour, 1 unit of electricity is consumed, which is also measured as 1 kWh (1 kWh = 1 unit of electricity).

Appendix XIX

Seating Arrangements in Banquet Room

Seminar styles

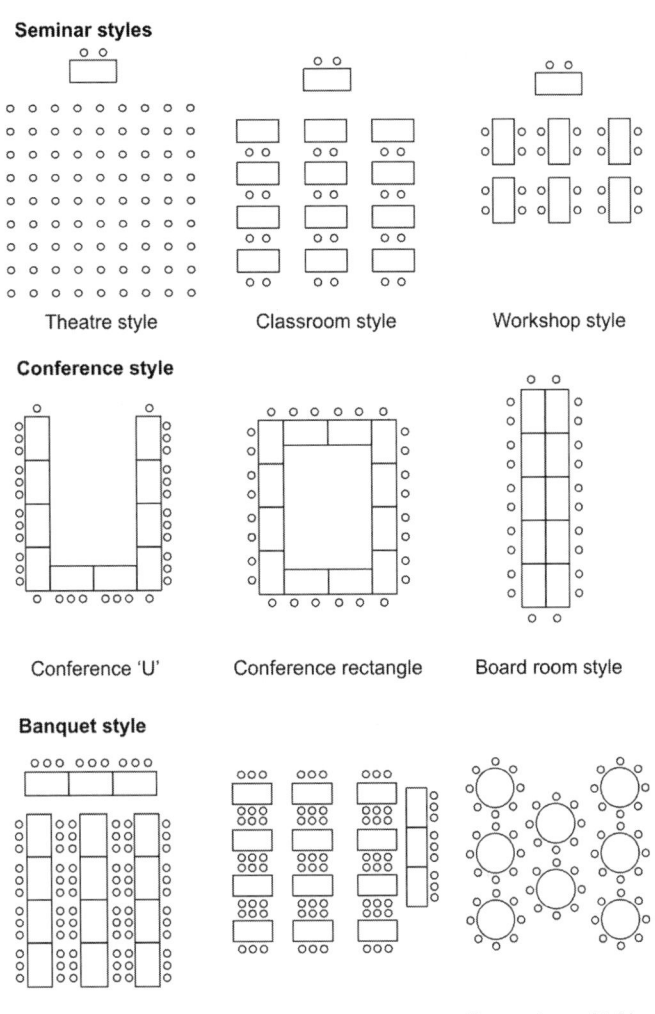

Theatre style   Classroom style   Workshop style

Conference style

Conference 'U'   Conference rectangle   Board room style

Banquet style

Banquet 'E'   Banquet individual   Banquet round table

Index